Great Expectations

Great Expectations
The Psychology of Money

HENRY CLAY LINDGREN

William Kaufmann, Inc.
Los Altos

To Charles Dickens, who not only
inspired the main title of this book,
but who knew more about
the psychology of money than most writers,
both of his age and ours.

Library of Congress Cataloging in Publication Data

Lindgren, Henry Clay, 1914-
    Great expectations.

    Bibliography: p.
    1. Money—Psychological aspects.   I.   Title.
HG221.L5468   332'.01'9   80-14177
ISBN 0-913232-82-3

Printed in the United States of America

Contents

Foreword by Authur V. Toupin vii

Preface ix

1 Why does money matter? 1

2 Money begins to matter 8

3 Money in the modern world 32

4 Money, status, and power 58

5 Money and self-worth 83

6 The rich and the poor 100

7 Giving money away 124

8 Money motives, sex, and guilt-edged anxiety 137

9 Money the manipulator 156

10 Money, work, and achievement 172

11 Money and mental health 195

Appendix: Analysis of the Reader's Questionnaire . 223

References 229

Index 237

Foreword

Although most people will agree that money, or the lack of it, is one of the important motivators of human behavior, there has been no prior comprehensive treatment of Dr. Lindgren's subject, "The Psychology of Money." Writings on the subject by psychologists and psychoanalysts, beginning with Freud, are fragmentary. Economists have had little to say about it. Dr. Lindgren has integrated what has been written and has added experiences and observations from his personal research to create a lucid, thought-provoking book. When Dr. Lindgren told me of his plan to write this book, I was uncertain whether it would be possible to assemble the variety of relevant information that would be needed for a fresh and interesting treatment of the subject. I was accustomed to the academic, esoteric, essentially boring treatises on the subject of money most often written by economists. Could he command the attention of the average man, who each day adds to his own stock of personal experiences about money and who usually is his own expert?

The answer is yes. Dr. Lindgren has succeeded in creating a readable, nontechnical book. He writes about money in a manner every reader can enjoy, helping us to comprehend our own responses to the host of situations in which money affects our lives: getting, borrowing, lending, spending (both wisely and improvidently), giving, budgeting, saving, investing. The author's observations and the case studies he uses invariably call to the readers' minds their own personal experiences with money. He deals effectively with the relationships in our society among money, the perceived worth of an individual, and social power, and with the passive attitudes toward life often exhibited by those with little money.

The moods, attitudes, behavior patterns, the joy, excitement, depression, anxiety, hostility and guilt associated with the acquisition and disposition of money are all covered with sensitivity and understanding. Throughout, the author writes with a subtle humor derived from a sure knowledge and years of professional experience in the psychology of people's responses to money.

Dr. Lindgren selected money as a subject because so many people, lacking understanding, make it a scapegoat for their problems, an easy rationalizer of complex events they don't want to examine carefully. His goal was to display the "why" of money—the reasons for our behavior toward and with money. He has handled the task skillfully and ingeniously.

For a banker like myself, steeped in conventional writings on money subjects—from money supply statistics to foreign exchange translations—this is a useful, impressive, and enjoyable book.

Arthur V. Toupin
Vice Chairman of the Board
Bank of America

Preface

Part One

This is a book about the psychological aspects of human behavior toward and with money. Money is a subject on which we all have pronounced views, in some respects negative, in some respects positive. Before going on with the preface, you may enjoy responding to the following questionnaire, in order to determine where *you* stand on money. Inasmuch as many of the items in this questionnaire are treated directly or indirectly throughout this book, you may want to answer the questionnaire again or reconsider your initial responses after you have finished reading the book. If so, record your responses the first time on a separate piece of paper, which you might use as a bookmark, in order to have them on hand when you take the questionnaire a second time.

Attitudes toward Money: A Questionnaire

Directions: Please circle the response that best expresses your feeling about each of the following statements.

    SA strongly agree
     A agree
     ? uncertain
     D disagree
    SD strongly disagree

SA A ? D SD   1. Money is the root of most evil.

SA A ? D SD   2. Money is an absolute necessity in the functioning of any modern society.

SA A ? D SD   3. Most of the pathological problems of the world are either caused or aggravated by money.

SA A ? D SD   4. It is reasonable to put a money value on the responsibilities that employees bear toward employers.

SA A ? D SD   5. The introduction of money into a human relationship inevitably worsens it.

SA A ? D SD   6. People who have money tend to be happier than people who do not have any.

SA A ? D SD   7. Money is or symbolizes the ultimate obscenity.

SA A ? D SD   8. Whatever economic democracy we have in Western society is made possible by money.

SA A ? D SD   9. The abolishment of money is prerequisite to the establishment of the ideal society.

SA A ? D SD   10. Money provides a reasonable basis for a status system, if we are required to have one.

SA A ? D SD   11. Money corrupts whatever it touches.

SA A ? D SD   12. Thanks to money, the world is a better place.

Directions for scoring: The above statements have been arranged in such a way that odd-numbered statements are anti-money in tone, and even-numbered statements are pro-money. The responses are scored in a pro-money direction, as follows:

Odd-Numbered Statements		Even-Numbered Statements	
Response	Value	Response	Value
SA	1	SA	5
A	2	A	4
?	3	?	3
D	4	D	2

The mean or average score made by San Francisco State University professors, who completed the questionnaire anonymously, was 40.69. A completely neutral score (averaging out to a "?" for all items) would be 36; therefore the professors tended to be somewhat favorable, but not strongly so, in their attitudes toward money. If a score of 48 (12 times 4) represents a definitely favorable attitude toward money, their mean score of 40.69 stands at less than half the distance between a neutral 36 and a positive 48.

About a third of the professors scored below 36 and therefore held unfavorable attitudes. Another third scored 45 and over. Here are the mean or average scores for each item (remember that over 3 signifies a positive stance; under 3, a negative one):

1.	3.1	4.	3.5	7.	4.2	10.	2.5
2.	3.9	5.	3.5	8.	2.5	11.	3.8
3.	3.5	6.	3.5	9.	4.0	12.	2.6

The answers to Statements 7, 9, and 11 indicate that the professors tended to reject the idea that money is obscene, that it should be abolished, or that it is inevitably corrupting, and their answer to Statement 2 shows that they were inclined to think of it as a necessity. But they also tended to reject the idea that money makes economic democracy possible (Statement 8), that it makes the world a better place (Statement 12), or that it is a reasonable basis for a status system (Statement 10).

The statements are loaded, of course, but they do reflect in one way or another, views or beliefs that are commonly held about money, and by making it possible to react to them according to graduated degrees of acceptance and rejection, the questionnaire does provide a rough index to how people feel about money, a topic we shall explore in depth at a number of points in this book. For a further analysis of this questionnaire, see Appendix, pages 223–227.

Part Two

In a world that is operated by and largely for adults, children have relatively little power. What power they do have lies in their claim on adult responsibility and in their ability to charm or annoy—sources of influence that are not very reliable and that can have unpredictable results. Money is the first form of dependable, impersonal power that is put into their hands. Through spending it, they learn how to get people outside their families—strangers—to do their bidding and grant their wishes. A child with five dollars to spend is as important in economic terms as an adult with five dollars to spend. Through using monetary power, the child learns something of what it is like to be an adult.

I was six years old when my uncle handed me my first silver dollar. It seemed enormous. I wanted to spend it, but my parents insisted on depositing it in my savings account. I found their decision depressing. At that age, money was to be spent, not saved. Money that was banked disappeared, never to be seen again.

I spent the next dollar I was given for candy. My family disapproved and chided me for being improvident. I felt guilty.

When I was about seven I began to receive an allowance of ten cents every Saturday. I remember agonizing over how best to spend the weekly stipend. When decisions were especially difficult, my weekly shopping spree could last two hours.

When I was eight I sold newspapers and learned that money earned is infinitely more valuable than money received as a gift. I saved some of my earnings, not to bank them but to spend them on obsolete American coins—broad copper cents, flying-eagle pennies, two- and three-cent pieces, and half dimes. I also bought a few Confederate notes and marvelled that a hundred-dollar bill could be purchased for twenty-five cents. My early interest in old money has in recent years reappeared in the form of the study of ancient coinage.

In high school, my knowledge of money became more sophisticated. A social studies teacher asked us to select a stock listed on the New York Stock Exchange, observe its price changes for a few weeks, and try to explain them in terms of current events. I picked a company called Grigsby-Grunow and followed its career for a number of years. It disappeared in one of the market shake-outs of the 1930s. This was my introduction to the Wall Street "money game" so exuberantly described by "Adam Smith." Over the years I have found that the Wall Street money game has few peers as a spectator sport. Nor am I alone in this: Witness the millions who have watched Louis Rukeyser's "Wall Street Week" on Public Television every Friday night.

I have always found my experiences with money by turns exciting, depressing, anxiety- and guilt-provoking, but above all, fascinating. Of course we all find money interesting, if only because our existence in today's world involves so much acquiring, possessing, and spending of it. But my interest in money has transcended conventional attitudes. I have been intrigued by the fact that money has a special effect on people's mood, attitudes, and behavior; I have observed that what people say about money is often at odds with their behavior toward and with money.

My first years as a professional psychologist were spent as a counselor, a role that gave me a valuable opportunity to do a great deal of thinking about the disparity between what people say and what they do. It often occurred to me that money figured in many of the difficulties that troubled my clients. Professional literature in psychology was of little help to me here. Although there was much that dealt with sexual problems, very little was concerned with the part played by money in neurotic patterns of thought and behavior.

As I moved out of the counselor role and became more involved in college teaching and research, I expanded and deepened my knowledge of personality and social psychology, investigating such areas as creativity, need for achievement, leadership, group processes, authoritarian attitudes, and the effects of crowding. My early interest in the part played by money in everyday life problems continued, and I kept on the lookout for material that might shed some light on the motives underlying attitudes toward and with money. I also conducted a few studies on my own. In the course of my periodic monitoring of the psychological research literature, I encountered no general discussions of the psychology of money, but I did find a number of studies in which money figured as an incidental element—for example, as reward or reinforcement, as incentive, or as indicator of self-esteem. Over the years I have collected these odds and ends of data and have found them useful in developing concepts of the psychology of money.

In recent years, a few books that discuss psychological factors of money-related behavior have appeared. These have been written by authors having a psychoanalytic orientation, who treat money as a pathogenic element—a source of neurosis. These authors have ignored a fact that to me seems obvious—namely, that money is an artifact, like written language or the wheel, that is essentially neither good nor bad, that can be used in helpful or destructive ways, but that has on balance done a great deal to improve the human condition. While there is little doubt that neurosis and other forms of psychopathology often involve money, it is also true that money often facilitates healthy, creative, and integrative behavior. And it occurred to me that what was needed was a book that would present a *balanced* treatment of the psychology of money, one that would deal with a broad range of the ways in which money affects human behavior, and not only in psychopathological terms.

These considerations have been very much on my mind as I developed this book. I hope that it will give readers a better and more complete understanding than they now have of how money affects their own thoughts, feelings, and actions, as well as those of others. I hope, too, that it will convince its readers that the social and psychological conditions that are ordinarily attributed to money—differences in social status, for example—are not caused by money, but are the effect of fundamental behavior patterns that involve all of us without our awareness. Money does not cause human misery but is rather the means whereby we inflict misery on one another and even on ourselves when we are so inclined.

As we examine the part money plays in human behavior it should become apparent that the psycho-*logic* of money is not the everyday logic we use in much of our behavior with or toward money. Our everyday logic often leads us to misjudge the motives and behavior of others and of ourselves. These misjudgments are usually unimportant, but sometimes they lead to major errors that worsen our relationships with others or undermine our mental health and sense of well-being.

In order to present the psychological facts about money in settings that make them understandable, we must examine many aspects of money-related behavior. The psychology of money is embedded in a matrix of personality-and-social psychology. Hence we must discuss behavioral trends and patterns that at first glance seem unrelated to money but that underlie key money-oriented attitudes and behaviors. Inasmuch as personality-and-social psychology is concerned with the ways we interact and regard one another and ourselves, an understanding of the psychology of money should in the end lead to a better understanding of ourselves and others.

In writing this book I have been stimulated and encouraged by many colleagues and friends. I would like especially to acknowledge the advice and help of Charles Johnson, retired advertising executive and amateur classicist; C. Daniel Vencill, Assistant Professor of Economics, San Francisco State University; Robert N. Schweitzer, Associate Professor of Economics, San Francisco State University; Hubert J. Bernhard, Copy Editor, the *San Francisco Examiner*; Arthur V. Toupin, Vice Chairman of the Board, Bank of America; and Fredi Lindgren, my wife and co-researcher.

Henry Clay Lindgren, Ph.D.
Department of Psychology
San Francisco State University

1 Why does money matter?

Wine maketh merry: but money answereth all things.
—ECCLESIASTES, 10:19

Even the blind can see money.   —CHINESE PROVERB

Money is like a sixth sense—and you can't make use of
the other five without it.   —SOMERSET MAUGHAM

The cheerfully cynical lyrics of a song in *Cabaret* tell us that
"Money makes the world go 'round."

Like many other foolish-but-wise sayings that reflect what
we have feared but have been reluctant to express openly, this
claim contains more than a kernel of truth. The world—society
as we know it—would come to a grinding halt if suddenly there
were no money. The vast, incredibly complex mechanism of
our world is programmed to respond to money and to nothing
else. For example, a vending machine will produce a candy bar
only if the proper coins are inserted in the designated slot, and
drug-abuse clinics, reforestation projects, and municipal sewage
treatment plants must remain on the drawing boards until they
are funded. Would-be home owners must make a suitable down
payment and sign a promise to pay off the balance of a loan
before the machinery of lending agencies and construction firms
can be set in motion to supply them with the house of their
dreams.

The push that money alone can give does seem to make
the world go 'round. It is a small step from this disturbing
thought to the corollary that money makes *us* go 'round, too.

But despite appearances, money alone does not make the
world go 'round; not coins and bills, but people plus money,
have the power to do all the good or terrible things we men-

tioned. In and of itself money has no power, yet we respond to it as we do to nothing else. Why do we, the builders and operators of the systems and machines of the world, respond as we do to money?

The answer to this simple but fundamental question is incredibly complex.

Few people, experts included, have any idea why money turns us on and gets us to make the world go 'round. Many a sage has nibbled at the answer, but few have reached to the heart of it. Not until psychologists began to explore the substrata of man's social behavior were we in a position to frame explanations for money's effect on us. The psychology of money is an understanding of the effects money has on people's behavior. The effects appear in the way we evaluate ourselves and others, as well as in the value we place on rewards and goals. Money may facilitate or interfere with human interaction. It arouses and excites; but it also inhibits and depresses. Although it is we who have created money and given it its power, we often regard it as an element beyond our control—almost as though it were an omnipotent deity. In spite of the fact that money can be measured in very precise, specific terms—to the very penny—we remain unsure of how much power it actually has. The indeterminate nature of its power makes it possible for us to attribute all kinds of influence to it and to believe that it causes or can cure personal problems that are essentially unrelated to, and unresponsive to, money. Yet the psychology of money was not invented yesterday. History furnishes one example after another of those who seem to have understood why people respond as they do to money. John Law was such a man, as was Benjamin Franklin; more recent times have produced financiers like Jay Gould and John Pierpont Morgan. Today, too, individuals who are unusually competent in money matters exercise considerable power: They have a feeling for how much money it takes, and under what conditions, to get people to accomplish what is needed.

But those who understand the psychology of money never talk about it. They know that few would be interested in their insights; no one thinks he needs lessons to understand money. Yet rare is the person who is deeply aware of how money affects his behavior. Most of us, for example, could not predict how we would behave if suddenly possessed of a great deal of money or faced by a severe loss. And even if we could say *how* we'd behave, could we say *why?*

The individual who understands the "what" and the "how" of money has a definite advantage over his fellow citizens, but he is eclipsed by the person who also understands the "why," just as the electrical engineering graduate is no match for the engineer who also has his doctorate in physics. As in any field of human endeavor, the one who knows "why" has a special advantage.

In many areas of human experience—marriage, sexual relations, parenthood, career, health, etc.—the "experts" are eager to probe the "why" of our behavior. They may not agree among themselves, but the gurus are readily available, both professional and amateur. The passion to educate—or at least to advise—is hard to keep under control.

The Experts on Money Matters

There are many who want to advise us about money matters, and a few do it very well. In the newspapers Sylvia Porter gives down-to-earth advice on economic matters, and Milton Moskowitz's "Money Tree" tells us about struggles for power between and within giant corporations. Louis Rukeyser's "Wall Street Week" on Public Television is both entertaining and illuminating. In addition there are the financial sections of newspapers and magazines, and the several specialized publications like the *Wall Street Journal, Barron's, Business Week, Fortune, Forbes* and *Money*. But these sources, useful as they are, are preoccupied with the "what" and "how" of money's behavior; they rarely mention the "why."

Nor are professional economists of much assistance in helping us understand the "why" of money. They are generally preoccupied with the ebb and flow of forces in the marketplace and have little of value to tell the average person about money and motivation.

In their analyses and projections, economists treat money abstractly, as an element to be punched into computer cards along with other statistical data such as gross national product, housing starts, prime interest rate, and new unemployment claims. Our attitudes toward money, our belief about the part it plays in our lives, our responses to it, and our feelings about the relationship between work and money are not the province of the economist; nor is he much concerned about how ignorance and misperception of these motivational aspects of money warp our judgment and aggravate our personal problems.

For an understanding of the psychology of money, then, we turn from the professional and academic money people to the psychologists and psychoanalysts. A fair number of psychological studies have involved money, but few have focused upon it directly.[1] Money has been included as only one element among many others in investigations concerned with learning, altruism, decision making, and industrial morale.

Psychoanalytic theory, on the other hand, deals with monetary motives directly, but it is difficult for the ordinary citizen to apply such a theory to the events of his everyday life. For example, Sigmund Freud, the father of psychoanalysis, maintained that our attitudes and behavior toward money were determined during toilet training, when we established control over the anal sphincter. Habits of thrift, Freud said, were derived from the pleasure of retaining the contents of the large intestine; in symbolic terms, then, money, is excrement. We will have more to say about this theory in Chapter 8. For the present let us suggest only that Freudian theory puts the average person in somewhat of a bind when it comes to understanding the economic problems of everyday adult life.

The Why of Money

The scarcity of helpful information about the "why" of our behavior toward and with money is surprising, considering that money questions are at or near the top of the list for almost everyone. Our own common sense is of little help, and the experts have been singularly uninterested. Hence we find ourselves alone in our attempts to answer such questions as: *Why*

---

[1]A notable exception has been that of George Katona, now Emeritus Professor of Economics and Psychology of the University of Michigan. Katona has been primarily interested in the behavior of the consumer.

do we spend more than we should? *Why* can't we save? *Why* do we feel irritated by or hostile toward those who have more money than we do and guilty toward those who have less? Why do we feel both guilty and annoyed when we are asked for money? Why do we feel that we never have enough money no matter how successfully we pursue it?

The answers to these questions are complex because our attitudes and feelings about money are woven into the entire fabric of what psychologists call our "self-system." Our money problems involve elements deep in our personalities that often obscure the direct and decisive solutions we would like. It is no news that we sometimes deal irrationally with money. Let us consider a few examples:

Maria Santos lives in a dilapidated apartment with four children born out of wedlock and a man who is not their father. Her welfare support amounts to a little over $600 a month. Her rent is $200, and she spends between $250 and $300 per month for food, depending on the number of relatives and friends who share her place for brief or extended periods. She feels that the amount she receives from welfare is not enough to live on. During the five years she has lived in the apartment, she has bought food and household supplies at a small grocery store a block away. She could save about twenty percent on her grocery expenses—between $50 and $60 per month—by patronizing the large supermarket on her block. Her social worker asks her why she shops at the little store when she could save both time and money by going to the supermarket. Maria says it is because the people in the grocery store speak Spanish. The social worker points out that most of the clerks in the supermarket speak Spanish as well. Maria thanks the social worker for the suggestion but makes no change in her shopping habits.

It is in Maria Santos's best financial interest to shop at the supermarket and save. Nevertheless, she and millions of other poor people do not behave according to their best interests where money is concerned for reasons that seem inconsistent with common sense. We will have more to say in later chapters about the attitudes toward money of Maria Santos and her friends. Consider for the moment a second example—the story of Pamela and Carl Holmgren.

Mr. Holmgren is 55. A decline in sales has led his company to close the division where he has been employed for fifteen years. Rather than be laid off, Carl requests early retirement. As soon as his retirement has become effective, Mr. and Mrs. Holmgren prepare to take a two-month 'round-the-world tour. In discussing the forthcoming trip with family and friends, Carl and Pamela do not mention that the trip will reduce their life savings from $10,000 to $4,000. They seem almost not to realize that once the holiday is over they will be hard pressed to make ends meet on a pension of only $350 per month.

The Holmgrens' behavior, like that of Maria Santos, cannot be explained logically. Their motives are different from hers, however; we will discuss them in our chapter on money and mental health.

What Maria Santos and the Holmgrens share is the problem of insufficient funds. Surely we should not claim that it is irrational to "feel the pinch"—or should we? Comparisons between families at various income levels make us wonder. In 1978 the *San Francisco Chronicle* published a series of feature stories that told of the monetary difficulties experienced by families the editors had selected as representative of the economic spectrum, ranging from poverty to wealth. A family of seven on relief, as expected, said that they had difficulty in getting along on their annual allowance of $5,520. But another family of five said they had to economize in order to get along on $27,000 a year. The father moonlighted and the mother held two part-time jobs, and still they did not have quite anough money. A millionaire couple economized by buying used furniture in junk shops and said that they stopped buying beef three years ago because its price had risen to unreasonable levels.

The difficulties described by the families featured in the *Chronicle* stories resembled those that beset families surveyed by *Fortune* some thirty years earlier. *Fortune's* reporters found that families in the $25,000–$30,000 income bracket had as much trouble living within their means as did those at the $5,000–$6,000 level.

Incomes have changed markedly since the late 1940s, but people and their money problems have not. Families at the $12,000 income level think their budgetary difficulties would disappear if they could only raise their income to $15,000; but those fortunate ones who do reach that level quickly discover that what they really need is $20,000 a year, and so it goes. How much money is "enough" clearly does not depend on quantity. It depends, instead, on attitudes, values, and patterns of behavior that are remarkably similar from person to person. It is this similarity that enables psychologists to study human behavior and identify its fundamental trends.

Each of the individuals we have mentioned is troubled by money-related problems whose solutions seem ridiculously simple. Maria Santos would save money by buying at the supermarket; the Holmgrens would avoid much future difficulty by not taking the expensive trip; and people with average incomes or above should have little difficulty in deciding not to buy goods and services they cannot afford. These solutions are obvious, yet we know that the individuals involved will not apply them. The difficulty is, of course, that the solutions are simple but the reasons why they cannot be applied are complex. The people concerned do not feel free to take the steps they know will resolve their pressing problems and make life easier. The point is that what seems to be a money difficulty always turns out to be a problem involving both our psychological make-up and the social forces that bear upon us.

Yet there is no doubt that money plays an important role both in the problems we have described and in reactions of the individuals concerned. Money's effect on us is different from that of anything else we encounter. Yet it has no power in and of itself, as we noted at the beginning of this chapter. Therefore *we* must have given money its unique power to influence us, we who invented it in the first place.

How money was given its ability to influence its creators is an interesting story, or rather, a series of stories. We present them in the next two chapters, in the form of a psychohistory of money.

2 Psychological origins of money

He that loveth silver shall not be satisfied with silver, nor
he that loveth abundance with increase.
                                        —ECCLESIASTES, 5:10

Grace is given of God, but knowledge is bought in the
market.   —ARTHUR HUGH CLOUGH

The use of money is all the advantage there is in having
money.   —BENJAMIN FRANKLIN

It is easier to use money or to talk about it than to define it.
The British economist Sir Ralph Hawtrey (1928) said: "Money
is one of those concepts which, like a teaspoon or an umbrella,
but unlike an earthquake or a buttercup, are definable primarily
by the use or purpose they serve." The American economist,
Charles R. Whittlesy (1967), defined money as "the medium in
which prices are expressed, debts discharged, goods and services paid for and bank reserves held."

Whittlesy is of course describing modern money that can
be deposited in banks and transferred from one person to another or from one account to another by checks or even by
electronic means. Ancient money took a more concrete form—
that of commodity money—although societies that had banking
systems had bills of exchange that were in some respects similar
to the debt money in which most transactions are made today.

Most specialists in monetary history take the view that
money was developed in ancient times as a way of making barter
more efficient. This is a practical view that appeals to common
sense, but it is too narrow for our purposes, for it does not
explain why money became psychologically important. To an-

swer that question, we must return to modern research and theory in psychology and sociology.

Human beings are social organisms. Our drive or need to be with others has utilitarian value; it makes possible such cooperative activities as gathering, processing, and storing food, taking protective measures against an unfriendly environment, and implementing those interpersonal arrangements that ensure the survival of the species. But over and beyond these fundamental collective actions, we consistently invest time and energy in social activities that have apparently no practical value, at least in terms of survival. If psychology teaches us anything, it is that explanations of human behavior based on purely practical considerations are incomplete.

The fact is that much of our social behavior has little or nothing to do with survival. It appears that being with others is often its own reward.

Human beings are not alone in this. Much of the behavior of the other higher animals has nothing to do directly with hunting, food-gathering, physical comfort, or sex; it seems instead to meet a need to associate with others of the same species. Experiments with both humans and other animals show that a significant outcome of this purely social relationship is stimulation and arousal. We may not be aware that chatting with a neighbor or sitting cheek by jowl in a crowded bus is stimulating, but research shows that the mere presence of others produces a degree of hormonal activity not present when we are alone.

Still other studies have demonstrated that social stimulation is essential for normal development. If they are isolated from others of their kind, human young and the young of certain other mammals will develop subnormally in intelligence and in the ability to cope with new situations. But we do not need psychological studies to tell us how important the presence of others is, for it is widely known that solitary confinement is among the cruelest forms of punishment.

A case can be made that some of the most important human inventions—language, to name the most significant— evolved because they helped people get together. Certainly barter should be included among such inventions. At first glance, barter merely seems to be a practical device whereby we secure needed goods or services in exchange for goods or services surplus to our needs; but there is more to it than meets the eye.

Bartering for Fun and Profit

In a survey of primitive money and the social conditions preceding its use, Paul Einzig (1966) notes that barter is a major form of recreation and entertainment in many primitive communities. Participants appear to enjoy it for its own sake, aside from any practical gain they may derive by disposing of surplus goods and acquiring needed ones.

As a social transaction, barter is a flexible arrangement. It can be a clean-cut, open-and-shut affair, without dangling loose ends that require continued personal involvement and interaction. It is thus unlike transactions within the family or the political structure of the community, which often lead to new transactions and further involvement. If the participants wish, however, bartering can also serve as the basis for long interpersonal relationships: A satisfied barterer is likely to seek his favorite bartering partners when he has surpluses to be traded or when he wants only to socialize.

In these respects, bartering is psychologically no different from a great many transactions involving money. As purchaser and seller encounter each other, there is social interaction and arousal. Mail-order transactions may dehumanize such interactions by placing them on a higher level of abstraction, but even they have their share of arousal. The compleat gardener's thrill in leafing through the new spring seed catalog is matched only by the excitement of the mail order seed merchant who opens his post office box on a Monday morning and is inundated by a flood of orders. The fact that most of us engage in a great deal more purchasing than is necessary suggests that it meets a genuine need. In short, the need to encounter others and experience mild arousal is an important one, and commercial transactions provide a convenient way of satisfying this need. Economic activities satisfy other psychological needs, of course, as we shall discover later.

We should also note that one of the advantages of monetary

transactions over barter is that money enables people to buy and sell more frequently and thus experience more social interaction and arousal. In human behavior, the rule seems to be that if *some* is good, *more* is better. This is especially true of the stimulation and arousal we receive from social interaction. Constantine A. Doxiadis (1970), the Greek urban planner, has observed that of all the animals, man alone seeks to increase his contacts.

The coming together of our ancestors to form villages and, later on, cities was an expression of the human need to increase contacts. Money was especially suited to city life. The services that city folk have always needed and provided for one another do not fit a barter system very well; such services are exchanged more readily if they are priced and paid for with money. Rural people are less likely to need the services that city folk think are essential, and in ancient times what they needed could be secured as easily by barter as by money. Hence the use of money increased with the growth of cities, while barter lingered on in rural areas centuries after it had disappeared in the cities. But barter was the rule long before money made its appearance, and it was bartering that made villages possible in the first place.

We have very little information about the beginnings of barter, but we can speculate. Perhaps in earlier prehistoric phases a skilled maker of, say, flint tools, would seek out a successful hunter and haggle over the relative value of arrowheads and animal skins. As villages sprouted in localities where agriculture developed, markets were set up, and products that were frequently exchanged came to serve as standards by which other goods and services were valued. Villages sharing common languages often became federated; they organized into states whose governments developed standards—modes of conduct, religious values, and measures to be employed in the exchange of goods and commodities. Specified quantities of foodstuffs were often used as general measures of value. Observation of the trading customs of primitive tribes today suggests that such standards can be used in simplistic ways. Einzig, for instance, notes that even in the recent past, primitive peoples lacking a well-developed sense of value sometimes traded bowls for the amount of grain or oil they held, or exchanged slaves for their weight in salt.

As communities in ancient times developed standardized measures of weight and volume, barterers were able to take a significant step toward a monetary society. Measures of grain became the accepted standard of value in many early civilizations. This meant that goods and services of all types could be priced in terms of what they were worth at the grain market. A metal worker who wanted to obtain a sheep could set a value, in terms of units of grain, on a sword he had made and exchange it for sheep having the equivalent value in grain. It was not necessary to convert the sword into grain and the grain into sheep.

Once the problems of day-to-day survival were solved, the people of many early communities invested their energies in the expansion of commercial activities. They devised systems of extending credit and recording debts. The accepted standards of value—baskets of grain, head of cattle, metal ingots of a certain size, or whatever—became units of account in which such transactions were recorded. In fact, written language owes its beginnings in large part to the necessity of recording commercial transactions.

Slaves, and Other Commodities

The goods and other items employed as standards of economic value have varied widely over the millenia and in various parts of the globe. Einzig notes that hogsheads of tobacco served as the unit of account in Colonial Virginia, almonds were used in India during the 15th and 16th Centuries, beaver skins were employed in transactions among North American Indians and traders during the 18th and 19th Centuries, and butter was the standard unit in medieval Norway. The slave girl, or *kumal*, was the unit of value in Ireland during the early years of its history. The *Tain*, the Irish epic poem said to be the first to appear in Western Europe, referred to a chariot worth thrice seven kumals, and St. Patrick reported that he had to pay the economic equivalent of fifteen slaves in exchange for a safe conduct when he visited Western Ireland.

Cattle tallied by the head were a common unit of value in

ancient times and still serve in that capacity in certain areas of Africa today. Indeed, we have derived a number of money-related words from ancient words for cattle. The Latin word for a head of cattle is *pecus*, and the word *pecunia* indicated "wealth, means, and property." *Pecuniary* is a modern English derivative, as is *peculiar*, which still carries some of its earlier meaning of "exclusive property or privilege." Latin, like most European languages, descended from a much earlier group of languages, commonly termed Indo-European. No one knows where the original Indo-Europeans lived, but scholars agree that cattle played an important part in their economy. The northern offshoot of the Indo-European word from which *pecus* was derived appeared eventually as *Vieh* in modern German and as *fee* and *fief* in English—words that both denote economic concepts.

In retrospect it seems inevitable that metal should have become a unit of value; but this apparent inevitability may only reflect the bias of our own culture, which takes metal objects for granted. Ancient societies used little metal; they made far more use of bone, stone, shell, and baked clay.

A number of ancient societies continued to prefer commodity-based units of value even after the appearance of the lumps of metal that constituted early money. Egypt is a good example. As early as the Third Millenium B.C. the Egyptians found that expressing value in terms of a specific weight of copper,[1] termed the *deben*, facilitated barter. Some authorities maintain that the Egyptians may thus have used copper rings or coils of copper wire as a form of money. This view is supported by the fact that the concept of money was expressed in hieroglyphic writing as a bent wire. One would think that with this brave beginning the Egyptians would have been among the first to coin money, but they were not; instead they continued to use barter long after monetary transactions were the norm in other Mediterranean countries. One reason for this is that metals of all kinds were in short supply in Egypt, the closest source being the mines in the distant and dangerous desert of the Sinai Peninsula. In any event, the ancient Egyptians never

---

[1]Three ounces, troy.

used copper rings as money, for instead of counting them in making a purchase, they *weighed* them, thus treating them as a commodity.

The ancient Egyptians were not the only ones to realize the advantage of employing standard weights of metal as a measure of value. The Code of Hammurabi, a collection of laws in force in the Mesopotamian world at the end of the Third Millenium B.C., specified that surgeons, veterinarians, and skilled workers should be paid in silver, usually in ingot form, while unskilled laborers were to be paid in grain. The Code was insistent on the social difference between the two kinds of payment: The law specified that if a barmaid insisted on being paid in silver, she was to be arrested and thrown into the water.

In spite of the fact that barter was a rather crude and awkward arrangement for exchanging goods and services, the Egyptians under the Ptolemies developed a sophisticated system of banking based on units of grain. Bank headquarters were in Alexandria; farmers could deposit wheat in one of the branch banks and issue checks that were negotiable—i.e. that would be honored at any government granary. Why, then, did the Egyptians fail to develop a monetary system? The answer, according to Einzig, lies in the fact that everyday life in Egypt was to a considerable degree planned and controlled. An autocratic government saw to it that change and instability were kept to a minimum, and a conservative and essentially passive people collaborated willingly with authorities to keep things as they were. The spirit of this collaboration between governors and governed is reflected in Egyptian art, where a parade of stereotyped images, march in lockstep across monumemts and walls in a format that remained virtually unchanged for three thousand years. Egyptian culture resisted novelty, in either invented or imported form; it had no need for money, whose introduction would have been profoundly unsettling. This stubborn, peasantlike preference for barter persisted in Egypt long after the Greeks established mints in Alexandria and other major centers. Records cited by Einzig show that as late as the 7th century A.D., on the eve of the Moslem invasion, only a third of Egyptian farmers were paying their rents in money, while the others still paid in grain and other commodities.

The First Coins

If necessity is the mother of invention, then a taste for novelty, enterprise, and adventure must be its father. Thus we must turn to the Greek world, with its turbulence, excitement, and creativity, to find the first coiners of money—that is currency that could be accepted at sight.

By the 7th Century B.C. in the Mediterranean region the metal employed in commercial transactions changed hands in the form of *dumps*—bean-shaped lumps. It is not known who first stamped dumps with identifying symbols, but the best evidence points to the Greek traders in Lydia, a region in Western Anatolia that was ruled by King Gyges between about 686 and 656 B.C. Lydia seems to have been a quiet, pastoral country, not a very important place in the international scheme of things in that day; but through Lydia passed a major trade route between the West and East. Even more important than this is the fact that the gravel of Lydia's rivers produced gold. Indeed gold was a major commodity of the area.

The first coins were crude and unattractive. They were little oval blobs of electrum, a blend of gold and silver, with a striated, corduroy-like surface on one side and punch marks in the form of an oblong and two smaller squares on the other. Some of the punch marks contained a crude design: a running fox, a stag's head, or an X. A few years later, the striations were replaced by the forepart or head of a goat, facing cocks or cocks' heads, or a lion's head. Barclay V. Head (1911), in his authoritative review of ancient coinage, speculated that the lion's head represented the royal seal and that coins bearing the other designs were probably issued by wealthy traders or bankers to meet the needs of markets or fairs held in connection with religious festivals such as those celebrated in the city of Sardes during the reign of Gyges.

The Greek historian, Herodotus, writing in the 5th Century B.C., credited the Lydians with the invention of coinage. Herodotus also noted that the young women of Lydia offered themselves as prostitutes in order to earn money for their marriage dowries, but he does not make it clear whether this unusual practice had anything to do with the invention of coinage.

For thousands of years before the first coins appeared in Lydia, governmental authorities in all civilized countries had regulated the weights and measures used in trade and had specified the amount of metal or other commodity to be employed as a standard of value. The silver ingots of the Babylonians that we mentioned earlier were probably much like the dumpy little coins that appeared in Lydia 1500 years later. But the Lydian inventions met with a degree of acceptance that was not accorded the Babylonian commodity money. The Greek merchants and their customers were psychologically ready for a medium of exchange that carried what amounted to an ancient version of the *"Good Housekeeping* seal of approval," an exchange medium that could be accepted at sight.

The coinage of money was clearly an idea whose time had come, for within a few years kingdoms and city states on both sides of the Aegean Sea were minting similar coins. During the final years of the 7th Century B.C. they tumbled forth in rich and varied array, bearing images of animals, birds, fish, fruit, weapons, and household utensils. Most of these coins were of silver, rather than of electrum or gold, for reasons that we will discuss later in this chapter.

Coins as Propaganda

The designs used on the coins minted by the Aegean states and their imitators represented the civic symbols or "trademarks" of the states that issued them. Inasmuch as the line between secular and religious authority was blurred or even nonexistent in that period, the symbols had religious connotations, too. Each of them referred directly or indirectly to the god, goddess, or nymph whose sponsorship the local population believed it enjoyed. Within a few years, many states were issuing coins stamped with the physical representation of their divine sponsor. Athens, for example, issued handsome silver coins that bore on one side the head of Athena, helmeted and ready for battle, and on the other, her mascot, the owl. Other city states also abandoned earlier, nature-oriented designs, and issued coins bearing images of Zeus, Hera, Apollo, Poseidon, or Artemis, as well as lesser divinities, among whom Hercules and Tyche (the goddess of luck or fortune) were favorites.

To the extent that a coin identified its city-state it also served as a bit of propaganda, proclaiming throughout and beyond the Greek world the status and power of the authority that had minted it. In order to prevent confusion, since some gods served as patrons of a number of states, most mints soon began to mark their coins with the names of the cities in which they were issued. This practice further enhanced the propaganda value of the coins. The coins also bore a psychological message for the citizens of the states that issued them. The owl-stamped coins handled by the people of Athens were a daily reminder of their identity as Athenians. In this respect, the ancient city states were responding to the fundamental human desire to use personalized artifacts as a reassurance of personal reality. We all acquire and use objects that become aspects of our identity—clothing, purses or wallets, watches and rings, jewelry, automobiles, books, art objects and so forth. The psychological importance of these objects becomes apparent when they are lost or stolen. When the psychological support we gained from their frequent use vanishes, we feel bereft, as though missing a part of ourselves. Among the many other things that reminded the Athenians of their ethnic identity—traditions; rituals and ceremonies; shared interest in public events; and the buildings, streets, and other physical features of the city where they lived—the little silver owls (their own term for the coins) helped to integrate their community.

Nor was the propaganda value of coins lost on the great conquerors. The Persian kings, Darius and Xerxes, issued gold *darics* and silver *sigloi* depicting themselves in a fighting position, kneeling and drawing a bow. Their efforts were rather crude—the identity of the kneeling figure was not clear, and numismatists today have difficulty telling which coins were issued by which ruler—but nevertheless the Persian coinage had considerable economic, political, and psychological importance. It provided a money standard for the millions of people of diverse cultures in the Persian realm; it was a constant reminder that they were subjects of the great king; and if it did not give them the kind of identity they wanted or enjoyed, at least it placed them on notice that they had something in common with people in other parts of the empire.

The gold *darics* of the Persian kings are now quite rare. When Alexander the Great conquered the Persian armies, he melted down the unartistic darics and struck *staters* of elegant design bearing a winged victory. Silver from melted down sigloi appeared in the form of *tetradrachms* with the head of Heracles on the obverse and Zeus enthroned on the reverse. Both gold and silver coins bore the words "of Alexander the king." As instruments of propaganda, Alexander's staters and tetradrachms were much more impressive than the darics and sigloi they replaced.

Coins Get a Head

The Greeks had issued numerous coins bearing portraits of gods in human form, and some states had even included the names of their rulers. With a few minor exceptions, however, no state up to this point had issued coins bearing the head of a living person. History does not record the basis for this omission, but it was probably motivated by democratic considerations. The Greek city states were close-knit communities that seldom comprised more than ten thousand citizens. Relations with leaders tended to be on a personal, face-to-face basis. It is easy to see why the people would be reluctant to place on a coin the portrait of a head of state whom they saw as "one of us." Such a gesture would suggest that the ruler was the equal of the gods or demigods who had theretofore been so recognized. A leader's demand to be honored by a portrait coin would have amounted to boastful pride, or hubris, a challenge inviting the wrath of the jealous gods.

Alexander's dazzling success as a conqueror changed the ancient world in many ways. The city states became minor elements in a vast imperial scheme. The king was no longer "one of us," but became an abstract symbol of power—like a god. Alexander encouraged this belief. On one occasion he ordered his Macedonian soldiers to prostrate themselves before him, Persian style. They refused. They admired and loved him, but they drew the line at worship. Alexander's obsession with divinity persisted however. A few months before his death in

323 B.C. he demanded that local governments recognize his divine status. They complied, but the spirit of democracy still prevailed in some of the Greek city states. Sparta gave tongue-in-cheek compliance: The decree published there read, "Since Alexander wishes to be a god, let him be a god."

Once Alexander was dead, all doubt about his divinity vanished. Coins bearing the head of Hercules continued to be issued in Alexander's name by local mints, but Hercules now distinctly resembled Alexander. As far as the man in the street was concerned, the face *was* that of the deified Alexander. These coins, which circulated throughout the ancient world for hundreds of years, gave visible support to the Alexander legend.

Seleucus and Ptolemy, two of the generals who divided the empire after Alexander's death, quickly established their claim to the hearts and minds of their new subjects by issuing coins on which they replaced the Herculean Alexander with their own portraits, thus establishing a pattern followed by monarchs and dictators from that time onward. The descendents of Seleucus not only had themselves protrayed on the coinage, they also referred to themselves in divine terms—as "Dionysius the god made manifiest," as "Savior" (an epithet formerly applied only to the gods), or merely as "God."

If the coin legends did not actually say "Seleucus satisfies," or "Antiochus anticipates your needs," the message was there by implication. The principle that apparently guided these Syrian kings as they chose their titles should be obvious to anyone who has cast a critical eye on modern advertising: "Never bother with modest claims, but make them as extravagant as you can." And then, as now, the relationship between claim and product quality was dubious. The later Seleucid kings did not behave at all like gods. Instead, they let their country deteriorate while they occupied themselves with bloody squabbles against claimants to the throne.

History has its own way of dealing with braggarts. A comparison of the lengths of the Syrian kings' titles and the lengths of their reigns shows that the longer the title and the more divine virtues a ruler claimed for himself, the shorter was his reign and the bloodier his death. Clinical psychologists would not find this relationship surprising: Pomposity and pretension are always indications of insecurity. The uneasiness of the Syrian kings was thus a possible cause of their extravagant claims.

The divine pretensions of the Syrian kings obviously had little influence on the men who killed them. Perhaps the assassins were skeptical men; or perhaps they were illiterates who, unable to read coin legends, did not know they were deposing gods.

The Financing of a Civilization

The pre-Alexandrian coinage of the Greek world was simple but elegant. Lovers of antiquity claim that some of the earlier coins, especially those of Syracuse, are the most beautiful ever struck. The coins of the post-Alexander era are considered more handsome than beautiful and are generally more elaborate than their predecessors. Favored was the large silver four-drachm piece, the tetradrachm,[2] which became virtually the universal monetary standard in the pre-Christian era. Hundreds of millions of these attractive, flashy coins were minted. This vast amount of coinage underwrote the costly wars waged among the Seleucid kings, the other descendants of Alexander's generals, and the dozen or so princeling upstarts of the day, but the money also financed a vast amount of trade and economic development, and paid for the construction of port facilities, theaters, public baths, temples, marketplaces, and government buildings. Science, literature, philosophy, and the arts flourished as more enduring by-products of the economic expansion of the Alexandrine era. The era may be seen as a dynamic social movement, which swept up the elements of classical Greek culture and expanded and integrated them in a way that created a Greek-speaking civilization for millions of people from Hispania to the upper reaches of the Indus, in what is now Afghanistan.

None of this would have been possible without the flood of silver tetradrachms that expedited the flow of ideas as well as goods, and whose economic message was essentially the same in all parts of the known world. The commercial system based on silver coinage was a strong and resilient network or infrastructure, which made it possible for the Romans, a few cen-

---

[2]The tetradrachm weighed about .55 of a troy ounce.

turies later, to integrate the entire area into a single empire. But before we take up the psychology of Roman monetary practices, we should examine some important Greek developments concerning the relationship among the three metals used in ancient coins: silver, gold, and copper.

The Silver Standard

Silver coins were, as we have noted, the chief medium of exchange throughout the Mediterranean and Middle Eastern countries. The early electrum coins had been found to be unsatisfactory, for it was difficult to determine at sight what the relative proportions of gold and silver were. Although gold was an important commodity, and in ancient times was relatively cheaper in terms of silver than it is today,[3] its employment in coinage, at least until the Alexandrian era, was confined to special occasions—to financing a fleet when war was imminent, to distributing the loot resulting from a victory, or to paying off an indemnity imposed by a military defeat.

When silver stocks available to government authorities were insufficient to provide the coinage needed during an emergency, the gold decorations and sacrificial tripods in the temples were melted down; coins were struck off to meet the extraordinary demand on the public treasury. There was nothing slapdash about the gold coins issued under these circumstances, for they are among the most beautiful minted during the ancient period. Gold was considered the noblest of metals; it was revered, virtually worshipped. Its mystique rivaled that of a divinity. It is comforting to note that today, when religious practices are honored more in the breach than the observance, that the worship of this ancient and honored metal continues unabated.

The preference of the ancients for silver money may seem somewhat surprising, because of the widespread belief today that *all* money before the advent of paper currency was based

---

[3]The ratio between the value of gold and of silver in the ancient Greek world varied according to time and place, but a drachm weight of gold was generally worth from 13 to 15 times as much as a drachm of silver. As this is written, a troy ounce of gold is worth almost $500, or about twenty times as much as an ounce of silver.

on the gold standard. It is true that gold has been the international monetary standard ever since the Spanish began importing it from the New World, but silver has actually played a more significant role throughout monetary history. The words used in modern languages for money show how important silver has been. The French word for money, *argent*, also means "silver," and the Spanish word *denaro*, refers to a Roman silver coin, the *denarius*. The German word for money, *Geld*, might seem to be related to *Gold* (the same word as in English) but it is related instead to *gelten*, "to be worth" (cf. the English word "yield"). The word *gold* is instead derived from an ancient word meaning "yellow." Our own word "money" has nothing to do with either silver or gold, but comes from the Latin *moneta*, a reference to the temple of Juno Moneta, where Roman money was coined.

To return to ancient coinage, the Romans did create a monetary standard in which the *aureus*, and later the *solidus*, both gold coins, bore a fixed value in terms of silver and copper coins, but the aurei and solidi of Rome disappeared from Western Europe with the Western Roman Empire, and gold coins did not return until the Crusaders came back from the Middle East bringing Byzantine *hyperpyra* and Moslem *dinars* with them. But in the main, gold played only a minor role in the history of money in ancient times. Only in modern times have we come to think of it as synonymous with money. From a psychological point of view, however, our behavior toward and with money can be analyzed, studied, and explained without reference to gold, fascinating as it is.

Silver was the chief monetary metal in most countries in the ancient world and well into the early centuries of the Roman Empire. For one thing, the amount of gold available could not have supplied the commercial needs of the times. For another, coins struck from silver, a relatively hard metal, showed less wear than coins made of gold, a relatively soft metal.

People in ancient times were slow to recognize the economic efficiency made possible by the invention of coinage. To them, coins were still a commodity, and they were exchanged for goods and services in terms of their value as metal. In other words, a silver coin was worth about the same as an uncoined lump of silver of the same weight. The advantage of the official stamp or seal, of course, was that it certified the weight and purity of the metal and thus obviated the verification of its weight. In practice, of course, merchants and moneychangers often weighed coins as a check on possible forgery and loss of silver through wear, but undoubtedly the common practice in everyday transactions was to accept the coins at sight.

A typical small silver coin, like the Athenian *drachm*, weighing about a seventh of an ounce, represented a day's wage for a citizen during the 5th Century B.C. Small as the drachm was, even smaller units were needed for everyday transactions, like the purchase of half-dozen eggs or a handful of olives. To meet such needs, silver obols were issued, each representing a sixth of a drachm. But so low was the price put upon human labor and its products that even the obol represented too high a value for many transactions, and it was further divided into fractional coins. The tiniest of these, an eighth of an obol, was a minute pinhead of silver that bore the image of an owl on one side and an olive branch on the other and went by the sesqui-pedalian name of *hemitartemorion*.

Keeping track of these miniscule crumbs of silver must have been a headache for buyer and seller alike. We are told that tradespeople in the Agora, the marketplace of Athens, kept these fractions of an obol under their tongues, presumably because the coins would have dribbled out through the seams of a leather purse. And Zeus help the poor merchant who sneezed!

In spite of the awkwardness and inconvenience of these tiny coins, they must have been preferable to the known alternative—barter—for the Athenians continued to use them for about a hundred and fifty years, until a more practical form of money, bronze coinage, was introduced in the middle of the 4th Century B.C.

Copper: The First Fiat Currency

The Greek states of Sicily were the first to mint bronze coins, early in the 5th Century B.C. At first they attempted to tie the value of the coins to equivalent weights in uncoined metal, but after a few years the authorities discovered that smaller, short-weighted coins were accepted readily in place of the larger and heavier ones. Eventually most of the city states of the ancient world issued bronze or copper coins that possessed token, rather than bullion, value. These coins were the first forms of fiat currency—money whose value is arbitrarily set by government decree, without regard to the economic worth of the material of which it is made. The bronze and copper fiat coinage of ancient times was the money of the poor. These coins, which represented small fractions of the value of the more important silver and gold coins, enabled the poor to participate in the economic life of the day. It freed them from barter and enabled them to accumulate savings against the proverbial rainy day or for investments in enterprises that offered the promise of a better life.

History does not record the name of the genius who discovered that governments could magically convert a copper disk worth virtually nothing into a coin worth something. Whoever he was, his success at convincing his fellow citizens that something with no intrinsic value could be used to facilitate the exchange of things possessing real worth may at first seem to make him one of the greatest con men of all time. But he was actually one of the world's greatest benefactors, for he freed us from dependence on the availability of gold and silver bullion for our supply of money. This freedom is a two-edged sword, of course, for while it enables authorities to provide their constituents with as much money as they need, at the same time it enables governments that have difficulty living within their means to issue increasing amounts of money to finance their deficits.

No records indicate that ancient peoples objected to being hoodwinked when governments supplied them with small change having little intrinsic value. By then they had come to accept as coins of the realm any metal disks that bore the official stamp of the minting authorities. Money had become integrated into their lives; its daily use and acceptance had become a norm.

The social and economic advantages gained from silver coinage were thus further enhanced by the introduction of copper coins. As for the governmental authorities, they had discovered a way of raising money without the imposition of taxes, for they could now convert, say, an obol's worth of copper into coins having the buying power of a silver drachm. But the Greek authorities employed reasonable restraints on the issuance of bronze or copper fiat money and usually minted only enough for normal commercial needs: The city states and kingdoms of the pre-Roman world competed commercially with each other in the most vigorous terms, and there was no advantage in flooding the markets with a currency that would raise questions about a country's financial stability and responsibility.

The Romans: Inventors of Inflation

The Romans took a different view of things. Their drive to expand in a military and political sense was stronger than their need to compete economically. Wars, however, cost a great deal of money, and Republican Rome was chronically short of silver and gold. Their first monetary system was based on copper, but conducting transactions with sackfuls of huge coins that weighed as much as a pound apiece was little better than barter. They attempted to set up a ratio of exchange between silver and copper, but quickly ran out of money as a result of the expenses of the wars with Carthage. The next step was inflationary. The ratio between the silver and copper coins had been one to six; it was increased to one to ten. Then it was increased still further to one to sixteen. The weight of the copper coins was reduced to an ounce and then to a half ounce, to stretch the supply of copper even further.

The standard silver coin, the *denarius*, was supposed to be pure silver, but some of the minting authorities tampered with its content. They covered a copper disk, or flan, with thin sheets of silver and then struck a coin with regular dies. The result was very much like the American silver-sandwich coins of the 1960s. The Romans evidently borrowed the sandwich idea from the Athenians, who had been forced to issue copper tetradrachms covered with a thin sheet of silver after their disastrous defeat in the Peloponnesian War. This mode of manufacture had also been employed by Greek forgers, and many ancient coins have been found that bear deep chisel cuts inflicted by bankers who wanted to be sure that the silver was more than skin deep.

In Republican Rome, it was common practice for the leading families to operate their own mints, and the government had great difficulty controlling them. The more troubled the times became, the greater the demand for money, and these private mints were happy to oblige. During the Social Wars of the early 1st Century B.C., all of Italy was flooded with silver-sandwich denarii issued by private mints and enterprising forgers.

The presence of all this debased money only whetted the public appetite for good silver, and many mints met this demand by issuing denarii notched around the edge to prove that their content was pure silver. Then the silver in the coins was alloyed with copper, so that no one knew what his money was worth in bullion. Inflation was rampant and both the State and its citizens were on the verge of bankruptcy.

The democratic party, which for the moment was in the ascendant, resolved the issue by decreeing that debts would be paid at one fourth their nominal value and that thenceforth the coinage would be pure, trustworthy silver. The reform did not last long; it was repealed when the patrician party came back into power, and before long the private mints were again issuing silver-copper sandwiches.

It is interesting to note that the conservative patrician party in Rome supported easy-money policies, while the more liberal democrats favored hard money. Politicians still squabble about these issues today, but the positions of liberals and conservatives have been reversed. The fact that in ancient times the poor reacted more strongly than the rich to the cheapening of the currency indicates how important for their welfare the monetary system had become.

The democratic party eventually prevailed. About sixty years later, Octavian, the adopted son of the assassinated Julius Caesar, became the first of the Roman Emperors, taking for himself the title of Augustus; and *denarii* issued by Augustus and his immediate successors were of good, solid silver. But once having tasted the giddy pleasures of inflation, the Romans could not long resist. Nero reduced the size of both the *denarius* and the *aureus* (which had become the standard gold coin); at the same time he alloyed the denarius, making it 10% copper. Gradual debasement of the denarius continued unabated for the next two centuries. By the middle of the 3rd Century A.D. it had become a tiny copper coin and had been superseded by a larger coin, the *antoninianus*. This coin was first issued at 60% silver; it entered the 4th Century A.D. as a miserable copper coin with a light silver wash to give it the appearance of respectability.

The Romans, like everyone who has followed them, found that inflation, once started, is difficult to stop. In 301 A.D. Diocletian attempted to stem a runaway increase in prices by issuing a stern edict that fixed maximum prices for all commodities. It was a failure. Merchants and farmers withheld goods from sale or disposed of them on the black market, and prices went even higher. When the supply of money grows faster than the supply of goods, price increases are inevitable.

In spite of the fact that the Romans were never able to master the delicate art of matching the financial resources with the cost of maintaining and defending the Empire, they nevertheless got a great deal of mileage from their money. The ability of the Roman Empire to survive in one form or another for some 1700 years (until the fall of Constantinople in 1453) is witness to the fact that the Romans' inflationary policies were effective in political terms, even though they drove the population to the brink of bankruptcy at frequent intervals. If inflation can be seen as a form of enforced taxation, it becomes clear that the continuance of the Empire was financed out of the pockets of the common people, most of them poor. When we take into account the political options available to them then, however, this may not have been too bad a bargain.

Propaganda for the Empire

Of considerable psychological interest is the way in which the Romans employed coinage as a propaganda medium. The autocrats of the Alexandrian era made some propaganda use of coins, but they appear as amateurs beside the Romans. During the century before Augustus, the noble families of the Republic began modestly enough by displaying portraits of eminent ancestors on coins or by depicting historical incidents—the rape of the Sabine women, for example—in which their forebears had played prominent roles.

With the advent of the Empire, we find the portrait of the reigning emperor prominently displayed, surrounded by a legend citing his name and titles. One of Trajan's coins, for instance, tells us that we are looking at the profile of "the Emperor Trajan, Caesar [and adopted son of] Nerva, the Augustus, conqueror of the Germans and the Dacians, the highest of the high priests, the holder of tribunate power [essentially, the Chief of State], consul for the fifth time, and Father of His Country."

The reverses of imperial coins were used to advertise the Emperor's piety in upholding Roman traditions, his generosity in distributing money to the poor and reducing taxes, and his prowess in battle. Public works were announced on coins: the building of the Coliseum; the new harbor works at Ostia, the port of Rome; and the construction of highways. The Emperor's hopes of establishing a dynasty were also reflected on his coinage, where likenesses appeared of his Empress, his sisters, his son and heir, and his daughter-in-law. After the Emperor died, coins were issued commemorating his deification, depicting him being carried off to the heavens on the back of an eagle.

The reverses of coins were also used to publicize victories over the enemies of Rome. The most widely advertised of these was the victory over Judea, symbolized on coins of Vespasian and Titus by a dejected woman weeping under a palm tree. Why the defeat of this poverty-stricken little country received such attention is a puzzle, until we recall that Judea was the first Roman province to stage a major armed rebellion against the forces of the Empire.

The minting of so great a number of such coins—probably millions—doubtless had the intent of warning other peoples within the Empire against taking similar action. It is interesting to note that the suppression of the second Jewish revolt, some sixty-five years later, was ignored by the Roman minting authorities. The government may have found it embarrassing to admit that the Jews had refused to learn their lesson and had once again challenged the entire Roman Empire.

The reverses of Roman coins present a kaleidoscopic view

of the interplay between people's anxieties and official reassurances. When a coin appears showing two right hands clasped, with the announcement that the armies of Rome are of one heart and mind, we quite rightly suspect that when the coin was issued, all was not well and that legions had been fighting each other instead of a common enemy. And when we look at a typical coin of the mid 4th Century A.D., and read a legend announcing that "happy days are here again," we also recall that the Empire was at that time in a sad state of disarray as a result of the civil wars and barbarian raids that were overwhelming its crumbling defenses. The fact that the "happy days" coins depict the Emperor on horseback, spearing a fallen barbarian, suggests that their intent was to build up morale; but to pull the disintegrating Empire together much more was needed than this futile attempt to whistle in the dark.

Wretched Coins, Wretched People

By the 5th Century A.D. the Western or Latin half of the Empire was a shambles and the Eastern or Greek-speaking half, with its capital at Constantinople, was in a shaky condition. Metal was so scarce that copper coins, which had weighed as much as a pound during the First Punic War, seven hundred years earlier, had now dwindled to tiny disks, smaller than the head of a thumbtack. Gold and silver coins of good quality were extremely scarce and were used primarily to pay the army, who had traditionally demanded and received currency of higher standard than what circulated among the civilians.

We have reviewed the first thousand years of money's history, a period of trouble, instability, and brutality. It was a period marked by the pursuit of expansionist dreams—desperate attempts to establish military and political security, usually at the expense of one's neighbors. It saw the flowering and fading of the Greco-Roman civilization, which had enabled hundreds of millions of people to enjoy a way of life more challenging, interesting, and personally involving than anything that had existed before. In comparison, the lives of people elsewhere during this period, with the possible exception of China, were dull, brutish, and short. Greco-Roman civilization opened the eyes of people to the great possibilities that lay within themselves. It led later centuries to try once more to build a world order that would generate the exciting possibilities a civilization provides. The choice between the civilized and the primitive life is easily made: Most people would rather be stimulated to death than bored to death.

Every student of ancient history has his favorite theory of why the Greco-Roman civilization emerged and endured. As a psychologist, I am attracted to explanations that include the Greek concern about the individual—his personality, his struggles, his freedom, and his ultimate fate—and the Roman passion for organization, dedication, and involvement in group enterprise. The principles of democracy and personal freedom, though often subverted and repressed, were always in the background. The individual in those times was freer to make choices and had more choices to make than one who lived during the periods that came before or after.

In this chapter, we have noted how money played an important part in the development of the Greco-Roman civilization. Money was the catalyst that enabled societies to create, build, and expand. Money facilitated the progress of democracy; its abundance enabled common people, even the poor, to broaden and deepen their involvement in the social life of the community, in both its immediate and its extended sense. The decline of this civilization was reflected, perhaps in large part caused, by the deterioration of the monetary system. Civilizations are made possible by the collaboration of people, a collaboration that requires mutual trust, confidence, and a sense of communality. A common currency is one of the forces that makes such collective action possible, and when people no longer trust their money they lose confidence in one another.

Money has value only because people agree to accept it in exchange for goods and services. Such an agreement is an unspoken social pact that makes trade and many forms of social interaction possible. When the pact no longer functions, societies disintegrate. This was, in large measure, what happened to the Western Roman Empire. The Eastern or Byzantine part survived for another thousand years. It is significant that the first Byzantine Emperor, Anastasius, gave his reconstituted empire a strong start by reforming the currency and putting it on a firm footing. Silver had become very scarce, and Anastasius based his monetary system on gold. Byzantine money was accepted at home and abroad, and society in the Eastern Mediterranean revived, even as it declined in the West.

The Romans demonstrated that large-scale economies did not require commodity money in order to function and that they could get along reasonably well on fiat. They found, however, that the issuance of fiat money opened the Pandora's box of monetary inflation, releasing a host of unfamiliar and disturbing problems. Although the Roman copper coins that constituted the Empire's fiat currency were worth very little, they were, as scrap metal, at least worth *something*. In the next chapter we will examine the next stage in the development of money, in which money is created out of debts, which are, or seem to be, less than nothing.

3 Money in the modern world

> Thou wicked and slothful servant, thou knewest that I reap where I sowed not, and gather where I have not strawed:
>
> Thou oughtest therefore to have put my money to the exchangers, and then at my coming I should have received mine own with usury.   —MATTHEW 25:26–27

> Money and not morality is the principle of commercial nations.   —THOMAS JEFFERSON

> The universal regard for money is the one hopeful fact in our civilization.   —G. B. SHAW

The Roman empire did not really fall; it disintegrated. No thundering crash brought the palaces, temples, and law courts tumbling down. Instead, internal mechanisms labored and slowed down. This internal deterioration was accompanied by external pressure: Waves of infiltrators invaded first the distant provinces of the Empire and then those lying closer to Rome. Rome itself was entered eventually and sacked. The infiltration began in the form of peaceful migrations; then the tribes who entered the Empire from the area east of the Rhine and north of the Danube invaded, sometimes passing through the border areas en route to the next and hopefully wealthier province, but often settling down and demanding protection under the *Pax Romana* and asking local officials to carry on as before.

The invaders admired Roman civilization and tried to keep it intact. They learned Latin, giving up their Germanic dialects, employed Roman teachers for their children, and instructed the mints to coin money bearing the diademed portrait of the Roman Emperor. Many of their coins carried the motto, *Roma invicta,* "Rome invincible," implying that the invaders had not defeated the Romans but had merely joined forces with them.

But the Germanic leaders eventually quarreled among themselves and showed more interest in personal ambitions than in trying to make the *Pax Romana* work. What unity they possessed came from temporary coalitions formed to fight off additional invasions from the forest homeland they had so recently and eagerly abandoned. Roman legions, the real backbone of the *Pax Romana,* no longer patrolled the Western Empire. No power was present to force local governments to maintain the network of communication and services—the infrastructure—that had enabled the Empire to function as a more or less integrated, organic whole during the preceding five centuries or more.

But the legions and the roads of the vanished Empire had been only the surface manifestations of psychological forces that had kept it together. Its real cohesiveness had been provided by the shared Roman belief that Rome was sacred and supreme—worth living and dying for. This overriding belief had provided the motive, the "psychological gluon," that had distinguished the Romans from all who had gone before them.

But beliefs do not last forever, especially when their basic elements are eroded by disillusionment, despair, and mutual distrust. The Empire's wars came increasingly to be fought by mercenaries hired from the very tribes that threatened it; the middle class, maintaining the infrastructure that held the parts of the Empire together, were taxed more and more heavily to support ever-larger armies. After a while, the citizens of the Empire became more concerned about their personal welfare than about the common cause. Modern social psychologists have demonstrated in their laboratories that cooperation is impossible when individuals become preoccupied with their own interests, and Benjamin Franklin pointed out to his fellow revolutionaries that if they did not hang together, they would hang separately. The decline and eventual disintegration of the once glorious Roman Empire provides a dramatic confirmation of the validity of these observations.

Christianity and the Disdain of Money

The belief in the supremacy of Rome also suffered from competition with a newer idea: the belief in salvation through Jesus Christ. After Constantine the Great was converted to Christianity in 313 A.D., the veneration of *Roma Eterna* gradually diminished in importance until it became token ritualism, commemorated only on the reverses of coins.

Once Christianity received the imperial stamp of approval, it emerged as the dominant religion—even among the barbarians who were taking over one imperial province after another. Its effect on the economic life of the day, and especially on people's attitudes toward money, was dramatic.

Christianity was from the very beginning the religion of the poor. It glorified poverty and was contemptuous of wealth. For example, the authors of the gospels have Jesus telling his followers that a camel may more easily pass through the eye of a needle than a rich man may enter the Kingdom of God. And Lazarus the beggar is lifted up into heaven when he dies, but the rich, many of whom refused to help him, are consigned to the tortures of hell.

People who are convinced that poverty is beneficial are unlikely to initiate programs of economic development. Indeed, they are more likely to make it difficult or impossible for anyone to improve his economic status. In this the people of Europe during the early medieval period were quite successful, blissfully unaware that the Greek-speaking citizens of the Eastern Roman or Byzantine Empire had decided to ignore Christian notions about poverty and self-denial and were developing an economy that was as wealthy as Western Europe was poor.

Those few who did accumulate wealth in medieval Europe did not always enjoy it in comfort and ease. The poor often took part in riots and rebellions that ended in wanton destruction and bestial violence. Jeffrey Burton Russell (1968), in his survey of medieval civilization, points out that the activists of that era were more interested in destroying objects of value than in stealing them. Wealth was viewed by them as a crime against the Christian ideal of poverty. In this they were encouraged by Reformist heretics, like Savonarola, who ordered the "vanities" of Florence to be cast into bonfires in the public square. As Russell observes, "Society was to be saved, not by better distribution of wealth, but by its destruction."

The cult of poverty that prevailed during the medieval period, and especially during its earlier centuries—the Dark Ages—inhibited trade and fostered economic stagnation. The teachings of the church fathers may have satisfied the needs of the spirit, but they did little for the needs of the flesh. Poverty, ignorance, and apathy lay over the land like a cloud, stifling enterprise and growth.

The Uses of Usury

When Charlemagne came to power at the end of the 8th Century, he tried to rectify the situation by issuing decrees that he hoped would encourage economic development. He also stabilized the monetary system by making the wafer-thin silver *denier,* or penny, the standard coin for all of Europe. But he also inadvertently discouraged economic development by confirming earlier decrees against the practice of demanding interest on loans—what medieval law called "usury." The idea that usury was bad was evidently based on the reasonable fear that people in dire straits would be exploited and victimized by moneylenders. The proper behavior toward those in need was to share resources rather than take advantage of them by lending money at interest. Unfortunately this law, which was intended to protect the poor, also had the effect of discouraging trade and industry.

A few businessmen found ways of circumventing the decrees against usury. They went to those who possessed the largest sums of ready cash: the princes of the Church. As priests they felt exempt from both the condemnation of wealth and the decrees against usury. Over the years they had accumulated vast sums of money, but there were relatively few products and services they could buy with it. By making loans to businessmen—especially to heads of government—they not only earned the gratitude of the borrowers but also increased their own economic and political power. Thus the Church became ever richer by following paths forbidden to its adherents.

The Knights Templar, for example, profited from this

rather cynical coalition between the spiritual and the commercial. This religious order was founded by Crusader knights in Jerusalem, about 1120, for the purpose of protecting pilgrims from marauding bands of Moslems. The founding knights called themselves the "Poor Knights of Christ and the Temple of Solomon," a name that stood in ironic contrast to the wealth and worldly power the order eventually accumulated.

The Templars attracted wealthy adherents, many of whom donated their possessions to the order. In 1139, the pope exempted the Templars and their holdings from the control of local church authorities throughout Christendom, and thus the way was cleared for their rapid ascent to the heights of power and wealth. The kings of France and England donated lordships and estates, and Alfonso I of Aragon actually bequeathed his entire kingdom to the order. The bequest was not retained, but was magnanimously handed back to Alfonso's anxious successors in exchange for a handful of castles and lordships.

The management of their burgeoning wealth became a major concern to the Templars. The revenues from their growing number of rich estates were funneled into regional depositories, converted into gold and silver bullion, and transported to the Holy Land on the Templars' own ships. The effectiveness of this network of facilities quickly became known, and soon the Templars were functioning as bankers, accepting deposits of coin and bullion at their temples, shipping specie throughout Europe and the Mediterranean, and lending money at reasonable interest. The Templars developed a reputation for honesty and efficiency, and pilgrims to the Holy Land entrusted their estates to the care of the Order, knowing that the revenues would not only be collected but would be transmitted to them in the Holy Land.

But success carries with it the seeds of downfall, and the Templars' avowed dedication to poverty and to Christ did not exempt them from worldly troubles. The economic, military, and political power wielded by the Templars brought them into competition with other knightly religious orders and with powerful political figures both in and out of the Church. There were charges and countercharges, followed by confiscations and arrests, which quickly gave way to torture and bloody massacres.Before it was all over, scores of the Knights and their followers had been burned at the stake as relapsed heretics.

The final blow fell in 1312, when the pope decreed that the property of the order should be given to its archrival, the Order of St. John of the Hospital of Jerusalem, commonly known as the Hospitallers. Although the Hospitallers, too, had amassed great wealth, they'd had the good fortune—or the good sense—to avoid the banking business. They had concentrated on the care of the sick, instead. The Order of the Knights of St. John survives to this day and has branches throughout Europe and North America.

Lombards, Banks, and Gold Pieces

About the time the Templars were so rudely ushered from the scene, the international commerce of Europe and the Mediterranean had increased to the point that the need for dependable banking services was acute. This need was met largely by Jewish merchants, whose religion exempted them from strictures against charging interest. But the growing demand for banking services led authorities to relax the usury laws and to encourage the growth of banking houses, and soon the near-monopoly of the Jews was challenged by a new class of merchant bankers from Piacenza, a city in the Northern Italian Kingdom of Lombardy. The Lombards were joined shortly by bankers from Florence and other Tuscan cities. Since the first Italian bankers were from Lombardy, the bankers from other parts of Italy were also called Lombards. They established branches throughout Europe. The street in London's financial center where the Italians formerly did business is still called "Lombard Street."

Banking firms appeared in the Low Countries, France, and elsewhere in Europe, but the Italian bankers deserve the credit for systematizing banking practices and especially for the development of double-entry accounting procedures, which reflected the interests of both creditors and investors and enabled bankers and merchants alike to control their transactions with clients and employees.

The trade that bloomed and blossomed in the marketplaces of Europe created a need for an increase in the supply of money. The demand for money was supplied from three sources: the debasement of the coinage, the minting of gold coins, and instruments of debt. Debasement involved the adulteration of the silver penny *(denier)* with admixtures of copper and tin, reviving the practice initiated by the Romans a thousand years earlier.

The gold acquired in the Middle East by the Crusaders and the traders who followed them provided the second source of coins. Only a few issues of gold coins had been minted during the dreary Dark Ages. There had been little gold available for coinage, and the supply of silver pennies was generally sufficient for commercial needs. Indeed, many people in rural areas had slipped back into barter and had little need for money. But in 1252, the Republic of Florence issued a gold coin appropriately called the *florin*. Mints all over Europe followed suit, producing floods of similar coins, which they called *sequins* or *ducats*, depending on the local custom.

These new coins also served, as had their Roman and Greek forerunners as instruments of propaganda and exercises in self-esteem. They presented the portrait, titles, and territorial claims of the ruler who controlled the mint. The coins of the many city-republics bore no royal portraits, but each issue carried the name and heraldic device of the city that minted it and thus surved as a display of local pride and prestige.

The First "Paper Gold"

The third form of supplementary money supply consisted of bills of exchange drawn upon banking houses. Before the 13th Century, bank credit could be transferred by debtor to creditor only in oral form, before witnesses. This was of course both awkward and clumsy, and in the 13th and 14th Centuries debtors began to follow the more convenient practice of executing in their own handwriting bills of exchange made out to specific creditors. The form of transferring credit was gradually simplified, and by 1500 documents that served the purpose of the modern negotiable check began to appear.

These bills of exchange were not money, of course, but they took the place of money. A Florentine merchant did not have to carry a sack of silver deniers and gold florins with him when he set out on his journey to the great international fair in the province of Champagne in Northern France. Instead, he carried bills of exchange made out in his name and payable to bankers who set up temporary offices at the fair. When he had done his trading at the fair, he would carry back with him bills of exchange made out to Florentine bankers. Dealings in bills of exchange at the Champagne fair led the bankers to set up clearing houses that enabled them to balance off credits and debits with very little transfer of hard cash.

The bankers learned by experience that much more money was left on deposit with them than would be required at any given time to pay off bills of exchange. A banker could therefore lend the excess money out at interest, provided he was careful not to lend so much that he would be embarrassed on the occasion when he was required to honor an unusually large number of drafts. He could, of course, borrow from a fellow banker in an emergency, but there were limits to the willingness of bankers to bail out a fellow member, especially when his shortage resulted from a greedy eagerness to make more loans than was wise. When a banker could not honor the bills of exchange drawn on him, his *banca* (the bench or counter over which he conducted his business) was *rotta* (broken). The Italian word *bancarotta* was back-translated into Latin and appeared in English as "bankrupt."

Instruments of debt had existed long before the medieval period. We noted in the previous chapter that the Egyptians under the Ptolemies developed a system whereby individuals who had made deposits in a government grain depot could draw checks against their credit balance. Inasmuch as the checks were negotiable and could be presented to any government granary, they served as a kind of primitive debt money. Other ancient societies—especially the Greeks and the Romans—also developed and used banking systems that made use of instruments of debt, but these disappeared with the decline of trade during the Dark Ages. Hence the Italians and other bankers of the medieval period had to "rediscover" the advantages of debt money.

We are using the term "debt money" to distinguish it from commodity money (money whose value was derived from the metal from which it was made) and from fiat money issued by government decree (like the copper coins of the Greeks and Romans). Since the silver pennies or deniers of the medieval era were tariffed at the rate of 240 to the pound, 240 of them could presumably be exchanged for whatever a pound of silver could be exchanged for. Gold florins and ducats, too, had the trading power of a comparable weight in gold. The new instruments of debt, however, were simply written promises to pay. They had no commodity value; their value was based entirely on faith—that is, they were accepted to the extent that the maker of the bill of exchange and the financial house on which it was drawn could be trusted. There were many abuses of the system, with periodic government interventions to prevent and punish fraudulent activities. Unfortunately, governments were the worst abusers of the system, often overdrawing their accounts and sometimes ruining the banking houses that had trusted them.

These difficulties retarded the growth of the practice of using instruments of debt as substitutes for commodity money, but the practice spread, nevertheless. Indeed, except for brief pauses for wars and financial panics, the system has never stopped growing and developing. A generation ago, blue-collar workers received their weekly pay in the form of bills and coins stuffed into small envelopes—"pay envelopes" in America, and "pay packets" in Britain. Today wages are likely to be paid in the form of a check. The check is of course a lineal descendant of the bill of exchange.

Receipts for deposits also took on the function of debt money. In England this practice began after 1640, when Charles I, who could not get a rebellious Parliament to give him the money he requested for the army, seized 200,000 pounds sterling of the gold London merchants had deposited in the Royal Mint for safekeeping. The merchants naturally decided that use of the Royal Mint was no better than an open invitation for confiscation. The London goldsmiths possessed vaults, and soon the merchants began placing their gold coin and bullion in them, accepting receipts for whatever amount they had on deposit. The goldsmiths soon realized that it was reasonably safe to lend some of the considerable amount of gold in their vaults and earn extra income from the interest borrowers paid.

Next the goldsmiths saw that they could issue notes or receipts for fixed amounts that had no relationship to any particular deposit but that were simply promises to pay a given sum of bullion or money on demand. These receipts and notes were negotiable; they circulated as a form of debt money.

A number of the goldsmith-bankers had bruising experiences with Charles II, and some of them went bankrupt when their loans went unpaid. It became apparent that dealing with the government was a task too large and too risky for any private bank, and in 1694 the Bank of England was founded. As the central bank of the country, it acted as a stabilizing force, lending money to the government as well as to private borrowers. What is important for this discussion, however, is the fact that the Bank of England also issued paper currency—debt money.[1] By 1770 most of the private bankers (many of whom had been goldsmiths a century before) stopped issuing their own debt money and used the currency issued by the Bank of England instead. From a psychological point of view, the Bank of England's notes replaced their competitors because of the greater trust they inspired.

What Is Money Really Worth?

Economic historians make much of the changeover from commodity money to debt money, and indeed debt money and commodity money appear to be quite different. The acceptance of debt money implies a willingness to take the written or printed word of others at face value, while insistence on commodity money—gold or silver—implies hardheadedness, skepticism, and mistrust. Thus the willingness of businessmen to accept the new debt money does seem to have indicated a major change in their attitudes and behavior.

As is the case with many signal events in human behavior, appearances are misleading. The truth of the matter is that it required no great change, either of style or pattern of belief, to

---

[1]Credit for the first issuance of paper money belongs to the Chinese. The 13th Century Venetian adventurer, Marco Polo, reported that the Mongol emperor of China, Kublai Khan, issued money printed on paper made from the bark of the mulberry tree. This fiat money was exchangeable for gold or silver at the government mint.

accept credit money. For the greater part of the preceding two thousand years, people had used money whose commodity value was less than the value at which it was accepted in trade. As we noted in the foregoing chapter, the Greeks minted huge quantities of copper coins that could be exchanged for silver coins whose bullion value was much greater. The Romans followed the same policy, and the total volume of the bronze token coinage they issued was far greater than anything the Greeks dreamed of.

There was virtually no token coinage in the Dark Ages; the extremely low volume of commerce did not warrant it. When trade began to pick up during the Crusader era, only the more affluent countries of the Mediterranean issued copper token coinage; but governments did debase the silver *denier*, or penny, as we observed earlier. The addition of copper and tin to silver coins was termed "seniorage" or, more bluntly, "brassage"—the profit margin exacted by a ruler for the services of his mint. Hence a pound's worth of silver coins never contained an actual pound of silver. Yet they circulated freely, were sought avidly, hoarded greedily, and spent reluctantly, just as if they had been pure silver. And with the great expansion of international trade—and warfare—of the 16th Century, the great need for money brought back copper token coinage.

The point is that the use of money had always demanded a degree of faith—a belief that it was worth something. People's willingness to accept the coin of the realm for their goods or services was based on the assumption that others would also accept it when the time came to pass it on in exchange for goods or services. The psychological basis for value of money lies in the shared belief that it is universally acceptable.

Expansion, Debt, and Inflation

The era we have come to call the Renaissance was one of great adventures—intellectual, artistic, political, and commercial. All these adventures cost money, and money was chronically in short supply. Queen Isabella of Spain pawned her jewels to finance the expedition of Columbus. Michelangelo and Benvenuto Cellini complained continually about the stinginess of patrons who seldom provided them with enough money to pay for the purchase of materials and the hiring of assistants. The invention of gunpowder and the greater sophistication of military equipment increased the cost of large-scale warfare.

Where there is a will, there is a way. Much of the money needed for these ventures was secured through borrowing, and the royal heads of Europe ruined one banker after another in order to finance their expensive tastes, their political schemes, and their endless military campaigns. When they had exhausted their bankers, they turned to their wealthier subjects and took what money they needed through direct confiscation. This was hard on the nobles and merchant princes, but it did get a great deal of hoarded capital back into circulation. By such means did the rulers promote social change and contribute to the common good. But more often the borrowed and extorted funds went down the drain, lost in the blood and destruction of wars.

The Renaissance adventures in the New World paid off handsomely and made large amounts of money available for new and grander schemes. Although the gold coinage from the new Spanish possessions in America was significant initially, the bulk of the new money was silver. The advancement in mining and smelting techniques also made possible the development of important silver mines in Western Bohemia, at Joachimstal. The metal was minted in the form of large, handsome coins bearing the bust of the Emperor on the obverse and his coat of arms on the reverse. The coins took their name from the town that first minted them and were initially called "Joachimstaler," later shortened to "Taler." "Talers" arrived in England by way of Holland—the Dutch word was "daler"—hence our word "dollar." Crude dollar-sized silver coins issued by Spanish colonial mints also circulated throughout the Americas. In British North America the "Spanish milled dollar"—the eight-*real* "piece of eight"—competed successfully with the pound sterling to become the chief medium of exchange. Eventually it became the basis of the currency system of the United States.

Although debt money played a part in the economic life of Europe from the Renaissance onward, it was not a major factor until the 18th Century. Most business transactions, large and small, were conducted in terms of commodity money— sometimes gold, but mostly silver, with copper coins serving as petty cash. The fact that the European economic system was based on "hard money" did not, however, prevent inflation from occurring. John Kenneth Galbraith (1975) points out that prices in England increased two-and-one-half times between the late 1400s and the late 1500s. By the latter 1600s, prices had increased to three-and-one-half times what they had been in the late 1400s. Wages merely doubled during the two centuries, thus indicating that merchants had been in a better position to raise prices than workmen had been to secure increases in wages. It is only fair to point out, however, that during this period the number of available workmen had increased relative to the amount of goods. Hence goods were relatively scarcer and employees were relatively cheaper.

The same principle applies to the general increase in prices during the two centuries: The amount of money had increased relative to the amount of goods available. In a free market, people compete with one another to secure their share of the goods. If a community produces roughly the same amount of goods year after year but the supply of money in the hands of the consumers doubles, the price of the goods will double to reflect the amount of money the consumers now have to invest in purchases.

Thus the cause of the inflation during the two centuries in question is easy to determine: It was the direct result of the great increase in money coined from silver from the Americas and from Bohemia. But the amount of money in circulation is not, however, the only factor in price inflation, as we shall see.

Galbraith maintains that the monetary inflation of the 16th and 17th Centuries primed the pump, so to speak, for the early development of European capitalism. High prices and low wages produced high profits, which permitted the accumulation of capital and provided strong incentive to further investment. Inflation, he says, not only facilitated and encouraged trade but also made commercial ventures somewhat fail-proof "by rescuing traders from their errors of optimism or stupidity."

John Law: The Invention of Modern Banknotes

The 18th Century saw the first real flowering of debt money. Its first blooms were, indeed, somewhat exotic—more akin to the

Venus flytrap than the rose or potted geranium. The new era began with the appearance of John Law at the court of France in 1716. A Scotsman, aged 45, Law was a financial genius, the author of a book on banking reform, and an accomplished gambler. He was also an escaped murderer on the run from England, where he had fought an all-too-successful duel with a Mr. Wilson. Law had just come from Scotland, where he had been unsuccessful in convincing the financial community that the financial depression that lay upon the country would be relieved if the Bank of Scotland could be persuaded to issue currency based on the land of the country as security. The prevailing theory of the day was that the wealth of a country consisted of its store of gold and silver, but Law maintained that a country's wealth depended on its commerce. What was needed to stimulate commerce, he said, was a plentiful supply of money.

Law appeared in France at an opportune time. An audit of the country's finances after the death of Louis XIV the year before had indicated that national bankruptcy was imminent. Business was at a standstill, money had disappeared from circulation, unemployment and starvation were widespread. The annual interest on the national debt, combined with the expenses of running the nation, were over 40% more than the state's total revenue.

Law was presented to the state finance council by the Regent, the Duc d'Orleans, who had met Law in a gambling house some years before. Law proposed that a bank be organized along radically progressive lines: It would be empowered to issue banknotes backed by commercial credit (mortgages, bills of exchange, and loans). The availability of this new money, said Law, would bring immediate prosperity to France.

The Council permitted Law to set up a private bank authorized to accept deposits, make loans, and issue notes. From the very start, the State was the principal borrower. It used the banknotes Law issued to liquidate its more pressing loans and to pay current expenses. Notes could be used to pay taxes; since Law's bank offered to redeem them in gold and silver coin, they were accepted everywhere. Confidence was restored, trade began to move, and prosperity smiled on France, as it had not for many a year.

Law ran his bank carefully and judiciously. If matters had gone well, perhaps he, rather than Napoleon, might have had the honor of founding the Banque de France, for in 1719 his private bank became the Banque Royale, a state bank. But like many another successful gambler, Law could not leave well enough alone, and soon branched out into another venture that eventually ruined him, along with thousands of Frenchmen. This project was the Mississippi Company, or *Compagnie d'Occident*, whose intended activities were the development and exploitation of the colony of Louisiana. Inasmuch as Louisiana was a vast, unexplored territory, the possibilities were unlimited, as were the potential problems and hazards.

The price of shares in the Compagnie d'Occident followed a classic pattern. They were bid up slowly at first, then more rapidly, as the Company took over the national tobacco monopoly, the French East India Company, the Guinea Company, the China Company, the Santo Domingo Company, the collection of French taxes, the national mint, and the slave trade to the New World. There was much in Law's Compagnie d'Occident that parallels the growth pattern of a modern conglomerate.

Law added further to the excitement by declaring a 12% dividend at the first meeting of the Company, before it had any earnings. Money is a powerful stimulant, and Law, like many another before and after him, was a classic example of a money-holic. He wheeled and he dealed. He bought stock options, he offered rights, he sold stock on margin. The price per share went from an initial 500 livres (roughly $125) to 1,000 livres in forty days. Two months later, shares were selling for 5,000 livres, and two months after that they were 10,000 livres. For several months they fluctuated between 10,000 and 15,000 livres. In his history of money, Groseclose (1976) reports a French writer as soberly estimating (in November, 1719) that France was five billion livres richer than it had been a year before. Yet all that this fabulous increase actually represented was a few trading posts in Louisiana and slight increase in the number of ships trading with the East.

Prices of land and commodities did not at first increase as much as the price of shares in the Compagnie d'Occident, but as large amounts of money began to circulate, people began to trade and speculate and drive prices up. The price increases, which applied to the *chateaux* of the rich as well as to the bread of the poor, averaged about 75% per year during the period Law was running France's finances. Although Law's schemes had started the country back on the road to prosperity, the economics of his operations were careening wildly out of control, and he was unable to apply the brakes. Within a few months, Compagnie d'Occident, commercial credit, and public confidence all collapsed. In October, 1720, everyone recognized that the system was finished, and the paper money Law's bank had issued was declared null and void. Law fled the country two months later. His remaining years were spent in Venice, where he lived in poverty until his death in 1729.

Galbraith says that as a result of the John Law catastrophe, the French have been suspicious of banks ever since. Their suspiciousness, however, has been no protection against at least three additional major monetary inflations, as well as a number of minor ones, during the course of the following 250 years.

Learning Lessons from Law

There were two psychological lessons to be learned from Law's unfortunate venture. The first is that money need not be convertible into a commodity like silver or gold to possess economic value. If the money is issued by a creditable authority, like the national treasury or a respected bank, people will accept it and use it. Indeed, there may be a great advantage to having money that is not tied to a commodity. In his book on the dynamics of money, Robert A. Hendrickson (1970) says: "The more use a society makes of an intrinsically worthless medium of exchange the greater its wealth becomes. The human mind is capable of assigning much greater value to intangible hopes and fears than to tangible things." The value of money is thus based on expectations.

This lesson has been well learned by governments today and is national policy in every country. Only a few countries tie the value of their currency to anything tangible. Iran is said, for example, to use the very extensive crown jewels of the deposed Shah as collateral for the *ryal*. But everyone recognizes that such gestures have only ritual value. In essence, money issued by any national authority today is debt money. Sometimes the banknotes say just that: "The Treasury of the Republic of Utopia promises to pay the bearer on demand ten spondulicks in lawful money." Most central banks recognize that such a promise is a redundancy, for the ten-spondulick note is itself lawful money. Over the years, authorities have promised less and less on their banknotes, and today most of them promise nothing.

Whatever the banknotes say, however, they represent debts, which means that they are claims on something. Inasmuch as most banknotes these days are issued by a nation either directly by its treasury or indirectly through its national bank, the debt is by implication a claim on the country's resources. Anyone who holds one of the notes can exchange it for a tiny fraction of the issuing country's gross national product, or some of its real estate, or some service that it or its citizens can grant.

Americans have in recent years been forced to face up to the real meaning of their debt money when the dollars they have sent overseas to buy oil return in the form of claims that must be honored. As long as the claims are for products like wheat and automobiles, which we are able to supply in copious quantities, we make little complaint; but when foreigners use "*our* dollars" to buy controlling interests in American manufacturing concerns and banks there is an outcry. Workers say that they do not want to work for foreign bosses, and depositors are uneasy about entrusting their life savings to the care of a foreign bank manager, who, as far as they know, might just take the money and run. Nothing so quickly brings out the xenophobia that lurks within us all as the sight of our dollars clamoring for repatriation.

A number of countries (mostly poor, but a few wealthy ones as well) have attempted to protect their national assets against the claims of foreigners by preventing the importation of their own banknotes. Such tactics raise havoc on the foreign exchange markets, and the currencies involved always sell at a discount. Why there is any market for the disowned currency at all is an interesting question; it can be answered by currency smugglers and black marketeers. One might also ask how the inhabitants of the countries concerned feel about the low value placed on their money in the foreign exchange markets. The answer is that unless they are in the importing business, or plan to travel abroad, they are hardly bothered at all. The money of Communist China, the Soviet Union, and countless third-world countries has little or no value outside the borders of the countries of issue, yet economic life within these countries goes on just the same. People buy, sell, save, and spend the local money without any concern about its worthlessness on the world market.

The idea that the money we scramble for, cherish, and hoard is nothing but national debt is a sobering thought, but we can take a little pleasure in the Alice-in-Wonderland aspects of the monetary system. We receive these government debts in the form of income and deposit them in our local bank. The teller makes an entry in our bankbook to the effect that the bank now has a debt to us in the amount of our deposit. The bank then lends this debt to borrowers, and receives debt instruments from them in return. These debts appear on the bank statement as assets. The bank also buys bonds and notes, which are debts of the government and of corporations, and carries these debts on its books as assets, which it lends out to other borrowers in exchange for their debts, which also become assets. Except to economists and financial experts, this is all very confusing.[2] Alice in Wonderland is, by comparison, much simpler and more straightforward. The system works reasonably well, however, and for this we can thank the genius of John Law, who first introduced the world to the possibilities of debt money.

The Folly of Overdoing It

The second psychological lesson to be learned from Law's

---

[2]It is probably just as well that the general public is unaware that the assets of banks consist entirely of debts, for the equating of assets and debts is somewhat mind-boggling and might undermine people's confidence in the system. The confidence that banks enjoy is, incidentally, nothing short of phenomenal. A 1978 Gallup Poll reported that an estimated 55% of the American people have great confidence in the country's banks. This vote of confidence was larger than that received by the military or the public schools. Even the US Supreme Court rated only 39%, and the confidence expressed in banks was exceeded only by the 60% given churches and organized religion.

French adventure is the folly of overdoing it. Pumping too much money too fast into a country's economy causes people to compete with one another in bidding up the prices of goods and services. When they acquire more money than they are used to receiving, people feel excited and optimistic. But they may also experience a twinge of anxiety—"Is my good fortune *real?*" One way to determine its reality is to spend it. They then find out that other people have more money too, and this realization takes some of the fun out of it. They soon discover that their money will not go as far as it used to, and then their anxiety increases. Eventually there is panic; people lose confidence in the acceptibility of their money. Whereas formerly they may have been inclined to hoard money against a rainy day, they now hoard commodities, valuable artifacts, and real estate.

Galbraith (1975) maintains that inflation financed the American Revolution. The Continental Congress had no alternative to the issuance of money. Had the Congress authorized taxes, they probably could not have been collected—there was no bureaucratic machinery to collect them, and the people, identifying taxation with foreign oppression, would not have paid them. Few people would have been willing to lend the untried revolutionary government any money; the loans received from France and Spain were granted not with any expectation of financial return but because of the malice these countries bore Britain, their ancient enemy. The issuance of the Continental paper dollars was in effect a forced tax on the country's wealth.

Critics have dwelt not on the political and military advantages gained by the first American inflation but on its evils. Continental dollars, they tell us, eventually were worth nothing at all, and creditors went into hiding to avoid debtors. Alexander Hamilton eventually persuaded Congress to redeem Continental currency for a penny on the dollar, a gesture that benefited mostly those speculators who were shrewd enough to have bought them for much less.

Critics of inflation have plenty of other horror stories. In 1789, the revolutionary government in France came to power only to find the treasury empty. They were tempted to issue paper money to pay operating expenses, but the memories of the John Law fiasco were fresh in their minds. They hit upon the idea of issuing notes—*assignats*—that could be redeemed in hard money five years later when the lands of the Church and the Crown were to be sold. They felt absolutely certain that the assignats would not become worthless paper as John Law's livres and the American Continental dollars had become, because they were backed up by something really substantial—land.

Revolutionary governments are rarely endowed with self-restraint. The primrose path to financial ruin, so well marked by John Law and the Continental Congress, proved irresistible. One large issue of assignats was followed by others. By July, 1795, assignats were worth only 3% of their face value in hard money. Businesses were ruined, farmers could not sell their produce, starvation was common, and dissidents rioted. The government tried the ploy of issuing a new form of paper currency, the *mandat,* which was worth thirty times the discredited assignat, but the people were tired of such games. In February, 1797, eight years after the first assignat was issued, the government returned to metal coinage.

Galbraith points out, with his characteristic irony, that since the French Revolution could not have been accomplished without the *assignats,* they should be given as much credit for its success as the much better known guillotine.

The worst horror story in the history of monetary inflation is the experience of the German Republic during the early 1920s. Faced by the need to pay reparations to the Allied Powers, the German Government elected to balance its budget by issuing more marks, rather than by drastically increasing taxes, always an unpopular move. In essence, this was the same problem faced by the French in 1717 and 1789, and by the American Continental Congress in 1775. In 1922, the German mark, which in the years before World War I had been worth 4.20 to the dollar, dropped from 162 to the dollar to more than 7,000. On July 1, 1923, the mark stood at 160,000 to the dollar; by November 20 it had fallen to 4,200,000,000. Business came to a standstill, barter replaced money transactions, and food riots broke out. Individuals on fixed income were heavily hit and the drop in real wages stripped workers of their buying power, but farmers and others with mortgages on their property profited immensely. The social and economic trauma that resulted from the runaway inflation is often cited as a major cause of the rise of Adolf Hitler.

Galbraith observes that all the central European countries that, like Germany, experienced galloping monetary inflations in the years that followed World War I also suffered under fascist dictatorships a few years later, in the 1930s, and that most of them came under Communist control after World War II. Do overheated inflations, then, lead to fascism, and then to communism? Galbraith doubts that monetary inflations are bound to have such discouraging outcomes. He points out that Germany actually enjoyed a high degree of prosperity in the late 1920s, after it had recovered from its inflationary binge of 1922–23.[3] When economic problems again developed in the early 1930s, however, the German government showed that it had learned its lesson all too well, for it decreed that wages and prices should be cut by 10–20%. Within a year the unemployment rate stood at 20%, and a year after that Hitler came to power. In Galbraith's view, the overly drastic *de*flation set the stage for Hitler's rise to power, not the inflation of ten years earlier.

Fine-tuning a Creeping Inflation

We will have more to say about the psychological effects of a monetary inflation in the last chapter, which deals with money and mental health. Here let us examine some of the psychological dynamics behind inflations—especially today's "creeping inflation," which so far has shown no signs of causing a financial panic, but instead boosts the cost of living (the consumer price index) from 3–15% per year. This level of price increase is small enough to take today's inflation out of the category of John Law's Mississippi Bubble, but it is large enough to upset a good many people. It especially disturbs those who would like us to return

---

[3]History plays ironic games. The currency the Weimar government introduced in 1923 to replace the inflated mark was the *Rentenmark*; which, like the French assignats in 1789, were "secured" by the nation's real estate. But the Rentenmarks, unlike the assignats, were successful. The German people were psychologically ready for a change, and wanted desperately to reaffirm their faith in the monetary system.

to a gold standard—an arrangement where the dollar is convertible into a fixed amount of gold.

The assumption underlying the gold-standard argument is that inflations are produced when the supply of money increases faster than the supply of things it will buy. Since the Government prints the currency that goes into the money side of this equation, it seems reasonable that if the Government would stop printing money and would balance the budget, prices would stabilize and inflation would end. Much the same effect would be obtained if the Government set a fixed ratio between the dollar and a unit of gold, for then unless it obtained more gold the Government could not issue any more money; the amount in circulation would then remain the same, and prices would no longer rise. The Government would thus be forced to balance its budget because it would be unable to issue the money needed to make up a deficit.

The argument is plausible, but it does not take into account the realities of today's economics, which are infinitely more complex than anything John Law envisioned. Banks today actually "create" money by the process of pyramiding. As we noted earlier, loans become assets, which in turn serve as the basis for further loans. The money thus "created" is far greater than the amount of cash in circulation At the end of April, 1979, the amount of US currency in circulation was 113.5 billion dollars, but the amount of money deposited in checking accounts was 260 billion. These two figures together comprise what the Federal Reserve System calls M1—the nation's basic money supply. In its weekly statement to the financial community the Federal Reserve System also reports a broader measure of money, M2—the amount of currency in circulation plus all private deposits in banks—savings accounts, checking accounts, and all other accounts (except especially large ones represented by certificates of deposit). In April, 1979, M1 amounted to 374 billion dollars, while M2 stood at 903 billion, eight times the amount of money in circulation.

There is no evidence that the growth in cash money was alone responsible for increases in M1, M2, and the cost of living. The cause-and-effect relationship among these and other economic factors are complex; economists spend endless hours at their computers attempting to sort out the elements that have a signficant influence on the cost of living. The Treasury and the central banks use the resulting data to adjust the interest rates and to increase or decrease the availability of credit in an attempt to manage the country's economy. It is popularly believed that they are successful in these endeavors. We have not had a really bad monetary inflation for over a hundred years, and there has not been a severe economic panic since the Great Depression of the 1930s. Instead we have had creeping inflation, a fairly prosperous economy, and an unemployment rate of about 7% that simply will not go away.

The management of the economy is based on the predictions of economists. The management takes the form of what economists term "fine-tuning," a procedure involving the adjustment of the money supply to changes anticipated by the economists. Hendrickson (1970) points out that the predictions of the economists have actually been rather poor and that anything better than a 40% error rate is considered by them to be a better-than-average performance. He says that perhaps fine-tuning can be made to work, but results so far suggest that the forecasters are tone-deaf. The fact that we have had no major disasters may mean that the Government's management is better than the predictions on which it is supposedly based. Maybe we have only been lucky.

The Psychology of Inflation

The psychological factor that continually eludes the analysts and planners is the mood of the public. When people are optimistic, banks confidently pyramid their loans, expand the supply of credit, encourage business investment, and reap good profits. When people are pessimistic, they refuse to make financial commitments, do not invest, and limit their purchases to immediate needs. The Government's attempts to pump more money into the system at such times go unheeded.

When people feel positive about the future, they can create more money by increasing its velocity—the rate at which money changes hands over a given period. The power of the people to increase the velocity of the money they control is a factor completely overlooked by the monetary conservatives,

Using high-speed computers, the modern economic analysts do take velocity into account, but the psychological basis for its velocity still eludes them.

The index of Consumer Sentiment devised by George Katona (1960, 1964) of the Survey Research Center of the University of Michigan has shown that people's optimism or pessimism about the future is a significant predictor of economic things to come. The fact that our central banks have not been very successful in their attempts to control the velocity of money by expanding or contracting the availability of credit, suggests that the mood of the people may not be affected much by easiness or tightness in the money market. A drop in the prime rate does not increase the worker's pay check. To be sure, lower prime rates enable businesses to borrow more cheaply and may encourage expansion of trade, which may eventually increase wages. But businessmen are much affected by the public's mood, and if the mood is not optimistic, businessmen will not be encouraged by lower interest rates. Interest rates were extremely low during the Great Depression of the 1930, but businessmen showed little interest in borrowing.

Robert L. Heilbroner (1979), professor of economics of the New School for Social Research, is not at all sure that the factors most economists consider significant are really what is fueling today's inflation. He says that "We still do not know whether an increase in the size of money is the cause of inflation or merely its passive accompaniment." The inflation may be actually caused by a general pattern of behavior that affects consumers, business and industry, labor, and government alike, in that they engage in a sort of mutual conspiracy to bid up prices, wages, and costs as they compete with one another for small advantages. It is public mood that seems to produce inflation, rather than the availability of more money. The money is generated in various ways as it is needed to pay for higher costs and rewards.

Heilbroner believes that this mood stems from an atmosphere of speculative excitement, coupled with insecurity, that has always given capitalistic economies a degree of nervous energy that other economies—feudal and communistic—do not have. In the past, this speculative tendency was tempered by recurring depressions, but people today feel that the country ment, with its ability to spend, lend, control, encourage, and tax can forestall any general financial collapse. Since they feel able to dismiss the probability of the proverbial "rainy day" from their minds, people can then direct their attention to the one major certainty—that the cost of everything will keep on rising. And so they say, "We'd better buy (or travel or build) now; prices may be high, but they'll never be any lower."

The funds for these escalating expenditures can be secured with relative ease, providing one's credit is reasonably sound. People today can literally "create their own cash," through the use of credit cards, second and third mortgages, and other types of loans. Undeterred by double-digit interest rates, consumer credit continues to grow and to break existing records.

Banks, for their part, have in recent years discovered an important and relatively unrestricted source of lendable funds: Eurodollars. Eurodollars exist in the form of U.S. dollar deposits and credit instruments held abroad. Beginning in the 1950s, European banks accepted large sums of dollars as deposits made by international corporations, governments, and other banks. These dollars have through the years been recycled, pyramided, and multiplied to the point where they constitute the world's largest credit source. The growth in Eurodollars has been staggering. From the beginning of 1970 until March, 1979, the supply of Eurodollars increased 1,033%. By way of contrast, M-1 in the United States increased a modest 160%. Eurodollars flow in and out of financial markets throughout the world; many of them come to the United States to finance loans to Americans, and it is believed that the great inflationary surge that was experienced in the United States in 1979 was the result of a large influx of Eurodollars. Federal Reserve officials have expressed concern about the fact that the creation of Eurodollars lies outside their control. Although they can require American banks to maintain adequate reserves when they bring in Eurodollars, they can do nothing to keep overseas banks from lending money to Americans or financing non-Americans who wish to buy corporations, commodities, real estate, or other assets in the United States. Thus Eurodollars constitute a major threat to any attempt by American governmental authorities to discourage inflation (Jansen, 1979).

Money as a Catalytic Agent

In these and other aspects of our daily life money plays a minor but significant role, as it has throughout history. The industrial society of today with all its advantages and shortcomings, its satisfactions and frustrations, owes its existence and form to the invention, availability, and use of money. In the technological and cultural changes that have taken place since money's appearance some 2500 years ago, money has played the role of the catalyst, the element whose presence causes or makes possible changes in other elements—human behavior, in this instance—and whose form or identity remains unchanged. In these two chapters we have shown how money brings buyers and sellers together; how money finances public improvements, creative endeavors, and destructive wars; and how money's increase can create the excitement of economic expansion but can also lead to the disillusionment and depression of a financial catastrophe.

It is we who have created money and given it the power it possesses over us. In this respect, money resembles other human inventions that are part of our social environment and that have power over us—for instance, language, customs, rituals, social norms, and government. We can, of course refuse to put any faith in money and thus keep it from having any power over us, but this is easier said than done. Money is so much a part of the fabric of society that we can escape its influence only by going into seclusion in a remote part of the world. (It would not do to join a primitive tribe, because even they are linked to the modern world by economic and social interests that involve money in one form or another.)

As creators of money, we are also its masters; money is but a servant. Difficulties arise, however, when the servant obeys not its master's orders but his wishes. We often use money in an attempt to satisfy urges we neither understand nor recognize. It is the task of the psychologist to identify these motives and help us understand them. In the following chapter we shall explore some of the ways in which our behavior and our thinking are influenced by our own and others' use of money—ways that often escape ordinary awareness.

4 Money, status, and power

Money is the mother's milk of politics.
— ATTRIBUTED TO JAMES FARLEY
AND OTHER INSIGHTFUL POLITICIANS

As wealth is power, so all power will infallibly draw
wealth to it by some means or another.
— EDMUND BURKE

High descent and meritorious deeds, unless united to
wealth, are as useless as sea-weed.   — HORACE

Some of our most cherished illusions concern how we make decisions—especially those that relate to money. We imagine that we base our choices on facts, logic, and common sense; we deny being influenced by the behavior of others. But the fact is that our actions are continually subject to others' influence, often without our awareness. The study of this subtle and complex influence is the job of social psychologists, who perform experiments that they hope will enable them to predict the kinds of choices people will make under certain circumstances. Thus do they seek to discover what influences and what motivates us.

Consider this situation. As you leave the supermarket, a young man approaches you and asks if you can give him two nickels for a dime. In order to grant his request, you will have to dig down into your pocket or purse for the necessary change—not much of a chore. Can the young man influence you so that you will do this simple favor?

"Yes," you say, "probably."

"Assuming you have the two nickels, under what circumstances might you refuse?" asks the psychologist.

"Well," you say, "I might be in a hurry."

"Would you be in a greater hurry if the young man were obviously of a low social status?"

"Don't be ridiculous," you reply. "What does social status have to do with whether or not I change a young man's dime? To me, one person is like another. It wouldn't make the slightest difference whether he were Mr. Gotbucks from Seacliff Heights, or Mr. Stonypoor from Hungry Hollow, or a hippie from Farout Commune. Things like that don't influence me."

Social Influence

Influence is the essence of the social experience. It is the influence of other people that makes us human. The parent uses influence on the infant to socialize it and thus prepare it for a world composed of others. The smiles and tears of the infant in turn influence the parents to provide nourishment, comfort, and love.

This pattern of mutual influence continues throughout life. Our capacity to survive and to experience a degree of comfort, security, and enjoyment in a world composed of other people depends on our ability to influence them: They will tolerate and support us if we can convince them that we are worth supporting, or at least that the benefits they secure by tolerating and supporting us are greater than the costs. Others, for their part, are willing to accept us as functioning members of society because we can be influenced by them in return. All forms of positive social interaction—cooperation, collaboration, conversation, sex, dancing, negotiation, and even shopping—depend on our having a more or less predictable and reasonably rewarding influence on one another. The society we live in works because we can get others to do what we want, at least some of the time, and others can get us to do what they want or expect, at least some of the time.

Thus we all exert, and we all respond to, social power—the ability of an individual or group to produce a desired effect on the behavior of others. The patterns of behavior that a society decides are normal—social norms—are the instruments through which it exerts its power. It is not the usher but the social norm that compels us to drop money into the church collection basket; not the waiter but the norm possesses the power to extract from us the "expected" 15% tip. Social norms usually carry a hint of coercion: Our refusal to respond to these socially legitimate attempts to influence our behavior always involves some cost, whether the demands are made by someone who can punish us (a tax collector or an employer) or by someone who can only make us feel defensive or guilty (a brother-in-law asking us to guarantee a bank loan, or a United Crusade canvasser asking us to double our annual pledge).

Inasmuch as everyone enjoys some success in influencing others, everyone has some social power. The amounts of power differ from time to time, situation to situation, and person to person. Individuals who occupy strategic positions possess much power because they are able to influence many people and bring about relatively significant changes in behavior. Employers, for example, have more power than employees, partly because they determine the events of the working day, and partly because they evaluate—ultimately in terms of money— the work of employees. Employees whose work is covered by union or individual contracts are able to set limits on employers' powers, of course, and even employees without contracts have some power—if only the power of subtle sabotage and obstructionism.

There are many forms of social power. The ability to command the attention of others through speaking to them is one form. Taking up strategic positions within the social structure is another. We can also exert social power by initiating sequences of behavior with others—what Erving Goffman (1967) calls "interaction rituals"—sequences whose form is prescribed by social norms. Money often plays an important role in these interaction rituals. We walk up to a sidewalk newspaper vendor, give him a quarter, and he hands us a newspaper. Or money may appear in the terminal phases of the ritual, as when we examine an array of merchandise in a shop, select an item, and hand it to the sales clerk together with some money. In the first instance, the payment of money influences the vendor to give us a newspaper; in the second, the payment of money influences the sales clerk to let us take possession of the merchandise.

Money and Social Power

One of the most important kinds of social power is money (Lee, 1944). We can in many instances influence others by offering them money, and the amount we offer frequently determines the extent of our influence. Money can exert power by being lent and by being borrowed. The amount of money we possess may influence the behavior of others toward us, even though there is no expectation that the money in question will change hands. The coolness that a bank officer displays toward a loan applicant of obviously limited means is matched by the veiled hostility with which an obviously moneyed person is regarded should he wander into a working man's saloon.

Money differs from other forms of social power in that it can be measured precisely. There is no standard measure for the power we possess as a schoolboard member, a spouse, or the chairman of a committee to plan a P.-T.A. picnic. But we can tell, and to the exact penny, how much money we have, either in our purse or in the bank. Sometimes the nonmonetary forms of social power can be measured, as in the percentage of total votes we receive for P.-T.A. president or in the number of raffle tickets we can persuade people to buy at the P.-T.A. picnic, but such instances are exceptional.

Experiences at the marketplace teach us precision in estimating the amount of influence given quantities of money will have. Such experiences tell us how many cents are needed to coax MacDonald's into supplying us with a hamburger. A quick appraisal of our monetary resources tells us whether we have enough money on hand to persuade our favorite restaurant to provide us with dinner for ourselves and out-of-town visitors. Our familiarity with the going wage for babysitters also tells us whether we will have enough money remaining to convince a teenager to take care of the children while we are at the restaurant.

Social power occurs in other forms, of course—propaganda and argument; manipulation of interpersonal relationships; sex; personal charm and charisma; appeals to conscience and loyalty; invoking of legal sanctions; displays of the symbols of status and prestige; and offers to exchange goods or services for some

desired advantage. Each of these works better in some situations than in others, but money is potentially influential with a
greater number of people and over a wider range of circumstances than any other forms of social power. It usually gets
prompter results and is more dependably persuasive. Money
is, in effect, a form of instant power. Of all the forms of social
power, it is the one that is the most energetically sought and
eagerly accepted.

But like other varieties of power, money is unevenly distributed among us; at any given moment some will have more
than most, and some will have less. No one, of course, ever has
enough. The hourly wage earner goes on strike for an increase
that will lift his annual income from nine to ten thousand. The
salaried executive tells his wife that if he were a millionaire
they would take the 'round-the-world cruise she longs for, but
the millionaire cancels a week's holiday in Baja California—it
would have been his first in two years—in order to keep a
watchful eye on a stock offering that will increase his personal
capital by 10%. In this respect, money is like the other forms
of social power. Its possession whets the appetite for more.

We often defend this appetite on grounds of our need to
feel secure. We claim that we must have more money, status,
eloquence, approval, love, or whatever, to defend ourselves
against competition, the attacks of envious others, and the trials
and vicissitudes of life, or to give us the resources to face the
inevitable rainy day, when the eagerness of others to respond
to our desires may be noticeably dampened.

Each new gain in power is reassuring, but the security it
brings is temporary. The drive to continue the quest always
returns, as strong as ever. Acquisitiveness and ambition have
been condemned as neurotic and hence pathological by some
psychoanalysts and psychologists, as well they may be in many
instances, but there is much contrary opinion among other
students of human behavior, who hold that the drive to improve
one's condition is healthy. When is ambition normal and when
is it neurotic? The line that divides these two conditions is
blurred, but most psychotherapists would agree that ambition
is pathological if it is uncontrolled, is destructive of normal
relations with others, or is out of touch with reality. But equally

pathological is the behavior of the individual who takes an essentially passive and apathetic view of life, is continually used and exploited, and makes no attempt to improve his position in relation to others.

Money, Power, and Excitement

Among the psychological needs and drives common to us all, one is especially important in explaining our interest in acquiring and using money and other forms of social power, an interest that is, as we suggested above, so widespread as to be considered normal. The motive (need or drive) in question is our tendency to be attracted to situations that are intellectually, emotionally, or physically arousing. The pioneer work of D. E. Berlyne (1966) led behavioral scientists to realize that the need to be stimulated is a basic human motive. In fact, it is universal among animals. This need for arousal is especially strong after we have accommodated ourselves to a given level of stimulation. Our tendency to avoid extended social isolation and to seek the company of others appears to be motivated by the need for arousal. There are of course times when we withdraw from a stimulating social situation and seek peace and quiet, but a diminished level of stimulation over an extended period of time usually produces a sense of boredom or restlessness and the desire to return to the more stimulating environment of everyday life.

The need for stimulation probably underlies a wide range of behavioral tendencies, such as the restlessness that leads to change in physical and social environments; the enjoyment of idle and aimless conversation, spiced by a dash of gossip; the appreciation of art, literature, and music; and involvement in games, contests, and competition. In these activities, arousal results from exposure to environments characterized by complexity and change.

In many of these stimulating forms of behavior there is an element of "making things happen." Change is exciting, but we feel more comfortable when we are in control of the process. The use of power involves both elements: change and control. We first enjoyed the processes of change and control as infants, when we learned to move objects by pulling. About the same time we discovered the joys of social power by smiling at adults and eliciting answering smiles. Later we used a new-found ability to say "Mama" and "Dada" to evoke cries of approval and encouragement from our parents. At mealtime we experienced the delicious pleasure of tyranny—power without responsibility—by dropping our spoons on the floor again and again just to watch our disgruntled parents pick them up.

During the years that followed these early experiences in influencing the behavior of others we developed a wide repertoire of ways to employ social power. We found the use of these techniques challenging and demanding; sometimes frustrating and disappointing; but always arousing.

By the time we had learned the advantages of money as a way of influencing behavior, we had developed a decided appetite for power, an appetite limited only by the restrictions imposed by others, by the promptings of our conscience, and by our appraisal of what could or could not be accomplished.

Taking into account this developmental history and the advantages money possesses as a medium for the expression of power needs, it is hardly surprising that we find money so interesting, value it so highly, and pursue it so diligently.

The Difference that Money Makes

The interest we have learned to display toward money is easily transferred, by the process of association, to the activities that involve it. By the same token, activities that do not initially involve money may sometimes become more interesting when money is introduced. Here is an example of the difference money can make.

Finding that she had a great deal of time on her hands after her two children had gone off to college, Alma Hensill volunteered as a part-time receptionist for the Northeastside Center, a family service agency.

During the first two months, the work was fascinating (if a bit confusing at times). Then, as she developed some expertise in her role, Alma began to notice things she had previously ignored. The social workers seemed aloof and did not treat her as an equal, even though she had a degree in political science from a prestigious university and had also done some graduate work. As time went on, Alma began to feel that she was being taken for granted. No one seemed to appreciate her work, even though she had taken the initiative to straighten out the Center's files and had developed lists of addresses and telephone numbers of referral agencies. The job, which had been challenging and exciting, now seemed irritating and frustrating.

When she had first come on the job she had scheduled her other social activities around the hours she would be at the Center, but as the months wore on she found it hard to turn down social engagements in order to maintain her hours at the Center. And so she began telling the coordinator of volunteers at the Center that she would not be in on this or that day next week because "something had come up" that required her presence. The coordinator sometimes had difficulty finding a substitute, but otherwise her occasional absences seemed to cause no problem. The staff members never said they missed her.

After she had been working at the Center for five months, Alma heard of a geriatric clinic that was starting a program to train volunteer counselors. Although at one time she would have dismissed the suggestion that she work with older people, the prospect now seemed challenging and intriguing. But she never got the chance to volunteer, for the next day the director of the Center called her into his office and said:

"You've been doing an outstanding job for us, Alma. We appreciate it more than I can say. Therefore I'm happy to tell you that we're now able to make your position permanent. Our grant has come through. We can put you on a regular salaried basis, starting today, if you are interested."

Moments earlier, Alma had thought that few things would give her more pleasure than to leave the Center and to train to become a geriatric counselor, but suddenly her work as a receptionist took on an entirely different meaning. For the first time in months it seemed important, worthwhile, and interesting.

The fact that the Center was now willing to put a monetary value on her work dismissed all her doubts about its significance. The frustrations and disappointments she had experienced no longer seemed important.

The salary not only made the *work* seem more important, but it also gave Alma Hensill a greater sense of her own *worth*. One reason for this effect, of course, is that the work she did was psychologically a part of her, and whatever evaluation the Center made of her work was viewed by her as an evaluation of *herself*. The fact that the Center was now willing to pay for her work therefore enhanced her self-esteem.

The Price of Personal Worth

Two points are illustrated in this anecdote. One is that money can be used to give a task importance. The second is that we tend to value ourselves in proportion to the money that others are willing to pay for our efforts.

The latter is a troubling insight. We would all like to believe that our value as individuals has nothing at all to do with what we are paid for our services. For one thing, we resist the idea that our psychological worth, which is reflected in our self-esteem, is controlled by others and not by ourselves. For another, the existence of wide ranges in pay scales means that there are correspondingly wide ranges in personal worth. Both concepts contradict a basic credo in the American culture—a belief in the fundamental equality of individuals, a belief that is expressed in the Declaration of Independence and is embodied in the Constitution of the United States and the laws of the country. The legal codes of most other countries also affirm the equality of their citizens, even when their traditions, customs, and cultural values may not be especially egalitarian.

As we examine documents, like the Constitution, however, we are only partly reassured about our equality as individuals. In the first place, laws and declarations all refer to the individual's *legal* status, the rights to which he or she is entitled by law. They say nothing about social and economic value systems that create vast inequalities.

In the second place, constitutions and other legal statutes are in many instances expressions of the way things *ought* to be, not the way they are. Although we would like to believe that the legal status of the individual has nothing to do with his or her socioeconomic situation, the facts show otherwise. Donald Black (1976), in his survey of legal procedures throughout

THE PRICE OF PERSONAL WORTH 67

the world, noted that as a matter of general practice an offender is likely to be imprisoned if his social status is lower than that of his victims. If the offender's status is higher than the victim's, he is likely to avoid prison and simply pay a fine. The probability that a lawbreaker will actually be arrested, charged, and found guilty also varies according to his social status and his financial worth. The white-collar shoplifter has a good chance of escaping prosecution if when caught he claims he has never stolen before and promises never to do it again. The store manager characteristically requires him to make restitution and then releases him with a warning. The blue-collar shoplifter's similar protestations are likely to be doubted. He is more likely to be turned over to the police and the courts.

When an offense is so serious that even a white-collar suspect must be charged, he who has more money is in a better position to secure an able lawyer than he who has less. In addition, the white-collar person, by reason of his better education and his substantial claims to respectability, makes a reassuring impression on judge and jury and is less likely to be convicted. To be sure, widely publicized exceptions, like the cases involving the Watergate culprits and Patricia Hearst, may lull us into believing that equality before the law guarantees equal treatment in the courts, but general experience tells a different story. As Damon Runyon said, the race is not always to the swift, nor the battle to the strong, but that's the way to bet. And when charged with a serious offense, the best bet is the ablest attorney you can afford. In sum, then, while legal codes tend to ignore social and economic status, legal practices generally take them into account.

Of course, our feelings about ourselves are not molded by the wording of legal codes, but by our success in dealing with others in everday matters. This success may take many forms—for example, the ability to get others to listen to us and take us seriously, the satisfactions we experience in work and play, and the effectiveness with which we perform the tasks and rituals appropriate to our roles as parents, employers, neighbors, students, spouses, church members, or whatever. Success in dealing with others depends on a number of personal qualities, but the chief among them is the ability to influence behavior—social power. Because our opinion of ourselves rests to a large degree on our ability to influence others, it follows that the social power we possess plays a large part in determining whether our appraisal of ourselves is positive or negative. It is not easy to be routinely successful in influencing others and at the same time to harbor a thoroughly poor opinion of oneself, though there are some who develop a perverse expertise at this demanding task. (The occasional suicides of the extremely rich are grim reminders that money is no bastion against neurotic guilt and self-hatred.) Conversely, people who maintain an extravagantly positive view of themselves in the face of a chronic deficit in social power are conventionally viewed as being out of touch with reality and hence as prime candidates for intensive psychotherapy or long-term custodial care.

From our recognition of the fact that money confers social power it is but a short step to the assumption that money and other forms of social power indicate worthiness. How easily we translate income or monetary assets into indicators of psychological or social value—even into indexes of personal adequacy. This kind of classification is especially tempting when the monetary differences are large, as between a bank vice president and a teller, or between a $15,000-a-year social worker and a $5000-a-year welfare recipient. Of course we are careful to decry such comparisons as specious, undemocratic, unworthy, perhaps even immoral; yet we make them all the time, without much more than a thought. Such appraisals—and often they are self-appraisals—are backed by the full weight of social consensus.

So powerful a force is social consensus that we outdo ourselves in living up to, or living down to, the price tag that society has placed on us. The banker makes dignified pronouncements and sage predictions, at the proper time and before the proper audience. His occasional human errors are studiously ignored, covered up, forgotten. The long-term welfare recipient also plays a role—one consistent with the meager income he receives from the government: He is unemployed and apparently unemployable; even if he had a salable skill, he would not know how to look for a job. He arrives late for his appointments with his social worker and sometimes forgets to come altogether. Should he do something very clever, however, such as catch the social worker in a procedural error, he would be unlikely to mention it. It is not appropriate for a "welfare case" to be smarter than a social worker.

It is fascinating to observe how society sorts our various social, psychological, and intellectual qualities and sees to it that they are properly correlated with that personal attribute that can be most precisely assessed and most readily communicated: financial worth. No wonder money-worth broadcasts a signal, loud and clear, that often drowns out the messages from other indicators of personal value.

We noted earlier that money and other forms of social power are not evenly distributed in society. In explanation of this fact it is often argued that the inequalities of distribution are determined by either the practical or the social value of the services provided by individuals. The bank vice president's services, the argument goes, are of more use to us than those of the teller, and the social worker's contributions are more valuable than those of the welfare recipient. But a careful analysis suggests that often *psychological* rather than practical value determines the apportionment of financial and other rewards. Thus in Western society bishops, baseball players, and bookmakers—whose functions run to ritual or entertainment—have more power, influence, and money than do garbage collectors, grocery clerks, and garage mechanics, whose functions are more clearly related to our survival needs. Similarly, in primitive societies, shamans, priests, and soothsayers have higher status than food gatherers and toolmakers. The rationale underlying this seemingly illogical system is very simple: Once survival needs have been met, social-psychological needs become preeminent.

Financial Status and the Power Structure

Irrespective of why status accrues more to some than to others, the plain fact is that all functioning social groups—tribes, nations, unions, trade associations, political parties, clubs, communes, neighborhood gangs, and so forth—produce status systems in which a minority is more influential than influenced and a majority is more influenced than influential. Sociologists call this arrangement a *power structure*, a term that is now popularly but erroneously employed in reference to the affluent few at the top of the status pyramid. The more or less unconscious motive behind this common misuse of the term may be that of concealing from ourselves the fact that we all participate in creating and maintaining both the larger power structure of the society to which we belong and the smaller power structures of the other organizations and groups, both formal and informal, of which we are members.

Most people think they have a choice about whether they will cooperate or not with the demands of power structures, but this belief is without substance. Power structures exist as a result of the collaboration of all concerned. The official aspects of their operation take such forms as salary and wage schedules, rules and regulations, organizational charts, budgets, policy statements, white papers, and interoffice memos. These comprise the structure's superficial aspect, to which some of us react by saying, "To hell with what the power structure wants. I'm going to do what I damn well please," a threat that is seldom carried out.

But this portion of the structure is only the tip of the iceberg. By far the greater part is composed of informal interaction rituals, unenunciated but powerful social norms, unspoken expectations, and the unannounced group decisions that everyone silently obeys. We rarely are aware of how we and others support the power structures that form the invisible social network in which we function and interact.

Signals of Moneyed Importance

We use a number of conventions to inform others about our financial status, about the amount of respect or attention we believe is due us—in short, about our position in the power structure. Dress is such a convention. Psychologists have demonstrated the effectiveness of this signal in a field experiment, mentioned at the beginning of this chapter, in which an accomplice of the researchers asked passers-by to give him two nickels for a dime. The experiment was conducted outside the entrances of supermarkets located in middle-class and lower-middle-class residential areas near New York City. When the accomplice was neatly dressed in a business suit and tie, the supermarket customers obliged him much more often than when he was dressed as a hippie (Raymond & Unger, 1971).

Thus do we create systems based on symbolic indications of status and power. We judge the suited accomplice as more "acceptable" and permit ourselves to be influenced by him. We accede to his request. We assign him whatever powers of rank go with his costume. We judge the hippie as "less acceptable" and ignore or refuse his request. We thus deny his claim to social power and place him near the foot of the social ladder.

In a variation of the simple experiment just described, about two hundred persons were asked by the accomplices (male and female) of a psychological investigator whether they had found a dime (planted by the researcher) in the telephone booth they had just left. Sometimes the question was posed by a male accomplice wearing suit and tie, and sometimes by the same accomplice wearing work clothes and carrying something to identify him as a member of the blue-collar class, such as a flashlight, a lunch pail, or a six-foot rule. In their "high-status" pose, female accomplices wore neat dresses and either wore or carried coats. When they posed as low-status individuals, they wore skirts and blouses and were generally unkempt.

When the accomplice's dress suggested middle-class status, over three fourths of the persons asked returned the dime; the remainder lied, saying they had found none. When the accomplice was shabbily dressed, however, fewer than half the phone-booth users acknowledged finding the dime (Bickman, 1971).

There is irony in an additional finding. When the investigator described the experimental conditions to his university students and asked them to guess which type of accomplice— the "middle-class" or the "working-class"—would be lied to most frequently by the phone booth users, they replied that there would be no difference. After all, who would lie to a stranger for a mere dime? And especially to a *poor* stranger, who obviously needed the money. These students naively underestimated the effects of status symbols on social behavior.

Dress is only one of the ways we signal our claim to status and power and announce our worth in both financial and psychological terms. The cars we drive are also a very important means of telling others who we are. Social psychologists Anthony N. Doob and Alan E. Gross (1968) contrived an ingenious experiment to measure people's attitudes toward drivers of cars representing two markedly different levels of social status and affluence: a new Chrysler and an old, down-at-the wheels Rambler.

The automobiles were driven by one of the investigators, who wore clothes consistent with the presumed status level of the car he happened to be driving. He gauged his approach to intersections in such a way that the traffic lights would be red. The driver who happened to stop behind him thus became the unwitting subject in the experiment that began when the traffic light turned to green. Instead of proceeding immediately, the psychologist/driver waited at the intersection for a full twelve seconds. An assistant concealed in the back compartment of the automobile recorded how many seconds elapsed before the driver caught behind him honked.

The researchers found that drivers waited longer before honking when the car ahead of them was the new Chrysler than when it was the old Rambler. Furthermore, eighteen of the drivers honked twice when blocked by the Rambler, whereas only seven honked twice at the Chrysler. Some of the drivers were extremely patient and did not honk at all during the 12-second wait; but even this patience seemed to depend upon the affluence of the driver ahead of them, for only six never honked at the Rambler, and eighteen never honked at the Chrysler.

The researchers were especially intrigued by these findings because they were inconsistent with the feelings Americans often express about high-status individuals—especially about the rich. The circumstances of the experimental situation made it impossible for the researchers to poll the frustrated drivers, but they did sample the opinions of students at a nearby university, many of whom drove the streets in which the experiments had been conducted. They asked half the students to estimate how long they would wait before they honked at the driver of an old Rambler who did not move when the traffic light turned green; the remaining students were asked the same question about being stuck behind a new Chrysler.

The students' estimates of how they would behave stand in interesting contrast to the way the subjects actually behaved. The male students, on the average, said they would delay honking about 9 seconds for the older, cheaper car and 5.5 seconds for the newer, more expensive one. This expression of what was presumably greater consideration for the lower-status driver was quite different from the behavior recorded in the experiment, where male drivers delayed an average of 6.8 seconds before honking at the Rambler, and 8.5 seconds before honking at the Chrysler. In other words, the greater impatience the male students said they would feel toward members of the "establishment" (Chrysler drivers) was nowhere in evidence in the way male drivers actually behaved on neighboring streets.

This discrepancy may characterize the way many males behave in a power structure: They claim that they will not defer to the higher-status members, but in the end they do. Since they conveniently overlook their own conforming tendencies, they are able to go through life entertaining the myth that the stuatus system is imposed upon them and exists in spite of their forthright and steadfast attempts to frustrate it.

The estimates of the female students, on the other hand, were in accord with reality. They said they would delay honking longer for the more prestigious car, and that is just what the female drivers did in the experiment.

Prestige and Money

It is reasonable to assume that most of the drivers who served as unwitting subjects in the Doob/Gross experiment were in cars that cost less and that hence suggested lower status than did the new Chrysler. Hence the consideration they expressed by delaying their honking or by not honking at all may be taken as a form of deference to a person they assumed possessed status higher than their own.

People are entitled to *deference* by right of their superior occupational status, wealth, income, educational attainment, political or corporate power, and kinship connections, according to Edward Shils (1968), the political scientist. A sociologist, Donald J. Treiman (1977), tells us that entitlements to deference confer *prestige* on individuals who possess them, a quality that is synonymous with honor, regard, respect, and esteem. It is prestige that makes the use of power legitimate and thus adds to its effectiveness. By joining the board of directors of the Community Chest and thus allowing his prestigious name and title to appear on its propaganda, the president of a major bank places his stamp of approval on the annual fund drive, assuring any and all potential contributors of the drive's legitimacy.

There are various ways of acquiring prestige. The usual procedure is to select, prepare for, and seek entry into an occupation. Opinion pollsters have found that their respondents agree about the degrees of prestige associated with various occupations. Treiman has analyzed public opinion surveys of occupational prestige conducted during the past twenty-five years in the United States and in some fifty other countries. The American surveys covered over four hundred occupations, which were ranked by various groups of respondents from Member of the President's Cabinet at the top of the scale to Shoe Shiner at the bottom. Surveys conducted in other countries yielded results quite similar to those obtained in the United States, indicating that occupational prestige hierarchies are much the same in all countries. A list of fifty occupations, selected as representative, indicated that in the countries surveyed, Physician, University Professor, and Trial Lawyer ranked highest in prestige, and Janitor, Servant, and Street Sweeper ranked lowest, with Farmer, Electrician, and Insurance Agent occupying the middle of the scale.

When Treiman compared occupational rankings with income data from census reports, he found that the two sets of figures were quite consistent: In general, the average pay received in occupations higher on the scale was more than that received in lower-ranking occupations. Treiman also found that the average amount of education completed by individuals in various occupations was even more highly correlated to occupational prestige than was income, indicating that in all countries today schooling has become the accepted route to positions that offer status, prestige, and money.

Most of us, however, think of money and not of education, when we consider occupations at various prestige levels. We all know, for instance, that physicians must spend long years of preparation, but it is their ability to earn more money than most of us that comes to mind when the medical profession is discussed. The fact that money is, as we have noted, the most visible aspect of personal worth also leads us to think of occupational prestige in terms of money. Educational level may play a large role in a person's social influence, as Treiman indicates, but it is the money he or she makes and commands that usually attracts our attention. Hence occupational status and money become linked in our minds.

Because of this mental linkage, we are likely to be disturbed when we experience disparities between income and occupational prestige. A few years ago, San Francisco residents were upset, when publication of municipal employees' salaries revealed that street sweepers were making $17,000 a year. The average San Francisco taxpayer, who earned considerably less than that amount, was outraged, and many angry citizens wrote letters to the newspaper and the mayor complaining of injustice. Even people at higher levels of prestige and income were offended at the disparity between status and earnings, for it meant that "the system wasn't working." As a result of the outcry, street sweepers were "reclassified" and paid a lower wage.

One of the reasons for the widely recognized interlinkage between money and status is that status provides people with opportunities to make money, as Robert W. Hodge (1979), a sociologist at the University of Southern California, points out. The causal relationship works the other way as well, of course. Hodge notes that study after study indicates that people with high income are more likely than those with low income to hold membership in voluntary organizations, to participate in community affairs, and to gather informally with friends, neighbors, relatives, and colleagues. Although such activities cost money, the expenditure relative to other outlays is low, but the amount of time they take is considerable. Inasmuch as the time of these well-paid individuals is so demonstrably valuable, one might think that they would prefer to spend less rather than more time at activities having no visible rate of economic return. Nevertheless, this type of involvement in the end turns out to be both status-producing and status-maintaining, in that it enables them to make useful professional or business contacts and thus find opportunities for their economic betterment. Such activities also enhance their social image and, as a consequence, their prestige. Thus status, money, and prestige are potential determinants of one another.

Over the years, I have observed that those people I know who have been most successful in acquiring wealth were not the ones who made money their top priority, but those who gave their main attention to striving for success in their chosen fields. Those who were primarily concerned with money when I first knew them, twenty or thirty years ago, are still preoccupied with it today, but they have been less successful in obtaining it than those who concentrated on career goals. For the latter, a high level of competence in their career brought them the respect of others, prestige, and status. It also brought them money, but that seemed to come along as a natural consequence of status and position.

Recipes for career success are a commonplace; self-help books that promise the secrets of getting ahead sell by the millions, and the mass media offer articles and syndicated columns by the score that reveal formulas for upward mobility: aggressiveness, assertiveness, friendliness, astuteness, cleverness, and dozens of other essential -nesses. The fact is that every successful person's story is unique, and such uniqueness does not readily lead to generalizations. But I have observed that the one thing successful people have in common is what they have *not* done—that is, they have not made getting a lot of money their main concern. This does not mean that they have been *un*concerned about it; like most of us, they have their money problems and have to be careful with their spending. But money issues have been incidental to their main interests.

Money, Freedom, and Independence

Should we be among the majority whose financial status is consistent with our occupational prestige level, we are not likely to be content with it. We cannot keep from feeling a degree of envy for those, however more prestigious they may be, who have more money than we do.

Why are those who have more money envied almost universally? Part of the answer may be found in the fantasies we all have about coming into a great deal of money. We imagine that if we were really wealthy, we could escape from the restrictions that bind us to situations and relationships we find unrewarding, frustrating, or inhibiting. If we had enough money, we say, we would not remain tied down to a tedious job, worried about making payments on the house and having to scrimp, economize, and giving up major and minor pleasures in order to eke out a living within the restraints of an inadequate income. We suppose that an abundance of money would free us from our present restrictive environment and allow us to pursue attractive ventures, enjoy new experiences, and dissolve encumbering responsibilities.

In order to determine what rewards people see in money, I asked a group of university students to imagine that they had become "instant millionaires" and to list five important advantages they felt their newly acquired money would give them. Virtually all of the lists included at least one statement that involved freedom: Freedom from debt, freedom from the need to work for a living, freedom for self-development, freedom to live life more fully, and freedom to live how and where one pleased were the advantages mentioned most frequently. Altruistic outcomes, such as the opportunity to help others and to support worthy causes were mentioned by many, along with the pleasures to be received from things that could be bought, but the majority of the advantages listed dealt with freedom in one form or another.

Expectations like these are based on our general awareness that money can "buy" freedom, in the sense that it widens our areas of choice. Money can secure freedom more efficiently than any other social or economic resource. The migrant worker who comes into money through some quirk of fate finds himself free of the necessity to earn his livelihood through the bone-crushing drudgery of stoop labor in the fields. The seamstress who has spent long, tedious hours in a garment factory saves her money and buys a small dry-cleaning establishment. She must still work hard, but now she is free to decide the pace at which she will work, as well as her hours of work. She has also been liberated from the foreman's critical scrutiny and can stop to socialize with customers whenever she feels like it.

Money may widen our area of choice in dealing with a multitude of everyday problems. When our roof leaks, we can, if we have the money, buy the material to fix the roof, hire someone to patch it, replace the entire roof, or move to a house that is in better repair. Without money, we must run for pots and pans when it rains and pray that the roof will not develop more leaks than we have receptacles. The impoverished individual who has run through his money must take whatever job is available, even if it makes unreasonable demands on his health and energy, is inconsistent with his skills and interests, and is ill-located. With money in the bank, however, he has more possibilities: He can spend time looking for a more appropriate job, seek training for more suitable work, go into business for himself, and so forth.

Money also opens up escape routes for the restless, the bored, or the harassed. Sometimes all we need is a change of scene. Money helps here by providing the means to holiday in pleasant surroundings, to travel, to spend a pleasant evening at the theater, or to escape from the kitchen by eating in a restaurant.

The money young people earn frees them from dependence on their parents and enables them to set up their own households. The money earned by an increasing number of married women has undoubtedly contributed to the rising divorce rate. When wives are no longer dependent on their husbands for economic support, they are free to leave when marriage relationships become overly stressful.

The fact that money has the power to increase options and opportunities may also cause difficulties. If we are inclined to be anxious, we may become especially cautious about using our money even for necessary expenses. Or the range of options our money makes available may generate confusion and apprehensiveness while we try to decide what course of action is best.

But these problems are not the main issues here. There are instead two points to consider. First, freedom (whatever form it takes) is attractive to most people. Second, most of the arrangements that make freedom possible cost money. It may be, as the song says, that the best things in life are free, but in today's world freedom itself must be bought and paid for.

Money as a Universalistic Resource

When something is especially important to us or arouses much excitement or concern, we tend to coin substitute names for it. Liquor is therefore referred to as booze, grog, rum, rot-gut, and a dozen or two other euphemisms. We similarly coin and use a great variety of words in speaking of love in its multitudinous forms. Money, too, can be referred to by terms such as cash, filthy lucre, the wherewithall, gold, silver, pence, dough, bread, and shekels, to name a few of the long list of substitute words and phrases.

For all the colorful and romantic language that is used to refer to it, however, money itself remains essentially unromantic and neutral. Because of its neutrality, the social psychologist Uriel Foa (1971) has classified money as a "universalistic resource." Our attitudes toward it, says Foa, are universally the same no matter who offers it to or receives it from us. Other universalistic resources are goods, services, and information.

Our attitudes toward love and status—"particularistic resources," in Foa's terms—depend a great deal on who offers them. A kindergarten teacher may enjoy offers of spontaneous affection from her school-children, but will feel upset if the offer comes from an adult stranger. A nuclear physicist may be elated by an invitation to address an association of scientists but is likely to be annoyed by requests to appear on television "talk shows."

In order to distinguish the effects of universalistic from those of particularistic resources, Foa conducted a series of experiments in which individuals traded cards on which were printed descriptions of various resources. A participant was required to offer each of his cards in turn to his trading partner, who would decide what resources he would give in exchange. From the records of these transactions, Foa was able to determine the extent to which a given resource was exchangeable in terms of other resources. Love and status, the two particularistic resources, possessed the highest degree of compatibility, for they were most often exchanged, one for the other; but compatibility was nil between love and money.

Some universalistic resources were moderately compatible with particularistic ones—for example, 41% of the participants who were offered a card listing a service offered love in exchange—but in no instance was love offered in exchange for money. In simplistic, everyday terms, this means that doing things for others may evoke their love but that love can never be secured for money.

Applying his findings to life in large cities, Foa points out that urban circumstances favor the acquisition and exchange of the more impersonal universalistic resources: goods, services, information, and money. Of all these, money has become the most salient, fluid, and useful, and it is common practice to value the other three resources in monetary terms. Foa says that the emphasis on universalistic resources has led to urban dwellers' being short-changed with respect to love and status. Their inability to secure and exchange these particularistic resources, coupled with their preoccupation with universalistic resources, especially money, creates an atmosphere that encourages irresponsibility. Foa points out that the citizen of a small town who does not pay his bills or who beats his wife loses status even if he is able to avoid arrest. In a large city, where the emphasis on universalistic resources promotes anonymity, his misbehavior would stand a good chance of going unnoticed by fellow employees or by neighbors, even if it led to difficulties with the law.

When love and status are in short supply, people have to settle for money and the other universalistic resources. This substitution according to Foa, will always cause dissatisfaction. A person who needs love and cannot get it will never be satisfied with money, no matter how much of it he or she gets.

All resources, whether particularistic or universalistic, can be employed to influence others and hence are potential sources of social power. Money, however, is an especially *versatile*, readily *recognized*, and quickly *convertible* resource—an *efficient* medium of exchange. Although it cannot buy love, it can be traded easily for many other resources, including the types of personal freedom we mentioned earlier. Indeed, the relationship to freedom may be an important difference between money and love: Money can free one from some kinds of de- ✓ pendence, but love cannot. Love requires commitment, mutual responsiveness, shared responsibility, and loyalty, all of which restrict freedom. Love exerts its power through promoting intimate interdependence; the possession or use of money permits or encourages noninvolvement and anonymity. It is, in a manner of speaking, "clean,"[1] for it is devoid of entangling encumbrances. Purchasing power, unlike the influence exercised by love, requires no ties of loyalty. The use of money can be as impersonal as the use of electricity.

The fact that money can be used to secure freedom sometimes makes it a threat to love. Imagine a pair of lovers, one with a great deal of money, the other financially dependent on the first. Though they may vow eternal loyalty to each other, the imbalance in economic power means that one partner possesses the means to engage in a wide variety of activities that may weaken the degree of mutual involvement. The first partner's greater freedom to engage in such activities may make the other partner jealous. If the activities are shared, the partner who brought fewer resources to the relationship may come to resent the continuing need to play a dependent role. If the arrangement develops frustrations and tensions, as is the common experience, it is easier for the wealthier partner to escape. Most modern societies make an attempt to remedy this imbalance by requiring that some kind of shared property arrangement go into effect automatically when the love relationship is officially recognized through marriage.

Love is so important a human resource that we cannot imagine a world without it. It is almost as difficult to imagine

---

[1] That money remains unsullied regardless of its transactional history has bemused philosophers and delighted cynics throughout the ages. Suetonius says that Titus, son of the Roman Emperor Vespasian, reproached his father for taxing the public urinals. Titus felt that the levy was unseemly and inconsistent with the dignity of the noble office his father held. Vespasian, a bluff soldier with an earthy sense of humor, plucked a coin from the first payment, held it under his son's nose, and asked if it had any trace of a latrine odor. Titus had to admit that it did not. "You see," said Vespasian, "money has no smell." Modern Parisians, who have a keen sense of history and a genius for coining euphemisms, have celebrated this conversation by calling their public urinals *vespasiennes*.

a world without money as well. Because of money's universality and flexibility it has taken on a high degree of what psychologists term "reward value," a value that we learn to recognize and accept at about the age when we graduate from diapers into less bulky underclothing. By the time we have entered the mid-stream of childhood a set of generalized attitudes and feelings about money has been so securely built into our nervous system that we respond unconsciously and at times instantaneously to its prod. It is this complex of attitudes and feelings about money that enables a promoter to breathe an atmosphere of excitement into a ridiculous guessing game by offering prizes of fifty, a hundred, or a thousand dollars for those who survive a sufficient number of trials. And the same complex of attitudes and feelings causes a hush to fall over a lively dinner party when the waiter presents the bill. Our society programs us to feel that money, (or the expectation of its coming), is exciting, while money's going, (or the expectation of its departure), is sobering.

In today's society, attitudes and feelings about money have become integrated into our lives in a variety of subtle ways. In the next chapter, we shall explore the deeper layers of person-ality to see how far our concern about money has penetrated.

5 Money and self-worth

Let all the learn'd say what they can
'Tis ready money makes the man.
—WILLIAM SOMERVILLE

A son can bear with equanimity the loss of his father, but
the loss of his inheritance drives him to despair.
—MACHIAVELLI

The poor man's wisdom is despised, and his words are
not heard. —ECCLESIASTES, 9:16

The management of money is, in much, the management
of the self. —EDWARD ROBERT BULWER-LYTTON

Each of us is interested in the unique aspects of his own behavior, but the social psychologist is most intrigued by behavior
we all have in common, especially those aspects that are shaped
by social norms—the ways we interact, attitudes, beliefs, and
values. We learn these behavioral and motivational patterns
from those we grew up with and from our associates: our cultural
or subcultural group. Among many other things, we learn certain attitudes and beliefs about money.

Almost all of us learn that money is something very special.
As we noted in Chapter 4, money is associated with power,
status, prestige, and advantage. We learn that money gives us
the social power to influence others and to resist their influence
as well; a lack of money makes us weak and subject to the
influence of those who possess it. As noted in Chapter 2, money
facilitates socialization. Imagine that you have suddenly been
given a sum equal to a year's income—what will you do with
it? Take a long holiday? Pay off a mortgage? Invest it for future
income? Go on a buying binge? Whatever fantasy comes to
mind, the chances are that it involves some form of social

interaction. Whether your fantasies run to pleasure, helping others, or investment, they all involve dealing with others. Money tends to increase our social contacts.

Money possesses the power to stimulate and arouse, as we also noted earlier. The sudden appearance of power in any form excites or upsets us because it suggests that our situation is about to change. We are therefore aroused—on the alert—prepared for any eventuality.

In short, money may influence our emotional state. This is especially true when our monetary status undergoes an unexpected change. An unanticipated gain, such as winning a sweepstakes prize, will produce elation; a loss, such as an assessment from the Internal Revenue Service for a thousand dollars more than we had figured, may produce anger, depression, and even despair.

The Self and Its Money

Our money is, strictly speaking, a part of our environment and not a part of *us*. Yet we react to major changes in our monetary situation as though changes were taking place in ourselves.

This universal tendency to regard possessions and a great many other elements in our social and physical environment as parts of ourselves has led to the development of a branch of personality psychology termed *self-theory*. Self-theorists attempt to explain our behavior in terms of our *perception* of our environment, rather than in terms of the environment itself. Let us say that your monthly statement from the credit-card agency still includes an erroneous three-dollar interest charge that a company representative told you would be dropped. If your anger is intense, its magnitude cannot easily be explained in environmental terms—that is, in terms of the real threat posed by this miniscule error. Your outrage can be attributed only to how you *perceive* the error.

Although its roots can be traced back to the founder of American psychology, William James, self-theory has in recent decades been identified with the writings of Carl Rogers (1951), a humanistic psychologist. But it is the self-theory of Donald Snygg and Arthur S. Combs (1949), also humanistic psychologists, that will help us explain how people react to changes in their monetary situation.

A view of the self and its environment—a self-system—is schematically represented in Figure 1. Like each of us, I live in an environment partly known, but mostly unknown, to me. The outer line of the diagram encloses the area I am aware of, termed my "phenomenal environment." Part of this phenomenal environment I experience as related to me, and hence it is termed my "phenomenal self." At the center of this area lies my "self-concept": who I am or think I am.

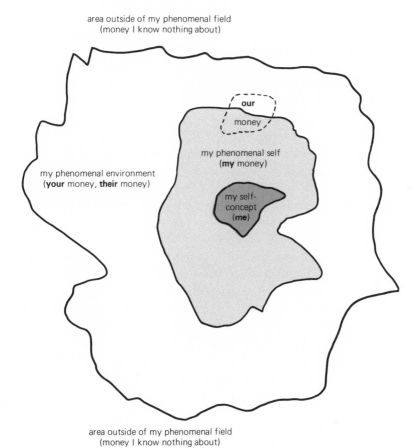

area outside of my phenomenal field
(money I know nothing about)

our
money

my phenomenal self
(**my** money)

my phenomenal environment
(**your** money, **their** money)

my self-
concept
(**me**)

area outside of my phenomenal field
(money I know nothing about)

Within the area of the phenomenal self are environmental elements that are not a part of my self-concept but still are things, persons, concepts, and events in which I am psychologically involved: e.g., my family, my home, my career, my ideals and values, my money, and my country. Anything that is not "myself," but which I can characterize as "mine," belongs in this area. The more I am involved with a thing, the closer to the diagram's central area—i.e., to the self-concept—would it lie; the less I am involved, the farther toward the outer boundary of the phenomenal self would it be placed.

The money in my checking account would lie in the phenomenal-self area. The check I have written for a local charity but have not sent lies further out on the periphery of the phenomenal self. It is still my money, but I have already bidden it farewell. Even after I have sent it to its destination, I maintain some interest in it, for I hope that it will be put to good use and I would be annoyed if it were used for "promotional expenses." In time my donation will disappear from my phenomenal environment entirely as it fades from memory.

Our self-systems are our unique versions of *reality*. Even though we base our impressions of the world to a large extent on the attitudes and actions of others, our individual experiences cause our views of reality to be different from those of every other person. Our decisions are based on the reality *we* perceive, not on someone else's reality.

Because actions based on a self-system in disrepair may turn out to be ineffective or disastrous, the maintenance and defense of our self-system are matters of high priority for us. If someone tries to alter our views, we defend our version of reality by reacting argumentatively. To change our views is to deny our own experience and judgment. Being told we are wrong threatens our self-systems and, ultimately, our innermost selves. This is why arguments over seemingly trivial issues may develop into serious quarrels.

Every self-system is unique, but this does not mean that each arises and functions independently. To some degree each self-system is the product of the others with whom it associates and identifies. The impossibility of experiencing everything in our environment means that we must all make use of a great deal of second-hand information in framing our views of the world and our concepts of reality. We are also responsive—much more so than we would like to believe—to the opinions others have of us. The assumptions others make about us have a subtle and irresistible influence upon the image we have of ourselves—subtle because it derives primarily from indirect and perhaps unconscious expressions of the roles they assign us in the scenarios of everyday living. Do other people attend carefully to us or do they ignore us; do they seek our company, or merely tolerate it; do they make demands on us, or do they permit us to influence them? In this social exchange of information and influence, we rarely recognize the full extent of the power of others to mold our self-esteem.

Money Games with Society

But the individual's self-system is by no means a merely passive product of the influence of others. Even while we are being molded by the open and concealed expression of others' attitudes, we are also busy seeking ways to make those attitudes favorable. Hence we play a game with society, in which the prize is the approval of others. If we win that approval, our self-esteem will rise, or will at least be able to maintain its integrity.

Money, as a particularly liquid form of social power and influence, plays several roles in the game. On the one hand, if we possess it we gain the respect of others. On the other hand, our monetary "winnings" may help others (and ourselves as well) to keep track of the degree of our success as we play the game.

Regardless of whether we buy and sell for a profit, work for wages, sell our services for a fee, gamble, or invest, we can be said to be playing the money game. If we come away from the game with more money than we began with, our self-esteem is thereby enhanced, for the gains we make in the money games we play carry with them a degree of implicit social approval. Societies throughout the world— communist, socialist, and capitalist alike—condone, encourage, and reward those who come out ahead in economic transactions.

In order to secure society's approval, we must of course play the money game according to society's rules. A game that deviates too widely from the accepted sets of games, that is too innovative or too creatively greedy, is almost certain to be regarded with disapproval and declared illegal. Social approval is also contingent on how profits or earnings—winnings—are invested. In a communist country, the government will expect a winner to put his extra money into government bonds but may reluctantly condone its being spent for consumer goods. In such countries the purchase of an automobile or a television set, should they be available, increases the owner's status and influence with neighbors, just as the purchase of a power cruiser or a swimming pool does in more affluent lands on the other side of the Iron Curtain.

The possession of money does more than increase social acceptance and self-esteem—it influences our characteristic mood as well. Opinion polls conducted by Gallup and similar organizations routinely report that people in the higher income brackets tend to be happier, more optimistic, and even more relaxed and tolerant—that is, liberal—in their views than those who have less. People in the middle and high income brackets are also healthier, on the average, than those in the lower brackets. The Health and Nutrition Survey, conducted a few years ago by the U.S. Department of Health, Education, and Welfare, reported that blood pressure is related to income: a relatively high proportion of respondents at or below the government-designated poverty level had hypertension (systolic blood pressure at least 160 or diastolic blood pressure at least 95). Respondents with middle-range incomes or higher were less likely to be troubled by abnormally high blood pressure.

The Fate of Losers

The individual who loses time and time again in the money games we all play with society is at first frustrated, then depressed, and finally apathetic. Lacking money, he finds his power-base reduced. The psychological result is lowered sense of self-worth. The loser also has the recurrent suspicion that he has been exploited, discarded, or somehow diminished both by the winners and by the system that enables them to win. The unemployed person whose money supply is shrinking sees on all sides those whose employment enables them to maintain an enviable degree of financial self-sufficiency. It is difficult for him to continue the tedious and frustrating search for work because his sense of self-worth has been undermined by the obvious contrast between his status and that of the regularly employed. His expectations for himself have been lowered.

In a society where paid employment is the normal adult condition, status cannot readily be obtained without it. Professors rank fairly high in prestige, but only if they are on a college payroll. Unemployed professors on welfare rank somewhere below employed construction laborers' and factory hands' prestige, and with prolonged unemployment, their sense of self-worth suffers accordingly.[1] Indeed, I have known unemployed professors who took jobs in factories and as construction laborers in order to improve their financial status. Although they saw such work as only a temporary pause in their attempts to gain academic employment, they acknowledged that merely being at work and being on a payroll did a great deal for their morale and sense of well-being.

Are We "Worth" What We Are Paid?

The young suffer most from combined financial, social, and psychological disadvantage in most societies. The young are most likely to experience the embarrassment of unemployment; when they are employed, their jobs usually rank lower than their elders, in both status and pay. Even when they work at the same job as their seniors, their wage level is likely to be lower. Beginning high school teachers aged 23 may do the same work as veterans of 35 who have been in the school system for twelve years, but their salary is likely to be at least a third lower. The salary increases that the younger teachers will receive over the years will be given on the presumed grounds that they are becoming more experienced and hence are worth more to the school system. Since the value of a teacher's con-

---

[1]Treiman's (1977) analysis, discussed in Chapter 4, gives college professors a rating of 78.3; construction laborers, 26.2; factory workers, 29.4; and persons on public assistance, 25.1. My comments on unemployed professors are based on conversations I have had with them over the years, conducted for the most part at psychology conventions, which they attend in search of academic positions.

tribution—quality of instruction—cannot be measured by any precise or reliable means, the explanation given for the annual pay raise lacks substance. A more reasonable conclusion is that the pay raises reflect increases in status, as the teachers move from the junior to the senior ranks of the faculty.

The widespread belief that an employee's pay reflects his value to his employer derives from our habit of equating "value" with "price." String beans are selling for about 75 cents a pound in San Francisco markets, as this is written, and a pound of cultivated mushrooms sells for about $1.50. Weight for weight, mushrooms are obviously "worth" twice as much as string beans to shoppers. (Note, however, that this does not means mushrooms have twice the value as a source of nutrition.) Thus if junior accountants earn $12,000 a year and department heads are paid $24,000, does this means that department heads are "worth" twice as much to their employers as junior accountants? If "worth" means "price," then the logic of our vegetable comparison makes the answer "Yes"; but if "worth" means "productivity" (ability to "nourish" the employer's interests), then the answer must be "Not necessarily."

In fact, however, the difference in pay between the junior accountant and the department head is better explained in terms of social status than in terms of their economic worth to their employers. Peter F. Drucker (1977) makes this point neatly in his analysis of the salaries of corporation officers. The presidents of General Motors, Proctor and Gamble, Exxon, and a number of other major corporations receive annual salaries of $500,000 or more. If executives were paid a percentage of the company's net, these large sums might simply reflect the profit-making power of their services. This is not the case, however. Such officials draw salaries of this magnitude even when their companies are losing money.

These large salaries are often rationalized by the "need to pay the market price" for top executives, but Drucker says that such an explanation is nonsense. He says that the real reason for the high salaries lies in the "internal logic of a hierarchical structure." The normal practice in many corporations is to pay foremen 30-40% more than each of the workers they supervise; the foremen's supervisors must be paid a similar increment in salary, and so on. Since a comparable percentage is added to the pay at each higher rung on the status ladder, the amount received by the top official is determined not by his impact on the corporate profits (this is an intangible, like teaching skill, that can never be measured) but rather by the number of levels in the status hierarchy. If production-line workers in a manufacturing company make $10,000 a year, and there are thirteen steps in the status ladder, then the top official must be paid something over $300,000 a year; if there are fifteen steps, his pay will run somewhere between $500,000 and $600,000 a year. Because of the powerful effect of money on the psyche, it is easy to see what a salary of such magnitude will do to the self-esteem of the official who receives it. And it is also easy to see what an income of $10,000 a year will do to the self-esteem of the employee at the bottom of the status ladder who reads in the morning paper what the top man in his company is paid.

People in middle management, says Drucker, recognize that the system operates to reward a specific type of creativity—namely, the ability to create additional layers of management. Drucker notes that many a manager has been able to jack up his pay by as much as 50% by "reorganizing" his division to require five levels of managers and supervisors where formerly there were only three. The 30-40% salary-increase rule will never be found explicitly stated in any company's personnel-practices manual, of course. But in playing money games, it pays to understand the implicit, unofficial, and sometimes unmentionable rules, which often carry more weight than the explicit ones.

The Dollar and Our Sense of Self-Worth

A great deal of our time and energy during the early formative years of our lives is spent in learning the explicit and implicit expectations that govern social conduct. These mutual assumptions—many of which amount to "rules of behavior"—tell us what to expect of others and of ourselves as well. Such expectations are not 100% accurate, because human beings are not completely predictable, but they work well enough in most situations for us to have confidence in them. If no one had confidence in the implicit and explicit rules of society, anarchy would result; negotiations of all kinds, financial included, would become impossible. Our survival as social beings depends both on learning the assumptions that govern social behavior and on coming to believe in them as rules.

Once we have learned a social rule, we tend to feel committed to it. It becomes a part of our phenomenal self, and we stand ready to defend it like anything else we consider ours. Our defense may take the form of evasive action, such as when we ignore or dismiss information that contradicts a rule we have learned. Permitting one of our rules to be challenged raises the possibility that our other assumptions may be faulty and suggests that we ought to reexamine our entire view of the world and of ourselves. Rather than consider such a major reappraisal, we reject the possibility that one of our rules may be invalid. Sometimes, however, the challenge overwhelms our defenses. Here are some examples.

For many years Americans assumed—believed in as a rule—that their dollar was universally acceptable as currency. According to this rule, the world was hungry for dollars. A cliché often heard in reference to foreigners was "All they want is our *dollars.*" For a good many years after World War II, assumptions about the universal acceptability of the dollar seemed valid, but recent years of monetary inflation and negative trade balances have changed the reality on which that rule had been based. As a consequence, Americans arriving at European airports have occasionally found their dollars to be unacceptable. These illusion-shattering experiences occurred on weekends during the early 1970s, when Washington announced one of its periodic reductions in the theoretical gold content of the dollar. The airport exchange offices would accept marks, francs, and yen, but would refuse dollars. Americans reacted first with shock and disbelief, and then with exclamations of outrage. Their self-systems buckled and strained as they strove to cope with so massive a disconfirmation of what they felt to be reality. And many thought: "How dare these foreigners contradict the truth? And after all we have done for them."

Fortunately, cab drivers and restaurant owners were found who, as a very special favor, agreed to take dollars at ruinous discounts. Far from being grateful, however, most travelers were resentful. When Monday dawned, exchange dealers came to their senses and once again accepted dollars, though at a few percentage points lower than the previous week. Once the dollar was again respectable, Americans quickly readopted their rule; for them, "reality" and "truth," though slightly tarnished by their brush with near-disaster, were back in their places.

After a number of these upsetting incidents, Americans adopted new "rules" regarding the dollar, and today it is no longer fashionable for anyone to say "sound as a dollar," except as a joke.

Americans have not been the only people to suffer shocks that shattered their views of monetary reality, momentarily upset their self-systems, and shook their unquestioning belief in the integrity of their national currency. Within the last decade British, Scandinavian, and French travelers have all had the unsettling experience of finding themselves unable to change their money at foreign airports on weekends after their governments had announced currency revaluations.

Assumptions about the value of the currency, like those we cherish about our homeland, are deeply integrated into our self-systems. A Canadian couple I know felt humiliated when a sales clerk in a Portland, Oregon, department store disdainfully refused to accept their Canadian dollars which at that time had an exchange rate slightly higher than American dollars. Since American dollars were willingly accepted at par by Canadian merchants, they had naively assumed that American merchants would reciprocate. But the worst blow to their pride occurred when they happened to include a Canadian penny in payment for a tank of gasoline in California. The attendant looked at the penny, glanced at their British Columbia license plate, and then, laughing, threw the penny across the parking lot. He thought he had done them a kindness by not demanding an American penny, but they were outraged that he should treat their national currency like worthless junk. In psychological terms, a bit of the Canadians' self-concept was invested in the Canadian penny. When the attendant rejected their coin, he symbolically rejected them as well.

The Perils of Being Overpaid

Of course, even more than the coins we use, the jobs we do, as expressed through the products we create or the services we provide, are extensions of our self-concept. (We noted in Chapter 4, for example, how Mrs. Hensill's feeling of self-worth was enhanced when the agency decided to pay her for the kind of work she had been donating as a volunteer.) As a result of our employment experiences, we come to expect payment at a certain level in exchange for our work. Whatever this level is— $5 an hour, $900 a month, $25,000 a year—it becomes a part of our self-concept. Being offered less than we have come to expect is viewed by us as an insult, an attempt to devalue us. But what if we are offered *more* than we expect?

In an experiment conducted by Stanley J. Morse and his co-researchers (1976), female university students were asked to proofread while listening to distracting background noise through headphones. Initially, each student rated the difficulty of a sample task and indicated on a questionnaire how much she thought she should be paid. The experimenter covertly noted the expected pay rate and then told the student how much she would be getting for the work. To half the women he quoted whatever rate they had indicated on the questionnaire; to the other half he offered double their expected rate. Thus half the students were getting what they expected and the other half were grossly overpaid. On completion of the proofreading task, each student was again asked to rate its difficulty.

When the performance of the two groups of subjects was analyzed, it became clear that the overpaid group had taken the assignment more seriously and had worked harder at the task, for they had marked 14% more typographical errors than had the equitably paid group. The overpaid students were also inclined to rate the task as more difficult than they had expected, whereas the equitably paid subjects had found it easier.

The students who learned that they were to be paid double what they had expected apparently assumed that the experimenter thought their services extraordinarily valuable. Such an appraisal undoubtedly boosted their feelings of self-worth, but it probably left them a little anxious about whether they deserved this high degree of confidence. As a consequence they tried harder. Afterwards they justified their extra effort, as well as the overpayment they received, by deciding that the task had actually been more difficult than expected. Thus they confirmed the experimenter's supposed evaluation of their capability.

Our responses to being overrewarded are sometimes more complex than this, however, especially when the inequity is known to our co-workers. Under such conditions we are likely to feel embarrassed and even guilty, as though we have been caught taking what is rightfully theirs. Actually, we are in a state of conflict: On the one hand we report that we are disconcerted at our employer's eagerness to overpay us, but secretly we are pleased and would like to believe that our work really *is* worth premium pay.

These reactions appeared in an experiment conducted by Alba Rivera and James Tedeschi (1976). Pairs of female students were asked to solve a set of difficult anagrams. A third student, actually an accomplice of the experimenters, supervised the work of each pair. After ten minutes each subject was taken by the supervisor into a separate room, where she was told that she and the other student had each solved the same number of problems and that it was the supervisor's responsibility to divide a reward of one dollar between them. Some of the subjects were awarded half the money. Others, though, received ninety cents. (In these cases the co-workers who would have received only ten cents were again accomplices of the experimenters.) No explanation was given to the subjects who received an inequitable nine-tenths share. Half the subjects were then asked to fill out a rating sheet designed to reflect both their mood at that moment and their feelings toward the supervisor. (Of the other half, who did not fill out the questionnaires, more in a moment.)

By comparison with the women who were paid an equitable share of the dollar, those who received an unfair share were more inclined to say that they felt unhappy and guilty. They also expressed more dislike of the student who had supervised them and reported a disinclination to work with her on future assignments. These results did not surprise Rivera and Tedeschi, for they were consistent with other findings from similar experiments. The experimenters wondered, however, whether the rating sheets had elicited the true feelings of their subjects. Filling out a report blank is a semipublic act; the subject knows others will see what she writes. Hence there is a tendency for subjects to report what they think experimenters will consider appropriate. Perhaps the overpaid subjects said they were unhappy, felt guilty, and disliked their supervisor because they thought they *ought* to have such feelings.

In order to determine what the students *really* felt about being paid more than their co-workers, Rivera and Tedeschi asked the subjects who had not filled out the rating sheets to record their reactions to the same questions on a specially designed piece of electronic equipment. The students were told that the equipment worked in the manner of a lie detector and was designed to reveal their true feelings. The results obtained with this "lie detector" justified the experimenters' suspicions, for these subjects reported that they felt no guilt at all about receiving a grossly unfair share of the reward. These overrewarded students also said that they liked the student who supervised and rewarded them and would be pleased to work with her again.

The value others place on our work, as reflected in what they are willing to pay, influences our performance significantly. A reasonable explanation of this effect is that our self-concept, which determines our motives in large degree, is dependent on the attitudes others express toward us. The Rivera/Tedeschi experiment also shows something of the motivational conflict we experience when we are overpaid. Publicly we represent ourselves as democratic and fair, denying any right to overpayment; but privately we enjoy being overvalued.

Sex Differences in Pay and Self-Esteem

In the experiments we have described in the last few pages, the subjects were women, a fact that enabled the researchers to exclude sex difference as a possible source of influence on their results. In the real world, however, both sexes compete for monetary rewards—pay. In the real world, furthermore, women generally receive less pay than men do, even when they provide the same services. This practice is described frequently as the cause of an irrational, unnecessary, and demeaning status differential between men and women, though it could be argued that lower pay may be the *result* of lower status rather than its *cause*. Some claim that men alone are responsible for these inequalities; men, they argue, are threatened by women's competence and seek to keep them in a state of subjugation.

Experiments by Charlene M. Callahan-Levy and Lawrence A. Messé (1979) cast an interesting light on this topic. In one of their experiments small groups of college men and women worked individually for 50 minutes writing answers to questions about campus issues. When the task had been completed, each was taken to a private cubicle and asked to take the amount he or she desired as pay from an envelope containing $6 in bills and coins. The students were not observed while they decided how much to take; only their sex and the amount taken were recorded. In a second experiment the initial task was identical, but on its completion subjects were taken to private cubicles and asked to take from the $6 allotment an amount to be paid one of their fellow subjects, the recipient to be selected at random. The sex of the recipient was clearly indicated on the pay envelopes: Some were marked "Her Pay," the others, "His Pay."

Thus two experimental situations were created: one in which individuals determined their own pay, the other in which they determined the pay of an anonymous fellow subject identified only by sex.

An analysis of the amounts taken in the first experiment indicated that the women placed a lower value on their services, for they awarded themselves an average of $3.45, in contrast to an average for men of $4.26. Inasmuch as the decisions were made voluntarily and privately, the experimenters having no check on the subjects' identities, we must assume that the women's decisions to place a lower value on their work were made without external interference or influence.

The second experiment made it clear that in determining their own pay the women did *not* reason that women's services are intrinsically worth less than men's, for an analysis of the pay awards showed no significant difference in the amount allocated to women and men, nor did the sex of the allocator have any effect on the amount awarded.

If the price we place on our services reflects self-worth, then the women in this experiment may have been motivated by a level of self-worth lower than that of the men.

A third experiment sought to gather information about the age at which this self-depreciating phenomenon appears in women. Subjects were girls and boys aged 6, 9, 12, and 15. Each child was interviewed briefly, asked to choose activities and future occupations from lists scaled according to "masculinity" and "femininity," and then told to take his or her pay from an envelope containing $3 in dimes. (First graders, who were somewhat confused about the value of coins, were asked to pay themselves from a box containing 30 Hershey chocolate kisses.) The children were then asked to indicate how well they thought they had done at the "job" they had completed. In these self-ratings there were no sex differences. Girls felt they had done as good a "job" as boys.

An analysis of the self-payments showed that girls aged 6, 9, and 12 awarded themselves about 36% less pay than did boys the same age, but 15-year-old girls gave themselves 88% less. Thus the tendency for women to underprice their work, in relative terms, appears to begin in childhood, and becomes especially strong after puberty. It was interesting to note, however, that girls who chose activities toward the "masculine" end of the lists awarded themselves significantly more pay than the other girls did.

The researchers noted that their findings were consistent with those of most previous studies and with everyday observations: "Women tend not to behave in ways that maximally benefit them economically." They granted that this "feminine" orientation toward money has been characterized by some as being "more healthy," irrespective of whether it appears in men or women, but they also observed that "such an orientation literally is costly to those persons who hold it, especially since it makes them vulnerable to exploitation by persons who have more self-serving ideas about money and work."

The investigators did not view the girls' tendency to choose substandard wages as indicative of low self-esteem. But we

cannot overlook the well-known tendency of people to gener-
alize from the part to the whole. Women may not wish their
expected pay levels to reflect on their worth as persons, but in
a work-oriented world they may have little choice.

6 The rich and the poor

It's the same the whole world over—
 It's the poor what gets the blame,
While the rich has all the pleasures.
 Now ain't that a bleedin' shame?
                    —ENGLISH MUSIC HALL BALLAD

The love of money is the root of all evil.
                    —1 TIMOTHY, 6:10

Lack of money is the root of all evil.   —G. B. SHAW

There are envious people so overwhelmed by your good
fortune that they almost inspire you to pity them.
                    —EDMOND AND JULES DE GONCOURT:

Thou shall not covet they neighbour's house, thou shalt
not covet thy neighbour's wife, nor his manservant, nor
his maidservant, nor his ox, nor his ass, nor anything that
is thy neighbour's.   —EXODUS, 20:17

We use the terms "money" and "wealth" imprecisely in everyday conversation. Most of us, believing the two terms to be
roughly interchangeable, say that the difference between the
wealthy and the poor lies in the fact that the wealthy have a
great deal more money. But the professional economist makes
a nice distinction between wealth and money. In the economist's
terms, wealth consists of property that has value. Money is not
considered to be wealth, but is the medium that enables us to
measure and exchange wealth.

   Consider, for example, a family with five hundred acres of
rolling pasture about twenty-five miles from a metropolis. They
could sell the choicest parcels an acre at a time, but they prefer
to keep the property intact and dispose of it as a whole. Their
asking price of five million dollars is more than real estate

developers are willing to pay, but the family insists on getting what they consider full value for their land. In the meantime, because property taxes strain their income, they are forced to live thriftily. They drive an old car, live in a dilapidated house, and eat frugally. There is no doubt that they are wealthy, for their property has enormous value; yet they have little money.

It is not unusual for the wealthy to have little ready cash. These days whoever receives money beyond his ordinary needs is well advised to invest it in something that will appreciate in value or that will at least yield more than bank interest, which, after taxes, will not keep up with inflation. The prudent person, in other words, does not keep his assets in money but invests them in real estate, stocks, bonds, or business ventures.

Nevertheless, in this chapter we shall follow the conventional, if somewhat imprecise, practice of blurring the distinction between money and wealth, as most noneconomists do when they write about money. For this we have ample precedent. In his stimulating book *The Money Game*, for example, "Adam Smith" wrote about stocks, bonds, and commodity futures, which are not money but forms of wealth. They are, of course, readily convertible into money, which is what makes the game he describes so exciting.

Thomas Wiseman, like other psychoanalytic authors, is more interested in the drives that force people to seek wealth than in their preoccupation with money as such, though the title of his book, *The Money Motive*, might lead one to think otherwise. His book deals with the rich and the would-be rich. The money motives of the poor interested him little.

In this chapter, we consider the poor to be those who have little or no money or wealth; the rich are those who have much wealth or money. After all, it is not the economist's technicalities that make the rich and the poor psychologically interesting, but the differences in the expectations, attitudes, values, and behavior patterns that characterize them. The work of sociologists like W. Lloyd Warner and his co-researchers (1941), who studied the residents of Newburyport, Massachusetts, in the 1930s, has shown that education, occupation, leisure activities, and general life style are the characteristics that distinguish individuals at one social-class level from those at other levels. However, most people are inclined to say that such social-status differences as exist in America can be explained in terms of money.

F. Scott Fitzgerald once had a side-swiping collision with this popular view of the rich. According to Ernest Hemingway, Fitzgerald said "The very rich are different from you and me," whereupon someone commented, jokingly, "Yes, they have more money." Hemingway despised the very rich and disliked Fitzgerald, and it is possible that he made up the story. But Fitzgerald was annoyed, and his complaint about it in a letter to Hemingway suggests that the incident may have occurred after all. In any event, Fitzgerald's alleged view would have been closer to Warner's, whereas Hemingway's reported rebuttal was consistent with popular thinking on the subject.

The point is that social-class differences reflect a great deal more than money. Sociologists do not deny that money, or the lack of it, is important, but they insist that differences in wealth and income play supportive and hence only secondary roles in maintaining each person's position in our social status system. Nevertheless, the presence or absence of the things money can buy is the most visible attribute of status and is what the average person thinks of when the upper, middle, or lower class is mentioned.

How Social Systems Operate

The world is often described as a jungle, where the competition is fierce and only the fittest survive. This description is somewhat extreme, but there is a measure of truth in the view that in our social system, as in social systems everywhere, the strong grow stronger and the rich richer, while the weak grow weaker and the poor poorer. Jesus, in the course of the Sermon on the Mount, memorialized the process in these terms: "For unto everyone that hath shall be given, and he shall have abundance; but from him that hath not shall be taken away even that which he hath" (Matthew 25:29).

The operation of this social "law", if we may call it that, is more obvious in some societies than in others. Among the Pacific Coast Yurok Indians, for example, the division of a stranded whale was conducted according to a well-defined status system. Wealthy families took their cuts at the carcass first, followed by the members of poor families, who took portions half the size of those taken by the wealthy. Violations of this established procedure led to fights and even to killings (Spott & Kroeber, 1942).

Every kind of monetary transfer seems to follow the rich-richer/poor-poorer rule, even taxation. An editorial writer for the *Wall Street Journal* (1978) observed. "It is not the rich who have the toughest time paying the costs the government is continually imposing on the economy through higher taxes and stifling regulations. The rich have not only the financial resources to get by, but also have the wit to push some of their burden on the weak. As the economic squeeze gets worse, the squeaking at the bottom of the ladder intensifies."

The Evasive Rich and the Elusive Poor

Of all the segments of the American status system, the very rich and the very poor receive the most attention. These extreme classes are studied avidly by novelist, politician, and sociologist alike. But despite this disproportionate focus upon them, the "rich" and the "poor" are not easily identified. In the first place, few people admit to being rich or poor; the terms always seem to apply to someone else.[1] In the second place, definitions of the terms vary widely. To an unemployed inhabitant of government housing in San Francisco's Hunter's Point district, "rich" might mean anyone who is working. To the owner of a $250,000 condominium flat on Nob Hill in the same city, "rich" might refer to Texas oil multi-millionaires. In fact, one of the several John Jacob Astors remarked, "A man who has a million dollars is as well off as if he were rich."

The word "poor" is equally hard to define. Even those who are far below the Federal government's "poverty level," know someone who is worse off than they, just as the billionaires at the very top know someone better off than they are.

---

[1]The reluctance of Americans to describe themselves as either "rich" or "poor" is analogous to their similar attitudes regarding social class. Irving Kristol (1979) notes that the overwhelming majority of us, regardless of economic or educational status, claim to be "middle class," and that "only a handful of eccentrics describe themselves as either 'upper class' or 'lower class.' "

One of the reasons few will admit to being rich or poor is that both terms carry a considerable load of disdain. This is of course most obvious with "poor," which not only signifies a low economic level, but also implies incompetence, inadequacy, and unworthiness. This is shown by the variety of phrases we use to soften the impact of the word.

Victorians spoke of the "deserving poor," who were hardworking but unlucky and were distinguished from the "undeserving poor," who refused to work and could easily be tempted by a life of crime. Tales told to children also featured "poor *but* honest" farmers and woodcutters, implying thereby that the poor were normally dishonest.

Today we try to avoid the use of "poor" altogether and instead seek refuge in euphemisms. People employed in various governmental programs designed to ameliorate the lot of the poor refer to them as "ghetto residents," "welfare families," or "people below the poverty level," in order to avoid saying "poor." If there were to be a contest for such euphemisms, the prize would undoubtedly go to the U.S. Department of Agriculture, which recently coined the term "limited resource family."

The euphemisms also apply to countries. Countries that are poor by international standards are called "developing countries," "underdeveloped countries," or "Third World countries." (No one, it seems, knows of an *over*developed country or a *Second* World country.)

The complexities of the massive governmental intervention programs that attempt to prevent or at least mitigate some of the effects of poverty require that the definition of poverty not be left to chance, whim, or common usage. In order to provide a poor person with the aid the law permits, officials must determine where to draw the line that differentiates "poverty" (or the "low income level," as the Bureau of Census prefers to call it) from other conditions in society. In the spring of 1979, the Labor Department drew the poverty line at $6700 for an urban family of four and at $3400 for a single individual. These figures compare with $6200 and $3140 for 1978. The difference suggests that every year it costs more to be poor, a sentiment that those below the poverty line would heartily endorse. But the cost of poverty is not only to the poor, for it is borne by everyone, in one form or another.

Why Nobody Is "Rich"

With all the disadvantages that cling to the term "poor," one would think that the term "rich," would be quite the nicest thing we could say about anyone. "If only I were rich" is a wish that has touched off pleasant speculations for almost everyone; and the Duchess of Windsor, who is something of an expert on what it takes to be upwardly mobile, is reputed to have said "You cannot be too thin or too rich."

Many hope to be rich, some actually acquire a great deal of money; but if we can believe what wealthy people say about themselves, no one ever *is* rich. The wealthy may admit to being "comfortably fixed" or "affluent" (to use two of the current euphemisms), but the term "rich," like the term "poor," is reserved for others. Why this avoidance of what ought to be a complimentary term?

A possible explanation is that the wealthy have a modern-day concern about *hubris*—the boastful characterization of oneself as "lucky," "important," "powerful," or "successful." The ancient Greeks believed that such claims invited destruction by the gods, who were jealously watchful lest men lay claim to divine status. *Hubris* was thus an invitation to be demoted from the "fortunate" to the "unfortunate" category.

Today people do not fear the malevolent intervention of the Greek gods, but they are nevertheless apprehensive about anything that might terminate their good fortune. Such intervention could come from the everwatchful Internal Revenue Service, whose agents are the modern equivalent of the avenging furies and harpies of ancient mythology—at least so one might conclude from the talk at the 19th hole at Pebble Beach or around any swimming pool in Beverly Hills or Dallas. The IRS aside, many of us also suffer from the superstition that the best way to break a streak of good luck is to proclaim oneself lucky. Perhaps we have not progressed beyond the ancient Greeks, after all.

Another reason the millionaire avoids being labeled as "rich" is that this designation, like "poor," can evoke the hostility of others. Just as we are apprehensive about the poor in our midst—perhaps because their need threatens the security of our possessions—so are we apprehensive of the rich, whose power places us at a disadvantage. We must compete with them for everything that is desirable, scarce, and for sale—view lots and building materials, beaches and wilderness areas, political offices, smoked salmon, and caviar. In the competition to live a "fuller" life, the rich have a decided edge. Most of us resent it.

The common view is that the rich deserve none of the advantages they enjoy. The rationale of this position is simply stated: We all work together to maintain a social structure whose rules permit money to be exchanged for resources essential to survival and for the occasional luxury. The rich work no harder at this task than anyone else—many do not work at all—yet they seem to get more than their fair share of the benefits while paying fewer of the costs. The system requires us to play the game, dealing with the rich on their own terms, catering to them, permitting ourselves to be used and exploited. Underneath it all, we are resentful and envious.

The Envious Us; the Enviable They

Helmut Schoeck (1966), in his classic study of envy, says that such feelings are entirely normal and that there has never been a society completely free of envy. But envy though normal, should be kept under wraps. Social climates that are best suited to the fullest, most unencumbered expression of creativity in its broadest sense are those in which "accepted normative behaviour, custom, religion, common sense and public opinion are more or less agreed upon an attitude which functions *as if* the envious person could be ignored." This shared attitude enables society and its leaders to recognize individual differences in ability and even make unequal advantages available to overachievers to the end that "the community may benefit in the long run from achievements which initially, perhaps, only few are capable of attaining."

According to Schoeck, legal systems that legitimize the accumulation of private property express society's awareness that individual differences in wealth benefit everyone, not merely the advantaged. But some individuals are so consumed by envy that they are led to violate society's rules. Most criminals, says Schoeck, rationalize their behavior nihilistically: They believe that no one should possess anything of value. Envy is a primary motive not only in robbery; it also underlies juvenile vandalism and the violent tactics of terrorists, who bomb, kidnap, assassinate, and maim in their singleminded attempts to destroy possessors and their possessions.

Envy may also find public expression in the form of laws aimed at curbing the more visible pleasures of the rich. The *Lex Didia* of Republican Rome (143 BC) punished hosts who gave extravagant dinners and the guests who were invited as well. Schoeck points out that laws condemning luxury continued to be popular until the end of the 18th Century, when "the rage for legislative restriction of luxury and consumption began to die down in Europe and America, making way for the inception of an expanding and economically healthier free-market economy." This more sensible attitude was based on the growing awareness that luxury was difficult to define. Clean shirts, for example, were luxuries during the Middle Ages, but today we regard them as necessities. Furthermore, as soon as one form of luxury was supressed, people found something else to envy.

Politicians, playing the role of the social reformers, often find it advantageous to appeal to the envy present in us all by promising to redistribute wealth. Upton Sinclair, the social critic, failed in his bid to become Governor of California in 1933, when his EPIC program—End Poverty In California—was rejected by the voters, but in Louisiana Huey P. Long's Share-the-Wealth platform got him elected to the U.S. Senate and enabled him to found a political dynasty that still rules today.

Once elected, politicians find that redistribution of wealth is impractical, but they do sometimes make gestures that attempt to deal with the envy of the many for the wealthy few. The progressive income tax, according to Schoeck, is intended to penalize the highly paid in order to appease the envy of the average wage-earner. But envy can never be appeased; it flourishes among the members of impoverished primitive tribes just as it does among the citizens of the more affluent modern industrialized states.

Schoeck cites the observations of the 19th Century French anthropologist de Levchine, who lived among the nomadic Kazakhs of Central Asia. De Levchine marvelled that although the Kazakhs' requirements were minimal, they were so much consumed by envy and jealousy that they fought terribly over minor gains and losses. When they robbed caravans, they cut their booty up into absurd, useless fragments.

Similar motivation can be observed in peasant societies. When anthropologist George M. Foster (1967) first arrived in the Mexican village of Tzintzuntzan, he wanted to get an idea of the social structure of the community. He asked "Who are the most prosperous people here?" The answer everyone gave was the same: "There are no wealthy; here we are all equal." The villagers gave similar responses about other personal characteristics. When Foster asked which of the men were the most *macho* (tough and aggressive), he was told: "Here there are no *machos*; we are all equal."

The villagers believed, Foster eventually realized, that an improvement in anyone's situation threatened the equilibrium of the social order. In Tzintzuntzan, the individual "who acquires, or is believed to have acquired, more than his traditional share of good, must be pulled back to the level of all, lest the temporary imbalance in the distribution of good become permanent, and lead to serious consequences. And a person who falls behind with respect to his traditional share of good is also a threat to the community: his envy of others who have lost nothing may bring them misfortune."

Clyde Kluckhohn (1946), another anthropologist, made similar observations regarding the Navaho, an impoverished Indian tribe in the American Southwest. Navahos have nothing that corresponds to the Anglo concepts of "personal success" or "personal achievement." Nor can a Navaho have good or bad luck. In the Navaho view, the prosperity of any individual can be attained only at the expense of others. As a result, Navahos who are better off are under constant social pressure to be lavish in hospitality and gifts. They know that if they fail to do this, "the voice of envy will speak out in whispers of witchcraft," and life will be "strained and unpleasant. . . ."

In the highly urbanized and compartmentalized society of North America, our social exposure is not as great as that of the Mexican villager or the Navaho tribesman; hence we seldom confront the envy and resentment of those less fortunate than ourselves. We are nevertheless aware that such feelings are normal. We therefore feel somewhat tense, and a little guilty as well, when others become aware that our life style is significantly more desirable than theirs.

The fact that envy is universal means that each of us is the target of others' hostility. But the rich are the focal centers of the greatest envy. Many wealthy persons must wish they could avoid paying this psychological price. They could, of course, remove themselves from the target area by giving their money away, but few consider this drastic step. Apparently being rich compensates for the slings and arrows of the envious public and for the pangs of guilt as well.

The View from the Bottom

The poor, too, can be targets for resentment and hostility. Just as we feel unfairly used by the rich, we feel exploited and manipulated by this relatively unproductive impoverished sector of society.

The intensity of this feeling was demonstrated in a poll of Californians conducted in the late spring of 1978, a week before they voted themselves a huge cut in property taxes. The pollsters asked which community services should be cut in response to the anticipated loss of tax revenue. Welfare and other public assistance programs were the favorite target of the respondents. Over half—62%—wanted to cut these services; 41% also wanted to cut back on government-financed public housing. The residents of California enjoy a high per capita income, yet many were eager to cut back support for the poor.

Nor are Californians alone in their antipathy toward the poor. A majority of those polled in a public opinion survey conducted in England in 1977 said that the poor have it within their power to escape their condition and that the cause of their continued poverty is laziness.

Public hostility toward the poor is also expressed in other ways. In Chapter 4, we cited Donald Black's (1976) finding that legal systems throughout the world punish lower status—generally poor—offenders more severely than high status offenders. The explanation commonly given for this inequity is that crimes committed by the poor are more likely to be violent; in fact, however, the poor are likely to be punished severely even when the offense does not involve violence, as Black indicates. The disparity in criminal justice is consistent with a larger, more fundamental behavior pattern: In every society social status systems operate to the advantage of those at higher levels and the disadvantage of those at the bottom.

The Rich and the Poor as Social Deviates

Another reason we dislike both the poor and the rich is that we see their behavior as quite different from our own. In every society, certain patterns of behavior are considered "normal;" marked deviations from the norm arouse concern, anxiety, and even hostility in members of the conforming majority.

What makes the rich and the poor seem different from the rest of us? To some degree it is their life-styles—their dress, abode, use of leisure time, and visibility. The rich are naturally noticeable on account of their large homes and expensive cars, but they become even more visible when their activities are mentioned frequently by the mass media. Through such reports we know of $100,000 parties that launch debutantes, of enormous inheritances and divorce settlements, and of spectacular activities in high finance.

The poor are also made visible by the media, which dwell on the sexual liaisons of welfare mothers, on cases of child neglect and abuse, on the unemployed who refuse to accept available jobs, on the crime rate in slums, and on the low academic achievement in ghetto schools. Those who are neither rich nor poor—"the rest of us"—cannot read the daily newspaper without a sense of outrage: Both the lazy irresponsible rich and the lazy irresponsible poor seem constantly to be taking advantage of "us."

The rich and the poor are for the most part well aware of the hostility "the rest of us" feel toward them. Apart from the well-publicized splurges and indiscretions of the less sensitive members of the moneyed community, the rich maintain what has been called "a low profile." Millionaire ranchers in the American West, for instance, often wear worn work clothes and drive battered pickup trucks in an ,attempt to blend into the social scene, while their wives assiduously pursue bargains at the local markets. Although middle-class people often spend more than they earn and go into debt to "keep up with the Joneses," many wealthy people deliberately live below their means—what the British call "living down to the Atkinses." As a result, the life-style of these affluent Americans is not markedly different from that of the middle class.

The poor, on the other hand, have few means for becoming less visible. One, of course, is to achieve middle-class status through self-education and other bootstrap operations. Most poor people, however, face formidable obstacles to progress: the circumstances of poverty are not conducive to the perspective and the insight necessary to get ahead. Thus many poor people attempt to deal with the hostility of the rest of society by remaining in their own neighborhoods and limiting their social contacts.

The Psychology of the Top, Middle, and Bottom

Psychological, as well as economic, differences exist between poor, rich, and middle-class people. A middle-class person is not merely a poor individual who happens to have more money. Not only the life-styles but also the attitudes, values, and self-systems that appear at various economic levels are profoundly different. Some of these psychological factors derive from the economic experiences people have, but most of them are produced by the norms and expectations of others of the same class. We refer here to what behavioral scientists term *culture* or *cultural pattern*.

Culture is a concept originally used by anthropologists to describe the ways of thinking, feeling, and behaving that characterize ethnic or national groups. Thanks to the work of the sociologists mentioned at the beginning of this chapter, we now know that people at a given class level also tend to develop characteristic attitudes and values. It is thus meaningful to speak of an "upper-middle-class culture" or a "welfare-class culture."

During the last generation or so a great deal of research has been concerned with detailing the psychological differences among people at various social-class levels. Most of this work has concentrated on differences between the more educated white-collar or middle class and the less educated blue-collar or working class. In economic terms, these classes overlap somewhat; a good many blue-collar people have, through union bargaining, raised their incomes to levels above those enjoyed by many white-collar people. A survey conducted in 1977 by *Time* reported, for instance, that whereas assistant professors at Yale received $14,750 per year, garbage collectors in New York City were being paid $16,350. Most blue-collar workers, however, do not receive high wages; the average annual income of this class, which also includes most of the chronically unemployed and those on welfare, is considerably lower than that of the white-collar or middle class.

Relatively little research has been done on the upper class. This group, representing only a small portion of the total population—sociologists (e.g., Coleman and Neugarten, 1971) estimate it at one percent—is adept at evading investigators of any type, be they newspaper reporters, income-tax agents, or behavioral scientists. The great financial resources of members of this class enable them to place obstacles in the way of researchers and others who are regarded as invaders of their privacy. Nevertheless, the available data suggest that the values and attitudes of "rich" people are not much different from those of the middle class. Hence it is not surprising that the lower or blue-collar class has received the major share of attention from researchers. And much that we know about the middle-class culture has come through using it as a background against which to observe and compare lower-class attitudes and behavior.

Social-Class Attitudes toward Money

Researchers have found that one of the major differences between lower-class and middle-class people lies in their attitudes toward money. It should come as no surprise that lower-class people, who are more likely to be chronically short of money, respond more readily than do middle-class people to opportunities to acquire it.

Harvard psychologists Bruner and Goodman (1947) wondered whether economic class would affect children's perceptions of coin sizes. They speculated that the more intensely objects are desired, the more vividly they will be perceived. They tested this hypothesis by asking ten-year-old children both of poor and of affluent parents to estimate the sizes of various coins by turning a knob on an apparatus that adjusted the size of a circle of light. The results confirmed the researchers' hunch: In contrast to the more realistic estimates of the affluent children, those of the poor children tended to exaggerate the coin sizes.

This tendency of poor children to exaggerate the size of coins seems to be universal, for John L. M. Dawson (1975) of the University of Hong Kong got similar results when he asked children of poor and of affluent Chinese parents to make estimates of coin sizes. Nor is this tendency confined to children. The adults who govern poor countries seem to think along similar lines. Jan L. Hitchcock and co-researchers (1976) at Pitzer College compared the sizes of coins issued by eighty-four nations. Using gross national product per capita as a measure of relative wealth, the researchers found that poorer countries tended to issue larger coins than did more affluent countries. The difference was especially marked when the countries' lowest-value coins were compared. The governments of the poorer countries seemed to be using the principle that although the low-value coins (used more by the poor than the affluent) will buy very little, if they can be given substantial size and weight they will at least be psychologically reassuring.

Reward Value: Pittances versus Praise

If a small amount of money "means more" to the poor, we would expect it to have a greater influence on their behavior than on that of the rich. Many studies have confirmed this effect. Robert E. Pierce (1970), for instance, conducted an experiment with eighth graders in a small town in Tennessee. Two groups of students were selected: one whose parents were on welfare, and one whose parents were known to have middle-income status. At the beginning of a school term, both groups were told they would earn one dollar for each letter-grade improvement shown on their next report cards. When he subsequently compared the performance of these two groups with that of low- and middle-income groups who were not participating in the experiment, Pierce found that the reward had produced no effect at all on the middle-class group but that the grades earned by the lower-income children had significantly improved.

In a Canadian study, children aged 6, 10, and 15 from low- and middle-income families were asked to perform a simple, boring, and meaningless task: pressing a lever repeatedly. The investigators, Swingle and Coady (1969), encouraged some of the children in both groups from time to time by saying "good"; others in both groups were given money; and still others received both verbal encouragement and money. Among fifteen- and ten-year-olds there was a decided tendency for poorer children to do more lever pressing when they were rewarded with small sums of money, while the more affluent children performed best when they were praised. There were no differences, however, between richer and poorer six-year-olds in this test. At age six, children had apparently not yet acquired the value standards characteristic of their income group.

And again, what goes for children seems to apply to adults as well. Maxine L. Reiss and her fellow researchers (1976) conducted a campaign (underwritten by the public health authorities of Florida) to get low-income rural parents to send their children to free dental clinics. The Florida officials, like public officials everywhere, had found that low-income parents do not respond eagerly to programs involving help for their children. It is difficult to pinpoint the reason for this reluctance. It may be that low-income parents tend to be suspicious of government programs. Some may feel humiliated by the suggestion that they need help of any kind; some may be preoccupied with more pressing problems; some may be forgetful or may not understand what is involved; and some may be too discouraged and apathetic to make the effort. In any event, the main problem in assistance programs aimed at the poor is that of getting the attention of the parents and then providing an incentive to action—a kind of pump-priming, so to speak.

Reiss and her associates tried a variety of techniques: (*a*) sending an informatory note home with the child, but doing nothing else; (*b*) sending the note, telephoning the parents, and following up with a visit to the home; and (*c*) offering the parents a $5 payment if they would send their children for treatment. As might be expected, the combination of note, telephone call, and home visit got more compliance than the note alone, but the $5 incentive got the best results. Furthermore, a higher percentage of parents who received the $5 incentive sent their children back to the dentist for follow-up treatment, even though money incentives were not offered for this additional cooperation. Thus, personal attention (a telephone call and a home visit) produced the desired results, but the monetary reward had the more lasting psychological impact. In addition, the $5 incentive scheme ultimately cost the health agency the least per client served.

There have been a large number of similar studies, but their results are much the same: poor people, adults and children alike, tend to react most favorably when rewarded with small amounts of money (for the effects of larger amounts, see below). Middle-class subjects, on the other hand, are likely to be comparatively unaffected by monetary rewards but respond well to praise. Middle-class individuals perform best, however, when they are rewarded with neither money nor praise but find the task worthwhile for its own sake. Thus, intrinsic and not extrinsic motivation works best for middle-class people.

According to students of psychological motivation (e.g., Rosen, 1959) middle-class individuals, in contrast to those from working-class or poverty backgrounds, characteristically enjoy tasks in which they can learn something about their own strengths and weaknesses. This interest in doing something merely for purposes of self-appraisal results from what psychologists call "the need to achieve."

The Risks of "Winning Big"

If low-income people respond favorably to small monetary rewards, would not larger rewards provide even better motivation? After all, the dream of "winning it big" through a lucky gamble is a common one in low-income communities, and there is reason to believe that the poor are the best customers of both the numbers rackets and the state-run lotteries.

But to the poor, large sums of money are the stuff that dreams are made of; handling wealth in reality is something else, and the occasional big winner is likely to find that his reality has turned unexpectedly stressful. In a lower-class culture where the norm is poverty, the person who suddenly wins a large sum of money becomes, by definition, "abnormal." The research of social psychologists shows that people who deviate from well-established group norms are pressured to conform, and this is exactly what happens to the newly rich resident of a proverty-stricken community. He is expected first to throw a big party for his friends and neighbors and then to distribute the balance of his winnings in the form of gifts or loans (which will never be repaid, of course).

It is possible that much of the generosity and willingness to share that characterizes life in impoverished societies is a defense against envy and possible rejection, as we noted earlier. The norm that no one should have more than anyone else in the neighborhood or village means that individual efforts at self-improvement are discouraged; assessments may even be levied against those who are believed to have more than others. Economist Thomas Sowell (1975) explains the higher food prices paid by the residents of poor neighborhoods in large cities as a result, in part, of the fact that merchants are expected to make frequent "voluntary" contributions to various "worthy causes." According to Sowell, these "contributions" are often "collected by tough young men or by others who speak with the actual or apparent backing of tough young men." This practice, part of the criminal or quasi-criminal scene in poor neighborhoods, plays a role in the "whittling down" process by means of which impoverished societies reduce their more affluent members to the "normal" economic level.

The poor person who providentially comes into money is best advised to escape to the outside world. Departure should be carried out stealthily, lest one's neighbors discover that the community is losing a prized economic asset. The financial success of a resident of one of the *favelas* of Rio de Janeiro led to outright hostility when she tried to leave. The *favelas* are stinking slums that cling to the slopes of the smooth stone hills surrounding one of the most beautiful bays in the world. *Faveleiros* live in shacks patched together from packing cases, scraps of tin and corrugated iron, and tar paper. Like the *barrios* that collect in festering swarms around the cities of other Latin-American countries, *favelas* house the illiterate, the marginally employed, the unemployed and the unemployable. The woman in question had been a part-time prostitute. More literate than her neighbors, she had over the years recorded her experiences and observations in colorful language on odd bits of paper. With her permission, an enterprising newspaper reporter edited her jottings and published them as a book. The book was very popular and brought the woman money and fame.

She quickly found that her neighbors expected her to be everyone's fairy godmother, whose magic wand was programmed to produce an endless stream of thousand-*cruzeiro* notes. But fairy godmothering formed no part of her dream. She longed instead for a more comfortable and secure way of life in an apartment whose roof did not leak in every tropical downpour. She decided to move out of the *favela*. She was not astute enough, however, to predict the effect her departure would have on her neighbors. As she tried to move her meager belongings out of the shack, her erstwhile friends, shouting curses, pelted her with stones and garbage.

The poor are generally long-suffering; they forgive one another's shortcomings, but they cannot forgive success.

Ratebreakers

The treatment of highly efficient factory workers is analogous. Such individuals are called "ratebreakers" or "ratebusters" by their fellow workers, who fear that management will use the higher production rate as a new standard of performance and hence will lower the wage per unit accordingly. (In some factories the fear is valid; in others, where wages are not tied to individual productivity, it seems to be unfounded.) The ratebreaker is the target of insults, practical jokes, physical harassment, and other expressions of peer hostility. This punishment is intended to make it clear to the overproducer that he has violated a norm, an often unofficial assumption about what constitutes a fair day's work.

A second reason for the rank and file's antipathy toward the ratebreaker is his "disloyalty." Employees, especially those working on production jobs in large establishments, are conscious of the status-differential that separates them from management personnel. The employee who voluntarily accepts management's goals of getting more production for less money is seen by his colleages as being with *them* and not with *us*. At worse, he is "a traitor in our midst;" at best, he is a dupe, albeit a potentially dangerous one.

Management, for its part, becomes anxiously concerned when it is known that a rank-and-file employee is being harrassed for subscribing to its goals. The natural reaction is to snatch the noble fellow from the clutches of his tormentors and reward him. The obvious reward is promotion to foreman or supervisor. Ratebreakers do not necessarily make the best supervisors, but both sides feel psychologically justified when the promotion occurs. Management feels that it has saved a loyal hand from an unkind fate, and rank-and-file employees see their former colleague's promotion as clear evidence that they were right about his disloyalty all along. And the ratebreaker, now foreman or supervisor, has made good his escape from the working class into the sanctuary of the middle class. He has gained status and is now in a better position to win in society's money game.

There is a third reason for the hostility the rank-and-file feel toward the ratebreaker: His superior performance makes them "look bad." His greater skill, higher intelligence, or better planning causes them to question their own value as employees. In short, he makes them doubt themselves, and undermines their feeling of self-worth.

Loyalty as Strength and Weakness

A sense of group identity, of loyalty, is at once the greatest strength and the greatest weakness of the poor. The awareness that "we are all in this together" and the norm that "we will share whatever we have" make survival in difficult circumstances possible and, at times, even pleasurable. But supportive social bonds can also be restrictive. They limit individual initiative and make it difficult for poor people to find more effective ways of coping with their difficult environments.

In our opening chapter we described the problems faced by Maria Santos, whose welfare income is meager but who ignores her social worker's suggestion that she shop at a supermarket where she would save money. To be sure, Maria has an economic reason for preferring the little *bodega* a block down the street: The owners provide credit between welfare checks, while the supermarket does not. But there are several psychological reasons as well: All her Spanish-speaking neighbors shop at the *bodega*; hence buying there is not only a group norm, but it also enables her to frequent a familiar, comfortable place where she can meet her friends. The proprietors of the *bodega* are people she feels at home with—her *socios*—and she feels a loyalty toward them that she does not feel toward the more impersonal clerks in the supermarket, even though they, too, speak Spanish. Thus buying groceries is for Maria Santos not merely a matter of economics, it is also a way of participating in the social structure of the community with which she identifies and which claims her loyalty. In short, although Maria Santos' economic situation might be somewhat improved if she shopped at the supermarket, she is not psychologically and socially free to do so. It would make her feel and appear disloyal and "different."

The fear of "being different" operates in other ways to raise the expenses of the poor. Milton Moskowitz (1977), in his nationally syndicated column "Money Tree," reports a survey showing that lower-income families living in inner cities are more inclined to buy the more expensive, nationally advertised brands of food products than the cheaper supermarket "house brands" that offer the same quantity and quality. The advertisements that appear on television and in other media are deliberate attempts to create social norms in buying habits. The more highly educated middle-class viewers seem better prepared to resist or ignore these attempts to channel their behavior into prepackaged norms and thus are able to decide for themselves where the best shopping values lie. The less-educated lower-class viewers feel safer and more comfortable buying the products television announcers have said are the most desirable. They are anxious to conform to social norms and to avoid being labelled as "different." "Playing it safe," they buy the more expensive, nationally advertised brands. As Moskowitz observed, "Any way you look at it, the poor pay more."

When Money Is "Unimportant"

Maria Santos and her neighbors do not shop where they could save money for yet another reason: In the lower-income world one often hears people declare that money is not important. "If you have health and friends," say the poor, "you don't need money." By means of such clichés the poor accentuate the difference between themselves and those who have money. Thus not having money, and by implication not needing it, becomes an important part of lower-class identity. Those who have money, on the other hand, seldom make a special point of denying its importance.

When a characteristic becomes a part of our self-concept, we are strongly motivated to make it a virtue. We have to live with ourselves, and it is much easier to live with a self we like and admire than with one we despise. This trait is universal, not peculiar to any social group or class. As a consequence, the depreciation of money becomes part of the social and psychological identity of impoverished people; it enables them to feel morally superior to those who have money and who presumably think money is important.

Of course, the daily experience of every poor person contradicts the notion that money is unimportant, but this contrary evidence has little effect on the norm. One of Freud's more significant discoveries was the psychological defense mechanism—the ability of human beings to ignore reality and to cling to fallacious beliefs in order to protect themselves from anxiety. In the case of the poor, the admission that money is really *very* important, and the recognition that the less of it you have the more of it you need, could generate a great deal of anxiety. By denying, through common agreement, that money is important, the poor reassure one another, prop themselves up with whatever resources they can call on, and face the world with courage.

Defense mechanisms enable us all, affluent and poor alike,

to endure the pain of living. The claim that money is unimportant enables the poor to reduce anxiety; however, since this defense mechanism is constructed of false data and self-delusions it also prevents them from thinking and acting realistically in money matters. For example, the supposed unimportance of money "excuses" Maria Santos and her friends having to save money by shopping at the supermarket. It also permits Maria to set up a time-payment account for a color television set, even though she is hard pressed to find the cash for daily necessities.

When Creativity is Discouraged

It is difficult for middle-class people to understand how success and creativity can be sources of anxiety for the working class and the poor. Yet the effect is noticeable even in kindergarten and elementary schools. When the teacher instructs the children to draw whatever they want, middle-class children enthusiastically give free rein to their imaginations. Children from working-class and lower-class homes, on the contrary, tend to hang back and look to the teacher for further guidance. They are happier when told what to draw. If the teacher refuses to give further direction, they reluctantly start to work, sneaking glances at one another's drawings in search of clues to the expected performance.

This tendency was clearly demonstrated in a set of experiments conducted in the Philadelphia schools by Emmy A. Pepitone and her co-workers (1977) at Temple University. Kindergarten and elementary school children from working-class and middle-class families were assigned to work at the task of assembling human figures using colored blocks of wood of various shapes, colors, and sizes. Each group was composed of three children of the same sex and social class. The experimenters encouraged creativity and individuality by telling the children to work independently, in order "to see which one of you three can make the very best picture." When the children were finished, they were all complimented by the investigators, who then photographed the completed figures for further analysis. Each of the figures was subsequently rated in terms of its creativity—that is, its complexity and originality—and its similarity to the figures the other two children had constructed.

The results showed that middle-class children at each grade level were demonstrating somewhat greater creativity than working-class children. Working-class children showed lower levels of complexity and originality, and imitation was common. The children had learned the lower-class social norm of "don't be different" and, instead of trying to see who could make the best picture, they copied one another's work. In many instances, the least creative child set the norm for the other two children. The implication of this experiment is not that lower-class or working-class children are inherently uncreative, but rather that one of the norms of their socioeconomic class inhibits the production of original work.

The fear of being viewed as different is an important reason children from working-class and lower-class families are reluctant to be creative and original, but it is not the only one. A generally passive attitude toward life makes people living at the lower end of the economic scale hesitant to tackle new and complex problems. Whether this passivity results from an overexposure to failure and disappointment, from trying to cope with life's problems without adequate resources, or from an attempt to conceal real or imagined personal inadequacies, it causes poor people to avoid challenges that are complex, abstract, and full of unfamiliar elements.

The Psychology of Diminished Expectations

The resigned pessimism of the working class and the poor is revealed in a set of surveys conducted in Mexico and the United States. Lower-class mothers in both countries were more likely than middle-class mothers to agree with statements of the following type:

> All a man should want out of life in the way of a career is a secure, not-too-difficult job, with enough pay to get by.
>
> When a man is born, his fate is already in the cards; therefore he might as well accept it and not fight it.
>
> The secret of happiness is to expect little and to be content with what comes.

Even if a person doesn't accomplish much, the best way is to enjoy life as he goes along.

In spite of what people say, life for the average person is getting worse, not better.

These days a person doesn't really know who can be counted on.

These statements express, in various ways, the philosophy that life is a bad bargain and that we can do nothing but make the best of it (Holtzman, Diaz-Guerrero, & Swartz, 1975). Everyone has felt this way at some time or other, but such feelings appear to be more frequent and more persistent among lower-class people.

Feelings expressed by mothers are likely to be reflected in the attitudes of their children. Hence it is not surprising that children from poor homes are more likely to lack self-confidence and initiative than are middle-class children. All children need to be encouraged and reassured, but teachers find that children from the homes of the poor need more encouragement and reassurance than most other children. Many of them display a behavior pattern that psychologists have termed "learned helplessness," a pattern characterized by lack of initiative, extreme dependency, and apathy (Seligman, 1975).

The obvious question is how the lot of the poor can be improved. Some believe that the poor would find life more satisfying and less discouraging if they simply had more money. The problem of how to get more money into the hands of the poor has challenged the world's thinkers and politicians from Jesus Christ to Karl Marx, from Julius Ceasar to Lyndon B. Johnson. Some of the psychological reasons why neither theory nor practice has been successful are examined in the next chapter.

7 Giving money away

We know that our salvation rests in sharing equally. The
message has always been the same, from Jesus Christ to
Karl Marx. But nature has fashioned us cleverly. Over
the long haul it has been easier for humans to take, than
to give or share. We have been programmed by our
biology to know that it is better to be "one-up" than
"one-down." —DAVID KIPNIS (1977)

Guilt is the repressed hatred of someone who has been
good to us. . . —ERNEST BORNEMAN (1973, trans. 1976)

Gratitude: a lively sense of favors yet to come.
—VARIOUS APHORISTS, INCLUDING
LA ROCHEFOUCAULD AND ROBERT WALPOLE

To either India see the merchant fly,
  Scared at the spectre of pale Poverty
See him with pains of body, pangs of soul,
  Burn thro' the Tropics, freeze beneath the Pole.
—ALEXANDER POPE

In their self-appointed task of explaining human behavior, the
behavioral scientists—psychologists, economists, sociologists,
and anthropologists—have done rather poorly with respect to
altruism. These scientists have modeled the human being as
self-centered, devoted to the pursuit of personal welfare and
satisfaction. Their research and their theories thus tend to explain generosity, sharing, love, friendship, and loyalty by assuming that people engage in such behavior only because they
have something to gain from it.

To be sure, the more experimentally minded behavioral
scientists are generally unconcerned about the motivational factors underlying atruistic behavior; they simply study the conditions under which people increase or reduce their donations

of money, goods, or services; volunteer or withhold help; or behave with concern or detachment. The results of these experiments tell us a great deal about the conditions that lead people in general—not unusual people or people in unusual circumstances—to behave altruistically or selfishly. But they provide few clues as to what motivates "unselfishness"—clues not very reassuring to those who want to believe that goodness is born into all of us—a belief that psychologists call *orthogenetic*. Experimental psychologists have little use for orthogeneticists.

The Problem with Goodness

Turning from the experimentalists to the theorists, we still find little support for the concept of innate goodness. The greatest of all personality theorists, Sigmund Freud, was profoundly pessimistic. He concluded that the best we can hope and work for is an edgy balance between our basic drives (which are essentially selfish and asocial, if not actually antisocial) and the demands and strictures of a heartless and impersonal society. Although some of his followers were more optimistic, they kept fairly close to Freud's self-centered model of the personality.

In this respect, Freud and his followers were not unique. Philosophers and other scholars who have analyzed human motives over the centuries have generally been critical, even derisive, of the idea that people might be innately altruistic. As we read the conclusions of scholars great and small we feel abashed and depressed.

Why do we read these unflattering descriptions of ourselves and our motives? There are several answers. First, critics get a lot more attention when they are negative than when they are positive, just as a pebble in our shoe gets our attention, while the shoe's stylish fit is taken for granted. Ill tidings are seldom welcome, but they sell more newspapers than good tidings, as any journalist knows. Hence books that tell us what is bad about ourselves and the society we have created are bound to sell better and be read more avidly than those that are reassuring and supportive.

Cynics and pessimists are popular, furthermore, because they confirm the free-floating guilt most of us carry around. We see things going wrong all around us, and we have a strong suspicion that it is our fault. The experts and scholars oblige us by seconding this impression, by specifying our deficiencies, and by telling us where we went wrong. By all reports, they find this exercise enjoyable and, judging from the sale of their books, profitable.

But if we push aside our neurotic need to have our guilt massaged by experts, and look at human and animal behavior objectively, we can see much that does not fit theories of selfishness, and much that is ignored in the experiments of psychologists. Parents, for example, make great sacrifices for their children, their only reward being the vicarious warmth of watching children enjoy themselves or young people succeed. Neighbors take hot dishes to families caught up in emergencies. We hear of an earthquake or a flood and send a check to the Red Cross to help people we have never seen and will never know. We donate money to a university to finance the education of youth or to endow the chair of a scholar.

Giving and helping are in a special class of human behavior; they should be fostered. In the following discussions we shall suggest that altruistic behavior is not always as selfless as it seems, but this is not to assert that altruism is always self-serving. Many manifestations of altruism presently defy categorization and are therefore not psychologically researchable, given the present state of the art.

Difficulties in Helping the Poor

Many who have had a deep sympathy for the poor have tried to devise plans and programs to alleviate their problems. The policy recommended by religious leaders for over two thousand years is that of charitable giving—outright grants of money. Medieval churchmen urged that alms be given as an expression of *caritas*—the love of God and the fountainhead of all virtues. Mohammed prescribed that the faithful give to the poor between 5% and 10% of whatever feedstocks have been held for a year. But he required that his followers give away only 2.5% of their *money*. This proviso must certainly be one of the earlier examples of a tax shelter for the wealthy.

Few people in the industrialized and urbanized areas of the world today feel religiously committed to charitable giving, and instead make donations out of a sense of civic responsibility or a moral commitment to human welfare. Personal asking—begging—and personal giving have almost disappeared. One psychological reason for this change is the fact that people usually feel ill-at-ease when they are asked for money or confronted directly with need. This discomfort has led to the institutionalization of charity, which now takes the form of tax-supported social-welfare programs and organized fund drives.

Why do we feel embarrassed when someone asks us for money? For one thing, such a request restricts our freedom (Brehm, 1966). We want to determine our own self-concept—who we are—and the request limits our freedom of choice by forcing upon us the choice of two unwanted identities: the "soft touch," or the stingy withholder of alms from the needy. Either we may give and perhaps feel angry at having been duped and exploited, or we may refuse to give and perhaps feel guilty. Often we try to find a compromise between these two unacceptable states of mind by giving somewhat less than has been asked.

It is psychologically interesting that when people volunteer money spontaneously they feel thereby ennobled; but the direct, person-to-person demand of a suppliant, by robbing our actions of their spontaneity and by thus preventing us from enjoying the full flavor of generosity, makes us feel put upon and exploited.

There is also the matter of guilt. We noted in our last chapter that people avoid being labeled "rich", partly because it makes them seem "different" and partly because the rich are traditional targets for hostility and envy. In addition, the ethical roots of our Judaeo-Christian culture lead us to associate wealth with sin and poverty with virtue. The request for money labels us as wealthier than the suppliant and tacitly accuses us of the sin of being rich. As a consequence we feel guilty.

Charity Begins with Guilt

The guilt we feel when confronted by the plea of an unfortunate member of society may originate far back in our evolutionary history. In her fascinating account of social life in a tribe of chimpanzees living in a Tanzanian jungle, Jane van Lawick-Goodall (1971) describes how higher-status animals, successful in their hunting, break off portions of meat and hand them to the lower-status members of the tribe who stand around begging.

In one episode van Lawick-Goodall tells of an aggressive young chimp, "Goliath," who was seated in a tree, gnawing at the body of a freshly killed baboon infant. "Worzle," an older but low-status member of the tribe, climbed up the tree, whimpering and begging for a share. Goliath resorted to evasive tactics, moving from one branch to another, but Worzle followed, whining and holding out his hand. When Goliath had pushed away the beggar's hand for perhaps the tenth time, Worzle hurled himself backward out of the tree and thrashed around in the bushes, throwing a tantrum. Goliath then gave half of the meat to the suppliant. It seemed clear that the commotion made by old Worzle had caused Goliath more discomfort than he could tolerate.

What Goodall observed, here, may have been the expression of mingled sympathy and guilt. Like Goliath, we are psychologically vulnerable to the suffering of others; we find ourselves sharing their pain, at least symbolically. We know that we are not the cause of the sufferer's problems, yet we feel somehow responsible—guilty, perhaps. Possibly we feel guilty because we have been spared the difficulties with which the sufferer is afflicted. Sharing or making a donation relieves our guilt. We then tell ourselves that we have done the best we can and are no longer responsible for the trouble we have seen.

A Balanced View of Tipping

Tipping those who serve is a ritual that affirms the higher status of those who are served. In our more or less democratic society, where we like to believe that status levels have been abolished, we are inclined to rationalize tipping by considering it extra payment for services performed promptly and willingly by waiters and waitresses, barkeepers, taxi drivers, and bellhops;[1] but upon examination, the logic of this explanation falters. For one thing, the individuals concerned expect to be tipped and usually *are* tipped, regardless of the quality of their service. For another, in many restaurants and bars tips are pooled and later divided, so that the reward given by a grateful patron to an especially attentive waiter immediately loses its personal significance. Hence the only explanations for tipping are these: It confirms the ritualized status differential between server and served, and it enables people with less money to share the good fortune of those who have more.

Woe betide the skeptic whose democratic inclinations cause him to forego the higher status ascribed to the tipper, and whose logical analysis leads him to reject the argument that tips are payments for special services. What does this democratic logician do when he is faced by the gloomy stare of the untipped waiter or the angry glare of the cab driver whom he has paid exactly what the meter reported?

For him, as for the rest of us, the pressures of tradition, custom, and social norm are more than the psyche can bear. He feels guilty. At the same time he is angry because his logic tells him there is no reason for guilt. But conformity to society's expectations has been bred into him; after a fumbling search for the right change, he hands over the tip, sometimes a defiant cut below the norm, sometimes a guilty tad above it. Then he goes his way, feeling victimized, blaming the extortionist, blaming himself, but seldom examining the social dynamics of his recent predicament.

In countries where traditions are cherished, tipping is unlikely to be an occasion for anxiety. Untroubled by a need for

---

[1]Popular belief has it that "tip" is an acronym for "to insure promptness", but it is actually related to the word "tipple." Traditionally, the tip was given the hardworking waiter or cab driver so that he could enjoy the luxury of a glass of beer, wine, or schnapps. The "tipple" interpretation is supported by the French word for tip, *pourboire* ("for drinking") and the German, *Trinkgeld* ("drink money"). The amount given also reflects the price of a drink. When drinks were a dime, the standard tip was a dime; when drinks went up to a quarter, the tip followed suit. Now that inflation has raised the cost of a drink to a dollar or more, a tip of anything less than that is regarded as an insult by most baggage-carriers and cab drivers.

simon-pure democracy, people there accept status levels as if they were natural phenomena; they feel neither outraged at being expected to tip nor demeaned if their social position designates them as receivers of tips. Most Americans, too, ignore the antidemocratic implications of the institution and tip without thinking.

Giving, Getting, and Sharing

We may find it awkward to deal with people who expect us to give them money, but we may not be aware that the askers also feel awkward. Even the very poor do not enjoy asking others for money—unless they happen to be professional beggars, in which case they regard panhandling as a form of paid employment. The great majority of the poor, like most other people, prize their dignity. They refuse to beg. Receiving charity is likely to be experienced as humiliating and demeaning, for it accentuates differences in status: The donor's status, whatever it may be, is elevated by his offer to give, whereas the prospective recipient's status is lowered by his need to be helped. By accepting the proffered gift, he signifies his acceptance of the difference in status; by rejecting it, he raises himself to a higher level than before.

An experiment involving status between givers and receivers was conducted by Fisher and Nadler (1976), who asked university students to participate in a stock market speculation game. Each student was ushered into a cubicle, where he was supplied with tokens representing money and was given information about fictitious companies affording opportunities for speculative investment. The student was told that the game was a competitive test of his ability as investor and that his performance would be rated against that of another student—his comparison-mate. Investments were to be made by means of a computer terminal in the cubicle.

None of the students knew that the results of the game were rigged so that after a series of speculations each player's money supply was reduced from thirty tokens to four, a situation in which he could be eliminated from the game after the next play. Half the students were informed that their comparison-mates had through wise investment increased their stakes from thirty to sixty tokens; the other half were told that the comparison-mates had not done well and that their capital had been reduced to sixteen tokens. At this stage in the experiment, all had lost badly and were as a consequence chagrined—especially those who learned that their comparison-mates had done much better than they had.

The players had been told that they might send notes to their comparison-mates, presumably for the purpose of exchanging information on investment strategies. The experimenters served as messengers. Although the students had thus been prepared for communication from their comparison-mates, each of them was surprised when he received an envelope containing a gift of four tokens, with no other message. The four-token gift was sufficient to enable them to make a comeback and restore their diminished self-images. The purpose of this manipulation was to make half of the students believe that the donor had been very successful and would hardly miss the handful of tokens he had tossed their way; the others were expected to believe that the donor was a loser who had chosen to share his meager resources with another unfortunate. There were no comparison-mates, of course; all aspects of the experiment had been secretly rigged by the experimenters. (Responses of the few subjects who suspected the hoax were dropped before the data were analyzed.)

The players were then informed that the game would continue but that the companies in which they invested were now to be real companies—Eastman Kodak, Proctor and Gamble, and the like. (The purpose of this announcement was to keep the students' interest high and to make the gift they had received all the more significant.) At this point, the students were asked to fill out an "interim report" on how they felt about the game, their comparison-mates, and themselves.

An analysis of the interim reports confirmed what we might expect: Students who believed that their comparison-mates were losers like themselves reported a higher degree of self-esteem than did students in a control group (players who had received no gifts). The students who got the four tokens from their fellow losers described the gift-givers as generous and said they were eager to meet them after the experiment.

Students whose donors had been very successful—rich—reported lower levels of self-esteem than did the control-group students who had received no gifts. They did not view the donors as generous, seeing them instead as power-seekers whom they would not care to meet after the experiment.

The experiment thus supports our impressions about the way receivers of charitable gifts regard themselves and those who give. The poor individual who receives money or other resources from another poor person suffers no damage to his self-esteem and may even feel affection and gratitude. Such a gift can be seen more as a sharing of scanty resources than as charity. The effect can be one of psychological comfort and reassurance.

Gifts from the rich produce quite different effects. The impoverished person now feels humiliated. He does not like his donor any better for the gift, does not feel especially grateful, and may even suspect the giver of using the gift to impress the recipient with his power. His mood is one of psychological discomfort, ingratitude, and distrust.

We might, at this point in our analysis, conclude that the rich should refrain from giving, leaving the poor to share among themselves their meager assets. But this is a short-range view. No one benefits, in the end, if the poor are doomed to remain poor. Poverty gnaws away at the structure of society and is a threat to the well-being of people at all levels. Urban poverty, especially, is an ever-present source of political and economic instability, crime, and social degradation.

We all want, or should want, the poor to help themselves. The experience of the last generation—President Johnson's antipoverty program, for example—suggests that outsiders cannot really solve the problems of the poor and that every well-meant gesture of help runs the risk of creating new problems. How can society best encourage the poor to initiate self-help?

The final phase of the experiment we have just described provides a possible answer. When the players were told to continue the game by investing in real companies, they were given brochures containing background data on the potential investments. They would be allowed only this one chance to familiarize themselves with the material. After they had finished reading and had signalled their readiness to continue the game, they could not refer to the investment data again.

The time spent by each student in reading the material was taken as an index of the strength of his desire to improve his investment strategy. If the student spent little time in preparation for the task it was inferred that he was discouraged and had concluded that further attempts to invest would come to naught. It was also assumed that the student who was optimistic and determined to try again would spend more time at the task of preparing for another round of investing.

We might expect that the psychologically comfortable student—the one who had received gifts from his "poor" comparison-mate—would spend more time in an effort to prepare himself for the second round. The results of psychological experiments, however, like the everyday events they are designed to reflect, often take unexpected turns. It was the psychologically *un*comfortable student—the one who had been humiliated by the gift from his "rich" comparison-mate—who actually invested more time in improving his situation.

What are we to make of this? It appears that psychological comfort, however gratifying it may be in the short run, may actually undermine the will to improve one's condition. Perhaps being helped by another loser confirms the feeling that one is "a loser, bound to lose" and thus lowers one's expectations. However, the person who has been upset by being an "object of charity" seems motivated to see that the need for charity does not occur again. There is something of the "I'll show them" spirit in his reaction.

As we have noted, charity in the form of personalized giving has in recent years been supplanted increasingly by government agencies. A small army of civil servants administers programs that provide aid on an equitable, nonjudgmental, and impersonal basis. The poor perceive the donor neither as another poor person sharing meager resources nor as a wealthy winner playing a power game. Hence there is neither the sense of psychological comfort that comes when an impoverished neighbor "gives the shirt off his back" nor the irritation and resentment that results from being "the objects of charity."

How Not to Help Gypsies

But the poor are not easily aided, irrespective of whether the help comes in the form of personal charity or from a government dedicated to eliminate poverty. The experience of Hungary's attempt to assist Gypsies is in many ways typical of the difficulties that arise when an impoverished minority group becomes the target of a government program of financial aid.

According to Jonathan Spivak (1979), a *Wall Street Journal* reporter, there are about 320,000 Gypsies in Hungary—about 3% of the total population. More than half of them live in remote rural areas. They are further isolated from other Hungarians by their adherence to Gypsy cultural patterns and values. Almost a third of them speak not Hungarian but one of the several Gypsy dialects or Romanian.

Gypsy problems begin in childhood. Half of the homeless children in Hungary are Gypsies, and most Gypsy children lag behind their classmates in school. There are only a dozen Gypsies among the 65,000 students who attend Hungarian universities.

As might be expected from this poor beginning, Gypsies are ill-prepared to cope with the world of work. Many will not take steady jobs, preferring to wander in bands. Those who do seek permanent employment must take poorly paid, unskilled work.

Hungarian government officials are embarrassed by the presence of impoverished Gypsies in a socialist state committed to the abolishment of economic class differences. They have therefore instituted special programs to meet Gypsy educational, economic, and social needs. Teachers are being trained to deal with special Gypsy problems and to teach classes in Gypsy dialects. Boarding schools are also being established to provide education for Gypsy children from remote rural areas.

A few of these well-intentioned efforts have backfired, however. Hungarian families with four children are entitled to government-subsidized flats. Some of the Gypsy families who qualify sell their right to the flats on the black market and then secure less-adequate housing for themselves, repeating the process every few years. Such behavior naturally upsets non-Gypsy

Hungarians, who already have a deep-seated prejudice against the Gypsies. This antipathy is further sharpened by the tendency of Communist Party officials to blame the Gypsy problem on the feudal society that existed before World War I and to deny that it is caused or aggravated by cultural differences.

Like poor minorities throughout the world, Hungarian Gypsies have a touchy sense of ethnic pride that often becomes a sticking point when others try to help them. Spivak gives the example of a social worker's attempt to get a forty-year-old Gypsy mother of six children to apply for $100 per month in government aid. The woman worked the night shift in a factory and did housecleaning as well. Her husband, a semiskilled workman, drank heavily and did not bring home his entire paycheck. The family's circumstances were substandard: Their income was about $250 a month and they all slept on two beds in a single room.

The Gypsy woman, who had refused to accept welfare payments in the past, agreed to apply for aid, but the social worker was not optimistic. "She'll change her mind. She has seven sisters, and five of them take no money from the state. She is afraid of what they will say."

The plight of the Hungarian Gypsies parallels that of Middle-Eastern and North African Bedouins, who resist with fierce pride governmental attempts to help them fit into a modern industrialized, urbanized society. As do poor minorities elsewhere, they seem determined to frustrate all efforts to guide them into channels of self-improvement.

In sum, there are no easy answers to the question of what to do about poverty, whether of individuals or of ethnic minorities. It would be inhumane for governments to halt self-help programs or to cut off the aid that keeps millions of the poor from starvation and exposure. But there is a general tendency for us to think that establishing such programs relieves us of all further responsibility. If the results of the second phase of the Fisher/Nadler experiment apply to everyday living, it would appear that gifts and other forms of help given directly to those in need stand the best chance of encouraging initiative and self-help. There are problems with this conclusion, of course. It may be that poor people would behave quite differently from the college sophomores who served as subjects in the experiment. In any event, we would require follow-up experiments comparing the effects of personalized gifts given by those with more, less, or the same resources, before we employed these findings in support of campaigns of direct giving.

Our present welfare programs do not appear to encourage self-help among the poor; indeed, it is often charged that they discourage it. A new approach is needed, even if the "new" approach is personalized giving—a form of sharing advocated by religious leaders since the beginning of recorded time.

8 Money motives, sex, and guilt-edged anxiety

Love and money make strange bedfellows. —ANONYMOUS

I think I could be a good woman if I had five thousand a year. —BECKY SHARP, IN W. M. THACKERAY'S VANITY FAIR

It is a kind of spiritual snobbery that makes people think they can be happy without money.   —ALBERT CAMUS

In spite of the fact that the money motive has become a major concern in some way or other for most of us, it is a relatively recent development. In Chapter 2 we noted that money first appeared in the 7th Century B.C. If the history of the human race were reduced to the span of a single week, money would have appeared on the scene only fifteen minutes ago. It has nevertheless penetrated and permeated the human psyche more than any other invention except language. The money drive has been blended so well into patterns of psychological and social behavior that it has become integrated into the expectations, plans, dreams, hopes, fears, anxieties, and disappointments of almost everyone.

The Money Motive among Primates

Although the money motive has to be learned, it is picked up easily. In one of the classic experiments in psychology, John B. Wolfe (1936), working at the Primate Biology Laboratories of Yale University, taught a form of the money motive to chimpanzees. The chimps learned to work for poker chips, which they could use to "purchase" grapes by inserting them into a slot in a specially constructed vending machine—a veritable "Chimp-o-Mat." Wolfe thus introduced the chimps to a monetary system in which a form of fiat currency—poker chips—was redeemable in fruit.

After the animals acquired this rudimentary money motive, they learned to save chips and spend them later. Then Wolfe added another touch. He introduced a new machine with a lever that was restrained by heavy springs. Its action was so stiff that it took three chimps straining together to make it surrender a single grape.

Once the animals had learned to operate the new device, it was altered so that it produced a poker chip that could be used to buy a grape at the Chimp-o-Mat. The change did not upset the chimps at all. Like their human counterparts, they collaborated energetically in order to earn the "money," which they then exchanged for grapes. As the experiments continued, the animals learned to identify special tokens that were good for two grapes instead of one. Different colored tokens were also introduced that could be exchanged for something to drink or for the opportunity to play with the experimenters. Again the chimps adapted.

Wolfe noted some strikingly human characteristics. One female begged for tokens from her "wealthier" friends "by whining and extending her hand, palm up." Given a handout, she hurried away to the Chimp-o-Mat and got the grapes she wanted.

The chimps competed with one another for opportunities to operate the apparatus. When no reward was provided, little work was done. When the chimps were given tokens outright, they took themselves off the labor market and refused to operate the lever. Like their human counterparts, they found it easier to acquire a taste for money than a taste for work.

The tests were conducted under time limitations. Wolfe observed that with such restrictions the more tokens an animal had earned through working, the less energetically it would work. But he suspected strongly that if the animals had unlimited time to accumulate their wealth, that trend would be sharply reversed. "Chimpanzees," he concluded, "can make a variety of discriminations between tokens having different reward values and can use them in harmony with their drives or motives."

Humans have even less difficulty acquiring monetary know-how and needs than the chimps. By the time they enter school, most children have a fairly sophisticated understanding of dollars and cents, or pounds and pence, and are already making active use of the monetary system of their society. And once monetary motives are learned, they rate high in our hierarchy of needs. Few sounds rivet our attention as does the tinkle of a coin dropped on the pavement nearby.

Money as a Reinforcer

Psychologists who study motivation recognize two types of drives: primary and secondary. Primary drives are those that are inborn: Hunger, thirst, sex, pain avoidance, sleep, and needs for arousal and activity are among the more prominent ones. Secondary drives are learned motives that initially were associated with behavior aimed at satisfying primary drives, but that may also develop "functional autonomy" and exist independently. D. O. Hebb (1949) has pointed out that eating a few peanuts does not satisfy the need for peanuts as nourishment; it actually creates the need for more peanuts. Like the need for peanuts, the money motive may also assume the status of a functionally autonomous drive, which may lead us to pursue money for its own sake. When the money motive becomes truly autonomous, it takes the form of what Karen Horney (1950) called a "neurotic need."

Edward Emmet Lawler III (1971), in his book on pay and organizational effectiveness, maintains that money is not so much the primary objective of a drive as it is a "reinforcer."

Reinforcers are elements in our environment that become associated with the satisfaction or reduction of drives and thus enable us to learn appropriate forms of behavior. Those elements that directly satisfy drives are primary reinforcers, while those that are less directly involved are secondary reinforcers. Food is a primary reinforcer when it helps infants learn how to get food into their mouths; but money is a secondary reinforcer when it helps us learn the behavior—paid employment, for example—that is needed to produce the means whereby food can be acquired in the first place. In Wolfe's experiment, just described, the tokens used to get chimps to operate levers would be considered secondary reinforcers.

Lawler maintains that the chimp experiments, though interesting, tell us little about human behavior toward and with money. Unlike the chimps, we do not usually think of money solely as something that can be exchanged for food. Money has instead taken on a much broader value for us, inasmuch as we have come to associate it with a great many other reinforcers: clothing, shelter, entertainment, social relations, security, prestige, status, and so forth. Unlike the chimps, furthermore, we need not experience personally all the particular outcomes that money may produce. In a delicately phrased example, Lawler points out that a man "may believe that if he enters a certain section of town, money will buy him the attentions of young ladies, yet he may never have actually experienced the association between money and female attention." In other words, what we know about money is based only partially on personal experiences; it also comes from what others tell us and from generalizations drawn from our observations of the way others behave toward and with money.

Lawler is also attracted to a theory of basic needs developed by Abraham H. Maslow (1954). Maslow thought of human needs as arranged in a hierarchy in which higher-level needs operate when lower-level needs are satisfied. Maslow's needs, arranged in order from the most basic, lower-level to the more complex, higher-level are as follows:

1. Physiological
2. Safety
3. Belongingness and love
4. Esteem
5. Self-actualization

Physiological needs, which include the need for water, food, oxygen, etc., must be satisfied if the organism is to survive. Almost as important for survival are the safety needs—the need to seek shelter from the elements and to keep out of harm's way. The need for belongingness and love is the most basic psychological need, followed by the need for esteem—the need to be accepted and respected by others. The highest-level need—self-actualization—may be satisfied by a wide range of activities, including self-development, the acquisition of new skills and competencies, and creative endeavor.

Lawler points out that money can be used to attain goals relevant to all the needs, although its function diminishes as we proceed up the scale from the lower to the higher needs. Money can buy food, clothing, and health care, but it cannot buy love, ✓ social acceptance, or self-actualization. Nevertheless it can play a supportive role in our attempts to meet these higher-level needs. The amenities it can purchase help us to satisfy needs for love and social acceptance. Self-actualization, too, is made possible by the purchase of tools with which to express ourselves. In any event, money is an aid or a facilitator and not an end in itself. Psychologists do not, Lawler says, "speak of a need for money," inasmuch as "money will not be sought unless it leads to other outcomes."

Lawler would probably hold that the individual who persistently pursues money, apparently for its own sake, is responding not to a "need for money" but to some neurotic need to be competitive, aggressive, or acquisitive.

Although Lawler's arguments are persuasive, we shall continue to speak in this book of a "money motive." Money may not, as he says, be an incentive—an object that "triggers" a drive and thus initiates an appropriate behavioral sequence—but it often seems to serve that function. Should we set up a sign over a storefront on a downtown street, offering to pay $10 for "five minutes of your time," a line of people eager for easy money would immediately form, even though they would have no idea what "five minutes of their time" would involve. Nor is it unusual, furthermore, for individuals to initiate a sequence of actions for the avowed intention of "getting some money."

There is no doubt that money has value as a reinforcer in real life, as well as in the laboratory, and we shall be citing some research in which money serves that purpose. But money's role as an incentive seems more prominent. We shall therefore consider those expectations, attitudes, feelings, and values that lead us to regard money as an incentive to be included in the "money motive."

Money versus Sex: Unequal Contest

In this complex, stimulus-laden environment of ours, we must decide how to distribute our time and attention among a variety of potentially satisfying objects and experiences. Although we strive to achieve a certain economy in our actions, meeting as many needs as we can in a single behavioral sequence, some motives will be "losers," no matter what we do. We may, for example, throw a party to which we invite family and friends, and thus satisfy needs for love and social acceptance, as well as food and drink, but by doing so, we may shortchange needs for self-actualization, sexual expression, and sleep. Hence we tend to order our needs, drives, or motives (we shall follow common psychological practice and treat them as more or less synonymous) in a priority hierarchy appropriate to each time and place. We try to balance the relative importance of each need against the chances of satisfying it. In our ordering of motives, we recognize that one class of needs—the biological—are more or less in conflict with a second class—the social. The opposition between these two classes of motives has concerned scholars since the dawn of philosophy. In modern times, the writings of Jean-Jacques Rousseau in the 18th Century and of Sigmund Freud in the 20th are among the better known analyses of problems created by this conflict.

Anthropologist Edward T. Hall (1976) describes how society's demands, in the form of time restraints, interfere with our biological nature. Hall says that man's first experiences with time were in the form of rhythms inherent in daily, monthly, and annual cycles. But now, he says, time "is imposed as an outside constraint and sends its tentacles into every nook and crevice of even our most private acts (bowel movements and sex are regulated by the clock and the calendar). As many of the young have discovered, our time system has done much to alienate Western man from himself. A reason for people getting sick is to escape the shackles of time and to return and re-experience their own rhythms, but at what a price!"

Of the various motives that clamor for our attention, social motives involving money are most in conflict with love, especially as it is expressed biologically in the sex drive. The two represent the classic examples of the conflict between our social and our biological natures. In its own way, each motive is intriguing, exciting, and demanding—so much so that most people find it difficult to pursue them simultaneously, with the obvious exception of those in the prostitution or the pornography business. For most of us most of the time, however, sex and money motives are in different compartments. As Foa (1971) demonstrated in the research we discussed in Chapter 4, people have difficulty in thinking of exchanging love for money, and vice versa. Love and money make strange bedfellows, indeed.

The fact that the sex drive occasionally wins out over the money drive in its competition for our attention should not blind us to the fact that we spend a great deal more time and energy in the pursuit of money than in the pursuit of sex. It is alleged that there are some for whom these priorities are reversed, but calm and objective evaluation of the evidence suggests that such allegations are more fascinating than true. For example, careful reading of the autobiography of Casanova, the 18th Century Italian adventurer whose exploits have served as a kind of high-water mark for those who like to boast of their sexual prowess, shows that he spent far more hours chasing ducats that he did in pursuit of bedmates. Indeed he might well have agreed with his British contemporary, Dr. Samuel Johnson, who said, according to Boswell: "There are few ways in which a man can be more innocently employed than in getting money."

Freud and his followers would probably dismiss as irrelevant most of what we have said so far in this chapter, but they would take marked exception to the sentiments expressed by Dr. Johnson. They would say, first of all, that *all* human behavior is involved with the sex drive in one way or another, and, second, that monetary motives are both degrading and unhealthy. Let us first examine their position on the matter of sex.

The Psychoanalytic View of Sex

The science of psychology appeared on the scene a hundred years ago. We have forgotten most of the early psychologists, but one stands out like a giant among the pygmies: Sigmund Freud. Freud was the founder of personality psychology and made important contributions to modern clinical, developmental, and social psychology. It was thanks to Freud that most psychologists today take it for granted that early childhood experiences have significant effects on interpersonal behavior and personality development—effects that continue throughout the life span. Freud demonstrated clearly that many of the most significant motives that underlie everyday behavior are unknown to us; they are in a manner of speaking, unconscious. Freud also delineated the role of anxiety in our lives. He pointed out that we engage in elaborate, almost ritualized forms of behavior—what he termed *defense mechanisms*—to shield ourselves from the distracting and at times painful experience of dealing directly with anxiety-laden experiences.

But no pioneering genius, however great, can be right about everything. Some of Freud's premises seem, in the light of what we know today, to rest on too narrow a base. His assumptions about the sexual basis of human behavior are now questioned frequently by behavioral scientists.

Freud and his followers constructed a theory on the principle that inappropriate and misguided behavior—neurosis—is an inevitable result of our attempts to misinterpret, distort, conceal, or repress sexual motives. The cure for neurosis lies in understanding, through psychoanalysis, how libidinous motives affect behavior. Patients must use this understanding as a basis for coming to terms with themselves and developing more effective styles of coping with the sexual side of life and its problems.

Freud and his interpreters built their theories and their practices at a time when public expression of sexuality was considered shocking and disgusting, Frances Trollope, in Philadelphia on the eve of the Victorian era, found that ladies and gentlemen were not allowed to view antique statuary in mixed company. A few decades later, Samuel Butler visited the Montreal museum and found that a nude statue of a Greek discus thrower had been hidden from public view because it was considered "rather vulgar." Prudery was equated with virtue and good taste in those unlamented days. Today, our nostalgia is focused on the Edwardian era, when Queen Victoria's son gave a guarded green light to sexual expression, at least as far as the aristocracy was concerned.

The campaign to drive sex underground was not initiated in the 19th Century. The authors of both the New and Old Testaments tended to take a rather raised-eyebrow view of sex. The Church's official position was (and still is) that sex is permissible only within the confines of marriage; even within this context it is not expected to be a form of entertainment. This rather stringent policy, however, has often been tempered by expediency and the need to deal with the realities of everyday life. Thus, the upper class has generally dealt with sex in a relaxed manner, and the working class and the poor, having few pleasures in life, have taken sex when they could, without much thought of the consequences in this life or the next; but the middle class has often attempted to put sex under wraps and to inhibit its free and easy expression. Martin Luther expressed their views rather well when he thundered: "Tis the devil inspires this evanescent ardor, in order to divert the parties from prayer." But, to give Luther his due, we should also note that it was he who is said to have sagely observed "Two times a week makes one hundred and four," thus setting a reasonable norm for an unreasonable age.

Freud's attack on the conventional façade of pretended sexual innocence and propriety was to some extent the impatient and somewhat vindictive gesture of an intellectual moving in for the kill. He had discovered a weak spot in the armor of his opponents—in this instance, the arrogant and self-satisfied members of Viennese middle-class society who had rejected and humiliated him. But the norms and values of the Viennese bourgeoisie were not very different from those of middle-class people elsewhere.

As Freud's ideas became more widely discussed, they gave conventional notions about sex a blow from which they have never recovered. Today, the revolution started by Freud rolls on, shaking the traditional institutions of courtship, marriage, and parenthood to their foundations.

The Psychoanalytic View of the Money Motive

The major drive according to Freudian theory is the *libido*, which is variously interpreted to refer to sexual craving, erotic pleasure, or "any *instinctual* manifestation that tends toward life rather than death, integration rather than destruction" (English & English 1958). Freud used "libido" in all three of these senses, but in general usage, which we shall follow, the term has come to refer exclusively to the sex drive.

Freud viewed the human problem as a struggle between the individual's libido and an implacable society that demanded the suppression of instinctual impulses. Although Freud recognized the need to come to terms with society, he tended to take a supportive stand regarding the individual's need for sexual expression, and he always saw neurosis as the result of social influences on the individual (Borneman, 1973).

Many of Freud's followers have tended to emphasize the sex drive and to regard society as the enemy. Money is especially evil because it plays a key role in the apparatus employed by society to keep the individual in bondage. The more important money becomes in our lives, the more we are inclined to repress the sexual side of our nature. The money motive is incompatible with libido.

Money, in the Freudian lexicon, is symbolic excrement. As a child becomes toilet-trained he derives a feeling of power from his new-found ability to control the expulsion of his feces; this pleasure is said to develop eventually into a feeling of power associated with success at making money. Activities such as saving money and budgeting are, in Freudian terms, identified with constipation, and those who are especially frugal and economical are said to have been "fixated at the anal-retentive level" in their early psychological development: when placed on the potty, as children, they derived more pleasure from stubbornly withholding their feces than from cooperatively and generously expelling them the way the normal child does. We are also told that children's interest in playing with their feces reappears in adult years as the pleasure in dealing with money.

This association of money with feces and of money-making with anal activity is a recurrent theme in the writings of Freud's successors. Sandor Ferenczi (1916), for instance, characterized money as "odorless, dehydrated filth that has been made to shine," and Thomas Wiseman (1974), in his recent book on monetary motives, maintains that Freud's "anal character is a cornerstone of modern psychology and affords the classic explanation of interest in money."

Ernest Borneman (1973) a German psychoanalyst, writes as follows: "The pleasure taken in property, which frequently manifests itself in looking at money or possessions, derives from the pleasure the child takes in looking at its intestinal products. When such a person pulls bundles of banknotes out of his pocket whenever he pays small amounts, we can be certain that we see here the regressed pleasure in manipulating one's own feces."

In their derogation of money, psychoanalysts take the view that the aim of all money-related behavior is the acquisition of money itself, ignoring the commonsense view that most people seek money because it is the means to other ends. Psychoanalysts seem to have overlooked the possibility that the average person might accumulate money in order to pay for a pleasant, carefree vacation or a backyard swimming pool. It could be argued that Freudians are concerned only about obsessive or compulsive behavior regarding money, but a scanning of psychoanalytic writing makes it clear that *all* money-related behavior is abhorrent to them.

The best explanation of the psychoanalytic rationale seems to be that Freud and his followers, as members of the intelligentsia, used the anal/fecal metaphor as a literary device to express their scorn of the bourgeoisie. Pragmatic values and the unabashed enjoyment of the marketplace have made the bourgeoisie the traditional target for the trigger-happy members of the intelligentsia, who have, at least since the days of Juvenal, delighted in characterizing them as loutish moneygrubbers.

It is to the credit of the later psychoanalytic writers, especially the neo-Freudians, that they rejected this equating of money and feces, but they did remain loyal to the intellectual tradition and hence did not regard money or its pursuit in a favorable light. Erich Fromm (1955), for example, wrote of the "alienating function of money," and the views of other psychoanalysts on money have ranged from the mildly critical to the downright derogatory. Wiseman (1974) reflects the characteristic psychoanalytic orientation when he reports that he was led to the study of money because it is "an institution whose 'sickness' is daily evident."

Norman O. Brown (1959), a psychoanalyst who has written extensively on history and economics, is scathing in his denunciation of both money and the work that produces it. Alienation, he says, is rooted in the compulsion to work, which "subordinates man to things, producing at the same time confusion in the valuation of things . . . and the devaluation of the human body . . . . It reduces the drives of the human being to greed and competition. . . . The desire for money takes the place of all genuinely human needs." In a later discussion, Brown says that money is condensed guilt and that guilt is unclean.

In his witty description of the Wall Street money game, the New York financier George J. W. Goodman, who wrote under the name of "Adam Smith" (1969), said that reading Norman Brown's books made him feel that he ought to be spending his afternoons fishing and drinking beer in order to escape the degradation of compulsive, guilt-ridden work. But then, said Goodman, "I have the sneaky feeling that while I am fishing Brown is working on another book."

Goodman's point was that his pleasure in the money game was such that playing it couldn't be all bad, even by the standards of Brown and other hypercritical psychoanalysts. Goodman said that he felt no guilt whatever when he was involved in the money game; he only felt guilty about money when he was reading Norman Brown.

Comfort, Joy, and Gobs of Money

Goodman's cynical comment about Brown's covert enjoyment of his work (and probably money as well) brings to mind the case of Alexander Comfort, a London medical biologist, whose 1972 book, *The Joy of Sex*, advocated a libidinous philosophy consistent with much current psychoanalytic thinking.

Robert M. Hutchins had for some years tried to persuade Comfort to take up residence at his Center for the Study of Democratic Institutions in Sant Barbara, California. Most people would have found Hutchins' invitation irresistible, for the resident fellows at the Center's villa received handsome stipends, slept in well-appointed quarters, and were served gourmet meals by the Center's highly trained culinary staff. Comfort repeatedly declined, however, until *The Joy of Sex* appeared on the best-seller lists and he suddenly found his substantial royalties subject to British income taxes, which are among the highest in the world. The chance to move to the United States, where income taxes are much lower, suddenly became more interesting.

Comfort took up residence at the Center and signed over to it the contract for *The Joy of Sex*, with the proviso that he would receive back 80% of the royalties, in addition to an annual stipend of $28,000. The arrangement worked to everyone's satisfaction for a couple of years. Comfort wrote *More Joy of Sex* and other learned treatises. Hutchins, for his part, considered himself fortunate to have so eminent a scholar in residence at the Center.

But even earthly paradises inevitably develop money problems. The sybaritic life-style enjoyed by the Center's fellows and staff was expensive, and costs ran far ahead of the generous income granted by an indulgent foundation back in Chicago. Hutchins was therefore forced to close down the villa and move the Center and its personnel to more economical and austere quarters in Chicago.

Comfort was upset at this turn of events. He had been content in Santa Barbara and had counted on staying there indefinitely. He refused to move, saying that his agreement had specified residence in the villa in Santa Barbara and that the Center's transfer to Chicago constituted a breach of contract. He therefore sued the Center for $93,000 in royalties, $63,000 in back pay, and $250,000 in punitive damages. Whatever Comfort's interest in the joy of sex had been, it certainly had not diminished his interest in money.

Comfort's case was tried before a Federal district judge, who found that the Center had indeed let Comfort down and directed it to pay him his back royalties and to return the rights to his book. But he ruled against damages and instead criticized both parties in scathing words for having entered into a "shabby pact" in which "Comfort untruthfully represented that he had written *Joy* in the United States and under the auspices of the

Center while using its facilities. . . . And the Center winked at the fraud."

The Comfort affair makes it clear that there is a great deal of money to be made in writing about sex, and suggests that "Adam Smith's" suspicions about the motives of psychoanalytic writers may have been on target.

Feeling Guilty about Money

These inconsistencies between psychoanalysts' official position on money and their all-too-human behavior in money matters seldom come to our notice. Whatever doubts they may raise are obliterated by the constant stream of books and magazine articles that urge us continually to feel happy about sex and suggest, directly or by implication, that we should feel guilty about our involvement in work and other money-related activities.

These views have had a strong appeal to the book-reading public and have had a considerable effect on the attitudes of college and university students. Most students have little money; the idea that those who do possess it ought to feel guilty is one they find attractive. Students sometimes go to elaborate lengths to deny that the money motive plays or ever will play a part in their lives.

The German sociologist, Helmut Schoeck (1966), says that such behavior is motivated by the students' envy of everyone above their own level. They consider escape into a life of poverty—"dropping out" of society—but this would lead to their secretly envying those in the class they have abandoned. Schoeck continues: "There is an obvious way out of this dilemma, out of these ambivalent feelings: the glorification of voluntary poverty in company with the genuine (or ostensibly genuine) poor and oppressed, whose utopia or planned social revolution promises that ultimately no one will be able to afford a pleasant life."

Schoeck wrote at a time when students were "trashing" classrooms and libraries or were leaving the university to take up lives of shared poverty in communes. Their negative position regarding money and work has melted somewhat in recent years, and more students are now taking courses in business and finance; but many still feel that the only meaningful careers for them are those that are relatively untainted by money and that are characterized by self-expression, self-discovery, and helping others. As a result, they flock into courses that will prepare them for careers in social work, biology, recreation, and creative arts, family counseling, clinical psychology, and education. The unemployment and underemployment that plague these fields do not seem to deter them. The reports showing that unemployment among teachers reaches a new high each year are dismissed by many students as irrelevant. They seek teaching credentials because teaching is a highly visible way of helping people, which is, in turn, the very antithesis of "dollar chasing." The fact that the teaching profession is notoriously underpaid means that no one can accuse them of being interested in money. Once they are credentialed and on the job, of course, they will strike for higher wages like everyone else. But during their training period they are preoccupied with "learning to help kids," and they cannot imagine that a few years hence they will be squabbling with school boards over the difference between the 10% increase in salary they expect and the 4% they are offered.

Losers Are Nicer than Winners

Over the years I have studied student views about money. In one experiment students were asked to read a 300-word description of a young man named Smith who leaves junior-high-school teaching to take a position as a civil rights coordinator of ghetto neighborhood organizations. At the end of a year, Smith takes stock of the satisfactions and dissatisfactions of his new job. He finds his work exciting and stimulating but very demanding. He also misses his teaching, sees very little of his family, and is concerned because his wife is talking about divorce. This profile of the ex-teacher presented such details in a sympathetic light and encouraged the students to identify with him. At the bottom of the description were six statements, such as "He is the kind of person I would like to know better," "I approve of his motives in taking the new job," and the like. Each statement was preceded by a five-point rating scale, ranging from "strongly agree" to "strongly disagree," designed to measure the degree to which each student liked and accepted Mr. Smith.

There were two forms of this profile, one headed "Joe Smith" and the other, "J. Smith." The two forms were identical in wording and appearance, except for one detail: Joe Smith received an increase in annual salary from $10,000 to $15,000 when he changed jobs, whereas J. Smith took a cut from $10,000 to $9,000. The two profiles were handed out randomly so that approximately half of the students reported their evaluation of Joe Smith, the gainer, and the other half reported the degree of their attraction to J. Smith, the loser. The students were not told that there were two different versions of the Smith profile.

After students had completed the questionnaires I compared the totals for the two forms. My prediction, based on what students have been telling us for the past ten years or so, was that they would like J. Smith, the $1000 loser, better than Joe Smith, the $5000 gainer. The results confirmed the prediction. In today's academic world, taking a cut in pay makes one more attractive than getting an increase. As far as economics are concerned, losers are more likable than winners.

The values implicit in students' evaluation of "J. Smith" and "Joe Smith" are consistent with those reported by Ronald J. Burke (1966). Burke asked college students to rank certain job characteristics in order of importance to them and to others. An analysis of the responses showed that men tended to rank "good salary" third, behind "opportunity for advancement" and "challenges ability," but they thought that *other* men would rank "good salary" first. Women said they would rank "good salary" second, behind "challenges ability," and believed that *other* women would rank "good salary" first.[1]

---

[1] In attributing these values to others, the students were like the group of three hundred American supervisors and technicians at ARAMCO who were asked to guess how their Saudi Arabian employees would rank eleven job characteristics. The Americans thought that the employees would give first place to wages, whereas the employees actually ranked wages in seventh place, after opportunity to obtain training and education, future security, opportunity for advancement, opportunity to get work experience, the supervisor's behavior toward subordinates, and benefits (Laurent 1962). The allegation that others are primarily interested in money seems to be a universal form of disparaging others and elevating one's own sense of self-worth.

When I conducted a similar opinion survey among my own students, I got results quite similar to Burke's, suggesting that college students had not changed much over the intervening years.

It is probably normal for us to think that *we* are endowed more than others with desirable human qualities, including good judgment and discriminating taste. What students were telling us, therefore, was that their superior judgment led them to put monetary return in second or third place among those job qualities they would desire for themselves. The fact that others were believed to value money more was indirect evidence of its lower value to the students doing the rating.

Money as "Corrupting Influence" and "Obscenity"

Where do college students get their attitudes toward money? They learn attitudes from a variety of sources—parents, peers, and media—but an important influence during the college years is the attitude expressed by professors. Accordingly, I prepared a set of twelve statements, six reflecting positive attitudes about money (such as "Money is an absolute necessity in the functioning of any modern society") and six reflecting negative attitudes (such as "Money corrupts whatever it touches," and "Money is the ultimate obscenity"). These same statements appear in the Reader's Questionnaire in the Preface of this book and are discussed in the Appendix.

The twelve-statement questionnaire was placed in the mailboxes of approximately one hundred university professors. Each professor was asked to indicate the degree of his agreement or disagreement with the views expressed in each statement. The replies were anonymous.

As I noted in the Preface, an analysis of the professors' replies indicated that their typical response was mildly in agreement with the positive statements, and mildly in disagreement with the negative ones. Considering the fact that the average salary of the group placed them in the upper fifth of the nation's wage earners, perhaps we should be surprised that their feelings about money were not more favorable. The same questionnaire, when given to a hundred undergraduates, yielded results substantially the same as those obtained from the professors.

These overall averages, however, conceal a number of interesting results. About half the professors rejected the idea that money has made a positive contribution to human welfare, and a quarter of them felt that money inevitably worsens human relationships. About one professor in seven took a consistently negative view of money, agreeing with statements that money inevitably damages human relationships.

These investigations are only small-scale "spot checks" of people's attitudes toward money, but they do suggest that negative feelings about money are fairly widespread among college students and professors. The results are, furthermore, consistent with our general impression that the attitudes of intellectuals toward money today are often tinged with guilt, hostility, and disdain. Although the number of psychoanalytic writers has been small, their influence on our thinking, over the years, seems to have been considerable.

If We Are Relaxed about Sex, Must We Feel Guilty About Money?

What we are faced with, then, is a marked reversal of values over the past century. Whereas the Victorians, like the Puritans before them, thought of work and money motives as praiseworthy and sexual motives as despicable, the modern trend is just the opposite. The irony of this reversal is compounded by the fact that in today's world, one cannot lead a full life without money. The belief that a great many people hold—that the pursuit of sex is far more important than the pursuit of money—is made possible only by a repression of monetary needs analogous to the Victorian repression of sexual needs. Every now and then a few foolhardy true believers set up a communal experiment to demonstrate that the pursuit of sex is essential but the pursuit of money iṣ not. Some of these experiments last only until the money runs out (apparently one never runs out of sex). Others continue only because monetary needs are met by contributions from relatives and friends and by food stamps and welfare checks.

There is considerable evidence that society's attitudes toward sex have taken a 180-degree turn in recent years. There has been, for example, a steady increase in venereal disease rates during the last decade or so, and the percentage of illegitimate births is high and continues to escalate.[2]

There is no doubt that "getting sex out into the open" has had its effects on mental health clinics as well. The classical neurotic symptoms associated with sexual inhibition are seldom encountered today, and clinicians say that they get few cases of the outright sexual repression and hysteria that made Freud's reputation. There has been, to be sure, a great proliferation of sex clinics, but their clients are primarily interested in improving their performance in this highly absorbing activity and are only marginally concerned with phobias, hysteria, excessive guilt, and other sex-related symptoms.

Most of the problems that psychotherapists treat today are concerned with self-confidence, self-esteem, and social competence—with "making a go of it" in today's world (Campbell, 1975). It seems obvious that such problems more likely involve money than sex. Money does, after all, help to create and maintain status differentials. By the very nature of the system, each of us is lower in the hierarchy than someone else. Brooding about such matters is hardly supportive of self-esteem.

The fact that we are inescapably committed to the money motive does make us vulnerable to manipulation, however. Money can be used as bait or incentive, as a way of arousing great expectations. The money motive may not reduce us to putty in the hands of the manipulator, but it cannot be denied that it gives him a distinct advantage.

In the following chapter, we will examine how money can be used to get people to do things they might otherwise have little interest in doing. And we will speculate on the surprising and persistent research finding that a little money is more persuasive than a lot.

---

[2]The 1978 *Statistical Abstract of the United States*, published by the U.S. Bureau of the Census, reports that the gonorrhea rate in the civilian population went from 145 per hundred thousand population in 1955 to 467 in 1976. Meanwhile, the number of births out of wedlock per thousand live births went from 183 in 1955 to 468 in 1976.

9 Money the manipulator

Against the talking power of money, eloquence is of no
avail.   —ERASMUS OF ROTTERDAM

Alle thinges obeyen to moneye.   —CHAUCER

Debt: An ingenious substitute for the chain and whip of
the slave driver.   —AMBROSE BIERCE

In spite of momentary or even chronic lapses, most of us respond to money in a positive way. We have a history of positive
associations with getting, having, and using money, coupled
with a history of unpleasant associations with its absence. The
pleasant associations include being rewarded for work accomplished, using money to entertain friends and loved ones, and
being able to spend it to acquire desired goods and services.
The unpleasant associations include losing money, being underpaid, being unable to offer it to loved ones who need it,
being embarrassed at the inability to pay a debt, and not having
sufficient money for desired goods and services.

In psychological terms, these experiences have *condi-
tioned* us to respond favorably to the prospect of acquiring or
having money and to respond negatively to the prospect of
losing or lacking it.

In most instances, the behavior we have learned to display
toward and with money operates below the levels of ordinary
awareness. We do not notice its effects on us any more than we
notice what causes us to shift from the gas pedal to the brake
and back again as we drive down a busy freeway. In most
activities we focus our attention on what is of greatest interest
and concern at the moment, and matters that have been thoroughly learned, like attitudes toward money and the use of our
right foot while driving, are ignored.

Money as a "Reinforcer"

Our characteristic inattention to the effects our money motives have on us, and money's usefulness as a reinforcer as well, can easily be demonstrated in the psychological laboratory. In one experiment college students were asked to discuss individually a variety of topics. While they talked, the experimenter gave them a nickel every third time they used an affirmative word, like "yes" or "agree." As a result, the students increased their use of affirmatives.

When the students were asked, after the discussion had continued for some time, if they knew what they were being paid for, they confessed that they were mystified. They were not aware that they were being rewarded for uttering affirmative words nor did they know that they had increased their use of such words (Koffer, Coulson, & Hammond, 1976).

The treatment employed by the psychologists in this experiment is termed "reinforcement" because what the experimenter does to the subject—giving him a nickel, in this instance—"reinforces" the behavior that preceded it. Reinforcement increases the probability that the subject will repeat the behavior. As we noted in our brief discussion of money as a reinforcer early in Chapter 8, we are programmed by a lifetime of favorable outcomes to respond positively to money. Hence the introduction of even a negligible amount of it is pleasant, and we seek to have the experience repeated.

The subjects in this experiment recognized that the experimenters, by paying them nickels, were expressing approval of something they had done. This is another indication that we have learned to associate money with social approval.

Still another point is worth mentioning. It was not necessary to pay the subjects *every* time they uttered one of the key words. They received the reinforcing nickel on every *third* affirmative word they uttered. This form of treatment is a type of what psychologists call *intermittent reinforcement*, a method that has been found to produce more satisfactory results than *continuous reinforcement*. The investigators might have been able to obtain even better results if they had not employed a fixed-interval (one-in-three) schedule, but had instead used a variable-interval schedule, in which reinforcement is done at random intervals, but still according to a predetermined ratio. The power of intermittent reinforcement, applied according to variable-interval schedules, has been long known to gambling-casino operators. The expectation of money gets even more action than money itself.

The Time the Park Visitors Really Cleaned Up

The power of partial reinforcement was demonstrated by a field experiment in which a team of psychologists helped the US Forest Service deal with a trash problem. The Forest Service was concerned with the increasing amounts of litter left by visitors in unsupervised forest areas. Authorities had tried to deal with the problem in the usual way—by posting notices asking campers and picnickers to deposit trash at designated garbage-collection areas. These notices, which bore the usual appeals to the conscience, personal pride, and altruism of the visitors, had little effect.

The psychologists suggested a different approach. In one forest area, notices were posted offering to pay park users 25 cents per bag for litter brought to area headquarters; in another area, the notices said that a ticket in a $20 lottery would be given for every litter-filled bag. The notices said nothing about the origin of the litter, and it was clear that a visitor could bag anyone else's litter and get paid off in quarters or in chances on a twenty-dollar drawing.

Only four out of every thousand visitors took advantage of the offers, but these few responded so enthusiastically that there was a noticeable reduction in litter in the recreational areas.

An analysis of the results showed that the lottery method was the cheaper of the two: It produced more work at a lower unit cost. Intermittent and uncertain reinforcement that aroused expectations was hence more effective than continuous reinforcement. The winners of the lotteries got the money; the losers' efforts were spurred on by hope (Powers, Osborne, & Anderson, 1973; Osborne, Powers, & Anderson, 1974).

Monetary Expectations and Sex

The monetary reward that reinforces behavior does not have to follow the behavior immediately. People have been known to work and wait patiently for years, sustained only by the hope of eventually receiving a sizable sum of money. The expectation of great wealth can also suppress sexual behavior. A survey of premarital practices throughout the world indicates that sexual intercourse between bethrothed persons is less likely to occur in societies where the families of the bride or the groom traditionally transfer large amounts of wealth to the newly wedded couple. In societies in which marriage gifts are relatively low in value, there seems to be little premium attached to self-restraint, and sexual permissiveness is more common (Rosenblatt, Fugita, & McDowell, 1969).

Whereas monetary incentives discourage sex among the unmarried in traditional societies, they have the opposite effect in the United States, where monthly payments are made to unmarried mothers under a social-welfare program entitled Aid Families with Dependent Children (AFDC). In 1935 Congress passed the Social Security Act, which provided that needy widowed mothers be paid monthly stipends based on the number of children under 18 who were in their care. The law has been liberalized and reinterpreted over the years so that payments may now be made to any needy parent with dependent children. Those who formulated the program probably did not anticipate that the meager allowance AFDC provides (an average erage of $238 per month in 1977[1]) would prove attractive to teenage girls, especially those from working-class homes.

The liberalization of the AFDC program in the early 1960s seems to have touched off a dramatic increase in the number of children born to unmarried teenage girls. In 1955, only 73,000 unmarried teenagers became mothers; in 1976, the number was 235,000—three times as many. In 1955, teenagers produced 39.5% of all children born out of wedlock; in 1976, they had 50.3%, an increase of 27%. The national birthrate had, in

---

[1]In June 1979 social welfare authorities in San Francisco were paying a single mother with two dependent children a subsidy of $356 per month.

the meantime, declined from 24.6 per thousand population to 14.8 (U.S. Bureau of the Census, 1978).

Most unmarried teenage mothers do not put their children up for adoption; indeed, it appears that they often become pregnant in order to be eligible for AFDC. These young mothers thus make a substantial contribution to the growing number of families receiving AFDC. Between 1955 and 1976 the number of families on the AFDC rolls increased from 602,000 to 3,571,000 (U.S. Bureau of the Census, 1978).

Money has not been the only reason for the burgeoning number of unmarried mothers, of course. The sexual permissiveness of the times is probably one factor. Another may be the youth revolt that began in the early 1960s; most adolescents have difficulties with their parents, and the growing tendency for teenagers to leave their families and set up housekeeping in their own apartments undoubtedly contributes to the trend.

It is difficult to put a figure on the degree to which these two factors—society's increased tolerance of sex in the young and youthful eagerness to escape from parental control—affected the surge in unmarried motherhood, but there is little doubt that money obtained from AFDC was the catalytic element that made it possible.

AFDC has not been equally attractive to all young women. Its meager allowance looks proportionately larger to those from poor families. Analyses of census data show that about 25% of working-class mothers are unmarried—about double the percentage of unwed middle-class mothers. A good many middle-class women are probably receiving AFDC, but most of them have other financial support available; therefore AFDC is less likely to be a strong incentive for them.

There is no question that AFDC is absolutely essential to the survival of millions of impoverished mothers and children, but we should not blind ourselves to the fact that through it we have created an arrangement that encourages sexual activity and pregnancy among teenagers and also rewards them, through allowance increases, for additional pregnancies.

Money and Mood

As we have shown in the foregoing section, money may influence the motivational aspects of people's lives through inhibiting or facilitating their expression of the sex drive. A number of research studies show that it takes very little money to produce an effect on other motivational patterns.

Two Pennsylvania psychologists, Alice Isen of Franklin and Marshall and Paula Levin of Swarthmore (1972), conducted a study using a technique similar to the experimental method discussed in Chapter 4, in which subjects did or did not admit they had found a dime left in a pay telephone (Bickman, 1971). Isen and Levin were not concerned about people's honesty. They were interested in the effect that finding a dime would have on subsequent behavior. In half the trials in the experiment they placed a dime in the coin-return slot of a public telephone; the balance of the trials were conducted with no dime in the slot. As each telephone user emerged from the booth, a woman confederate of the experimenters "accidentally" dropped a manila folder full of papers near the subject. Almost all (88%) of the individuals who had found the planted dime helped the experimenter pick up her papers, but virtually none (4%) of those who had not found a dime offered any help.

These results suggest that finding the dime was a pleasant surprise that put the recipient in a mood to help the woman who had dropped her papers. Perhaps the receiver of unexpected good fortune feels for a brief moment that he owes something to the generous Providence that has blessed him and hence "evens the balance" by helping someone in need.

Although the subjects were not interrogated about their motivation, it seems quite likely that they made no conscious connection between the dime they found and their willingness to help. As we noted apropos the experiment with the reinforcing nickels, small amounts of money may have a significant effect on people's actions without their being aware of it.

These are only two of a number of experiments that demonstrate the leverage of small gifts of money on our behavior. Here is another. One study of the returns of questionnaires sent out in mail surveys shows that the response rate can be substantially increased by including a gift of twenty-five cents. If survey operators find that such an outlay exceeds their budget, economies can easily be achieved by including the quarter only in the reminder letter sent to those who ignored the first appeal: experience has demonstrated that the strategy saves about half the cost without any reduction in the rate of response (Huck & Gleason, 1974). And still another pair of researchers found that including as little as a dime with the questionnaire may work almost as well, even with presumably well-paid business executives (Pressley & Tullar, 1977).

Why does payment of a paltry dime or quarter get busy people to drop whatever they are going to fill out a question-naire? There are several possible explanations. One is the "pleasant-mood" theory—the theory that we respond so posi-tively to money that the receipt of even minute amounts puts us in a warm and cooperative mood.

Surprise or shock is a second explanation. We do not ordinarily encounter unsolicited gifts of money when we open our mail. The unusual nature of the experience leads us to focus more than our normal amount of attention on the request that accompanied the payment. Our curiosity and interest are aroused, and we find ourselves reading and filling out the ques-tionnaire instead of discarding it as we would otherwise have done.

These explanations are not mutually exclusive: both may apply, along with the more complicated one we will now discuss, an explanation to which psychologists have given a label that is pure jargon: *cognitive dissonance.*

Cognitive Dissonance Manipulations: Getting More for Less

Cognitive dissonance theory is an attempt to make sense out of certain actions that seem illogical. In the type of situation cov-ered by this theory, individuals become aware of an incompat-ibility or "dissonance" between several of their own actions or commitments. This dissonance is bothersome, and the individ-ual characteristically takes steps, mental or otherwise, to elim-inate or reduce it. Often his behavior appears illogical to the observer, even though it may seem sensible and appropriate to the person concerned.

The classic study of cognitive dissonance was conducted by Leon Festinger and J. Merrill Carlsmith (1959) of Stanford

University. The experiment they devised differs in a number of respects from those we have presented so far. In the first place, money was not given to the subjects without explanation or as an unrestricted gift, but was, in effect, a bribe to tell a lie. In the second place, the investigators did not attempt to reinforce the subject's behavior or try to put him in a good mood. Their intention, instead, was to play a manipulative, Machiavellian game involving the subject's "motivational structure." In the third place, the experimenters were interested not in what the subject actually did but in what he thought of them and of the task they had had him perform.

Each student who had volunteered to participate in the experiment first spent an entire hour turning pegs on a piece of laboratory apparatus known as a "pegboard"—a task as dreary and tedious as any the experimenters could devise. The student was then told that another volunteer was waiting in the next room and that the experimenters were concerned whether this next subject would take the task seriously. Would the student help out by telling the other volunteer that the task was quite interesting and worthwhile? If he would, investigators would pay him for his help. Half the students were offered $1 for telling this bare-faced lie, and the other half were offered $20. Most of them accepted the assignment.

The "volunteer" in the waiting room who listened to the lie told by the student was in fact an accomplice of the investigators. When he expressed doubts on being told that the task was interesting, most of the students compounded their felonies by insisting that the experience was indeed worthwhile and was interesting "once you got into it."

The students then went to the departmental office to receive their pay. The clerk who paid them asked them to fill out a brief questionnaire which had the ostensible purpose of determining the availability of subjects for future psychological experiments. The real purpose of the questionnaire, however, was to yield data on the subjects' attitudes toward the peg-turning task. It obviously had been tedious and boring, but would the bribes make a difference in the way the students said they felt about it?

Common sense might predict that the students who received $20 bribes would rate the peg-turning experience more favorably than those who had been paid only $1. The results showed exactly the opposite, however. It was the students who had been *underbribed* who were inclined to say, in response to specific questions, that they found the task enjoyable, that the experiment was probably of scientific value, and that they would be willing to participate in future and presumably similar experiments. Students who had received the $20 bribe were much less positive. They were less likely to say that the task was enjoyable; they had more reservations about the experiment's scientific value; and they were less interested in participating in future experiments.

Festinger and Carlsmith explained these apparently illogical results along these lines: The student who had been paid $20 probably thought "It really was a dull task, and I can see why they would have problems in getting volunteers to go through with it. Well, it wasn't much of a lie, and I guess $20 is a reasonable payment under the circumstances." In other words, the overbribed student knew that the task really was dull; he had no problem explaining his lie to himself—he had been paid $20 to lie.

The "underbribed" student, however, did not have this defense. He may have reasoned along these lines: "Why did I tell this man that the task was interesting? It can't be because of what I was paid—a dollar is practically nothing. It must have been that the job *was* interesting. Yes, it must have been that."

The underbribed student finds it easier to explain his behavior to himself if he can alter his feelings and believe that the task was interesting. It is apparently important that we find our own behavior to be sensible and consistent, not "dissonant." We thus shift our thoughts and beliefs so that they are consonant with our behavior. Peace of mind is worth more than dollars, especially when we haven't received very many.

Cognitive dissonance may be of help in explaining why people are interested in filling out questionnaires accompanied by a dime or a quarter. Perhaps they reason along these lines: "A dime means nothing at all to me. It won't even buy a cup of coffee. In a way, it is an insult and I ought to return it. But it's more trouble to return it than to keep it. So I'll keep it. But l keep it, I have accepted it. Why have I accepted it? Perhaps because I think the questionnaire is worthwhile. I'll look at it. . . ."

In his attempts to resolve cognitive dissonance, the person receiving the questionnaire is moved to open the door to co-operation and participation. Through trying to rationalize his behavior to himself, he becomes involved in the task in spite of his initial resistance.

The "Foot-in-the-Door" Ploy

Applications of the cognitive dissonance theory are not fail-proof, but they do seem to produce interesting results in certain types of situations, especially when individuals become partially involved in a proposed undertaking and permit themselves to be maneuvered into making major commitments.

The foot-in-the-door technique used by door-to-door sales people represents a common application of the theory. The salesperson presents the householder with a small gift and then asks to enter the home to discuss the line of merchandise being offered. Accepting the gift gives the householder a sense of obligation, and he or she finds it difficult to refuse the request to enter the home. To accept the gift but refuse the request would generate cognitive dissonance, which the householder rationalizes by thinking "I wouldn't have accepted the gift if I hadn't been willing to cooperate."

Once the salesperson has entered the home, it becomes easy to make a sale because a refusal to purchase would create new cognitive dissonance for the householder, who now thinks "I wouldn't have a salesperson come into my home if I hadn't been prepared to buy something." Letting someone into our home is a gesture of hospitality; it calls for the expression of agreeable and cooperative behavior that we usually display to guests.

The foot-in-the-door technique has been the subject of psychological research. In one experiment, a young woman asked persons who answered their door bells if they would wear a plastic daffodil lapel pin the next day to publicize a fund drive for the Cancer Society. All agreed to comply with this request. The following evening a second woman solicited contributions for the Cancer Society both at the homes that had been canvassed the night before and at others that had not. (She did not know which houses had been canvassed.) In the homes where persons had earlier agreed to comply with the small request, 77% of the individuals approached by the second canvasser made a donation. In the control homes that had not been visited earlier, however, only 46% gave money. In money terms, the homes that had been visited previously made an average donation of $.92, whereas the control homes yielded an average of $.58 (Pliner et al., 1974).

The Cancer Society experiment was based on an earlier foot-in-the-door study, in which a telephone canvasser asked householders a few questions about the soaps they used in their homes. A few days later he made a more substantial request. He said that the survey was being expanded and that his employers wanted to send five or six men into the householder's home for two hours to classify and list all the household products being used. In order to complete this survey properly, the men would have to be granted complete freedom to go through cupboards and other storage places.

The fact that they had cooperated in the earlier and very limited telephone survey undoubtedly created cognitive dissonance for a high proportion of the householders, for over half of them agreed to grant this new and rather outrageous request. By way of contrast, only one in five of a comparison group of householders, who had *not* been asked the earlier questions, agreed to permit the two-hour inventory of household products (Freedman & Fraser, 1966).

We are more likely to behave in what seem to be irrational or ridiculous ways when we have publicly committed ourselves to a policy, a concept, or a choice. In one of the earlier cognitive dissonance experiments, children individually evaluated a number of toys. Two toys were then selected that the child had rated as absolutely equal in interest and value. When the experimenter had verified that the two toys were indeed equally attractive, the child was asked to select one for his very own, after which he was asked which of the two toys was the more attractive or interesting. In every case, the child said the toy he had chosen was the more attractive one, even though a few moments earlier he had said there was no difference.

The question evidently created cognitive dissonance for the children, which they apparently resolved by reasoning along these lines:

"Although the train and the truck seemed equally attractive before I made my choice, the train really must be more attractive—otherwise I wouldn't have chosen it."

Similarly, people who have recently purchased automobiles are more likely to read magazine advertisements for the make of car they have recently purchased than for other makes. It would of course be logical that *before* buying a car they would read advertisements for the kind that attracted them, but why should they continue to read them *after* the purchase?

The answer supplied by psychologists is that the car buyers were apparently trying to reduce the unresolved cognitive dissonance that still lingered after their decision. They were trying to reassure themselves that they had really done the right thing. Using this line of reasoning, the child who said that he had really preferred the train all along sought by means of this public statement to reassure himself that he had made the right choice.

The Purchase of Personal Commitment

The money deposit and its effect have been studied by a number of psychologists. In one experiment, women enrolling in an obesity study received a manual of instructions and were required to attend training sessions designed to encourage weight reduction. Some of the women were charged an initial deposit. The investigators initially were worried that the requirement of a deposit might backfire, for it could reduce participants' guilt feelings about breaking promises to attend. The concerns were groundless. The women who had paid a deposit had a better attendance record than those who received the treatment gratis; they also rated the instructional materials more highly (Hagen, Foreyt, & Durham, 1976). Similar findings were reported in another study of obesity therapy. Patients who paid the therapist's usual fee lost more weight than those who paid nothing (Stanton, 1976).

The principle in both these studies is the same: the individual who makes a personal commitment by paying out a sum of money is more likely than a freeloader to go through with a program of self-improvement. The money has considerable symbolic value. We noted in the chapter on money and self-worth that our money represents a portion of our perceived self. Individuals who pay the deposit or the therapy fee are placing a small part of themselves "on the line" and are publicly committing themselves to go through with the proposed program.

Public commitment is important, because our opinion of ourselves is in large measure determined by what others think of us. Reneging on a public commitment is more damaging to our self-concept than going back on a promise we had made only to ourselves. There is also an element of cognitive dissonance in the way we feel about a public commitment. We say to ourselves: "I must have been serious in my intention to go through with this or I would not have paid the money."

Like many other contractual arrangements in the social world, commitment has a price tag.

Manipulating Beliefs about Price and Value

The relationship between price and value is learned a thousand times over from childhood onward. Eventually we come to use price as an index to the quality of the items and services we purchase. In a world where decisions are often hurried and based on scanty data—sometimes out of necessity but more often out of habit—we ordinarily assume that more expensive items must possess higher quality than those that cost less. This mistaken assumption has been the subject of a number of studies in the field of marketing psychology. In one experiment, male university students were asked to grade what they were told were six different beers—two brands from each of three price levels: low, medium, and high. There were actually only two brands of beer involved—a low-priced brew, which a panel of experts had previously pronounced as of poor quality ("similar to apple cider"), and a brand that the experts had rated high in quality. The samples were served in plastic glasses, with no identification save price.

The students' judgments indicated that they were unable to distinguish between the two kinds of beer, for the differences in quality that they reported were entirely consistent with what they had been told about the retail prices of the beers (Valenzi & Eldridge, 1973).

A similar experiment was conducted in a supermarket, where shoppers were asked to rate three kinds of spreads which, unbeknownst to them, were butter, high-quality margarine, and low-quality margarine. As in the beer-tasting experiment, they were given false information about the prices of the spreads. The results showed that the shoppers were influenced partially by the actual quality of the spreads but that the supposed prices were the major factors that influenced their judgments (Cimbalo & Webdale, 1973).

These two experiments show that in judging the quality of goods, we often depend more on their price than on the evidence of our senses. When items are cheaper than we expect, we are therefore inclined to be suspicious of their quality. We have learned, rightly or wrongly, that "cheaper means poorer." Indeed, the word "cheap" carries connotations of substandard quality. Of course, merchants are aware of this; hence, when they cut their prices they attempt to reassure us of the quality of the merchandise being offered by noting that the discounted items are "nationally advertised brands" or by offering a plausible reason for the price reduction—"We overbought, and our loss is your gain; we lost our lease; this is a special, one-time anniversary sale."

The Cut-Price Fallacy

A merchant sometimes reasons that customers' eagerness to get quality merchandise at low prices outweighs their tendency to devalue low-priced items. It is therefore common practice to introduce new product lines at low prices in order to make them competitive with well-established brands. The idea is that customer resistance to the unfamiliar brand will be diminished by its attractive price. Once customers try the new brand and find it to be as satisfactory as the better-known makes, they will presumably continue to purchase it, even after its price is raised, once the introductory sale period is over.

The line of reasoning sounds logical, but it may be based on faulty psychology. In one investigation, psychologists studied the sales records of new brands of merchandise introduced by discount houses. In half the stores, the items were offered initially at a low price, which was raised to the expected level after the introductory period was over.

An analysis of the sales records of the products over a number of months indicated that the introductory discount was more detrimental than advantageous. The cut-rate items sold well, but sales dropped when prices were raised to more conventional levels. Sales of items that had been introduced at normal prices were poor at first, but they showed consistent growth; in the end, sales were higher than those of the initially discounted items (Doob, 1969). Customers must not have valued the discounted items very highly, even though their quality was equal to that of the higher priced merchandise.

Such experiments remind us that we react to the reality we perceive. In instances where we can compare prices, we often perceive a reality suggested by cost, not quality.

The Bargain-Seeking Complex

Merchants who make price reductions often attract confirmed "bargain hunters," rather than a representative sampling of the buying public. Everyday experience suggests that some people are more interested in price differentials than others. The possibility that such people may constitute a distinct "personality type" was explored by Charles Daviet and George Rotter (1973) of Montclair State College in New Jersey.

Daviet and Rotter devised a "Bargain-Seeking Attitude Inventory," which they administered to over five hundred college students. The students also completed both a questionnaire designed to provide information on actual buying habits and a general personality test. An analysis of the replies showed that the confirmed "bargain-hunter" does indeed exist. Bargain hunters appear to be people who like to plan, have a high need for order, and mistrust whim and impulse. They are not "sloppy consumers." When bargain seekers shop, they know they will not buy on the spur of the moment. They will weigh and compare; they will plan their shopping in order to get the very best deal.

The impulsive, non-bargain-seeker, according to Daviet and Rotter, uses the opposite approach. If he chances on a product that appeals to him, he buys it. He seldom, if ever, thinks of making a price comparison, unless the salesperson happens to mention it; even then he is more likely to be impressed by the personality of the salesperson than by what he or she is actually saying.

Bargain-hunting, if carried too far, may become an obsession. Edmund Bergler (1973) said that "all of the bargain hunters whom I have observed clinically have been orally regressed neurotics," a bit of psychoanalytic jargon describing an essentially infantile state of relating to the world.

Bargain-hunting, neurotic or otherwise, has this in common with the other forms of behavior we have described in this chapter: it is an example of the amount of leverage, in behavioral terms, that can be exerted by a small monetary reward. Perhaps the psychology of small rewards can be summed up in the popular buzz-phrase: "Less is more."

10 Money, work, and achievement

Work keeps at bay three evils: boredom, vice, and need.
—Voltaire

Half the working class is slaving away to pile up riches of which they will be plundered by the upper class. The other half is plundering the plunderers. —G. B. Shaw

Whoever wants to walk peacefully in this world must be money's guest. —Norman O. Brown (1959)

During the early years of this century, the watchword of the industrialist was "efficiency." "Efficiency experts" were hired to eliminate wasteful practices and thus to enable employers to obtain a higher return from their investment in plant and personnel. One of the first of the army of efficiency experts that descended on industry during this period was Frederick Winslow Taylor, whose *Principles of Scientific Management*, published in 1911, forthrightly proclaimed that much of the inefficiency in industry resulted from the practice of letting workers decide how a job was to be done.

Taylor's classic case was a Pennsylvania German named Schmidt, who was one of seventy-five laborers employed to load pig iron onto railway cars. The men loaded an average of 12.5 tons a day. Taylor believed that their output could be much increased with no greater output of energy, if only the work were properly planned. Taylor told Schmidt that he could earn more money if he did precisely what Taylor told him. When Schmidt agreed, Taylor accompanied him to the job and gave him specific orders—how to lift and walk, when to put the iron down, how long to pause, and so forth. By the end of the day,

Schmidt had loaded 47.5 tons of pig iron and continued loading this amount daily during the three years of Taylor's observation.

Two things made such phenomenal results possible: One was Taylor's skill at planning work routines to eliminate unnecessary motion. The other was Schmidt's eagerness to earn more money.

Planning + Monetary Incentive = Efficiency

In Taylor's view, all the employer had to do to get more production for less money was to have a scientific study done of work situations and set up a schedule of monetary incentives to be paid workers who followed the improved work routines. Taylor had no doubt that workers would be eager to cooperate, because they had only one motive: to earn money.

Taylor's principles of scientific management led to time-and-motion studies, to automation, and, simultaneously, to angry attacks from workers whose jobs were eliminated as unnecessary. No one criticized Taylor's assumptions about workers' motives, for they were in complete accord with common sense. It is interesting to note, however, that Taylor's principles and methods were used almost exclusively with production-line employees, not with supervisors and managers. The explanation usually given is that time-and-motion studies are appropriate when workers perform a restricted number of activities but are inappropriate when workers must carry out a complex variety of tasks such as are found at supervisory and managerial levels. It is possible, however, that the managers who were happy to have the tasks of their subordinates scrutinized and analyzed drew the line when it came to their own work. They may also have felt that Taylor's views of monetary incentives would not be as appropriate to managerial levels as they were to production levels.

Intrinsic versus Extrinsic Motivation

Taylor's ideas about efficiency and motivation in working conditions went unchallenged until the late 1920s, when a team of psychologists and efficiency engineers led by F. J. Roethlisberger and William J. Dickson (1939) conducted a series of studies at the Western Electric Plant located at Hawthorne, near Chicago. The researchers conducted interviews with over 20,000 employees, who were guaranteed anonymity so as to encourage frank expression of opinions regarding work, working conditions, and supervision. An analysis of the content of the interviews, which covered a wide range of subjects, showed that concern about pay appeared in only about one seventh of the eighty thousand comments recorded. By way of contrast, about one fourth of the comments dealt with aspects of the physical working conditions, such as the machines, ventilation, and washroom facilities, and another fourth were concerned with psychosocial aspects of the working environment, such as club activities, opportunities for advancement, and vacations.

The Hawthorne scientists also conducted a series of experiments, through which they studied the effects of various wage incentives and changes in different aspects of the work situation. The workers under observation maintained a steady increase in production during the two-year span of the experiments, but only a portion of the improvement could be attributed to their monetary reward. Nor did the changes in other aspects of the work situation contribute much toward their increased efficiency. The factor that played the most significant role was the increased interest the employees showed in their work. This involvement appeared to result from their awareness that they were playing key roles in an important experiment. Although the attention the scientific observers directed at them and their work can be considered a part of their social environment, the motive to improve performance came from *within* the workers. Their motivation to perform more effectively was thus the result of *intrinsic* factors and had little to do with *extrinsic* factors like changes in wage incentives and working conditions.

Frederick W. Taylor's theory that money and money alone motivates the worker was an affirmation of faith in the power of extrinsic motivation. The Hawthorne studies indicated that intrinsic motivation played a very important part in determining the amount of time and energy workers are willing to invest in their work. Although the Hawthorne experiments did not demonstrate that money rewards and other aspects of the work environment are irrelevant and unimportant, they did show that these extrinsic factors are only a part of the working scene to which the worker responds. Intrinsic factors—enthusiasm, belief in the importance of one's work, and morale—may be more important than the extrinsic factors on which employers have traditionally relied.

Until the Hawthorne studies were conducted, managerial tasks were relatively simple: Managers gave workers their orders, paid them the going wage, and provided a reasonable work environment. After Hawthorne, managers' tasks became incredibly complex, for they now knew they should take into account workers' morale, interest in their work, attitudes toward management, and feelings toward others in the work force—in short, a whole range of psychological factors that were difficult to measure, understand, and deal with.

Supervisors and middle managers, especially those with engineering background, expressed impatience and frustration when top management required them to take such intangibles into account. Most of them had neither training nor experience in such matters. The need for a different kind of expertise led to the creation of a new type of professional—the personnel psychologist, who trained managers and supervisors and helped find ways to identify intrinsic motivators that could be used to direct workers' activities into productive channels.

Money Rewards, "Common Sense," and Intrinsic Motivators

The Hawthorne studies did not bring in the millenium, however. The idea that money is the major motivator in work remains firmly embedded in what we call common sense. Today, fifty years after the Hawthorne studies, many managers still find it difficult to believe that intrinsic motivation plays much part in work. Opsahl and Dunnette (1966), industrial psychologists who have surveyed a large number of studies conducted in business and industry, report that when workers are asked to rank the importance to them of various aspects of their jobs, they seldom put pay at the top of the list; they usually place it somewhere in the middle. When employers, however, are asked to rank the same factors the way they believe workers do, they are almost unanimous in saying that workers would rank pay as number one.

This interesting difference is reminiscent of the research we reported in Chapter 8. When college students were asked how other students would rank the importance of job characteristics, they were inclined to say that "salary or income" would receive top priority. When they ranked the same characteristics for themselves, however, money was in second or third place, depending on the sex of the student.

It seems likely that if the managers had indicated what was important in *their* work, money probably would have ranked a poor fourth, as it did for the workers. Carrying the speculation even further, it also seems likely that if the employees had been asked how they thought the managers would rank the rewards received from *their* work, they would have said that the managers would place salary at the head of the list. As we noted in Chapter 8, it is always *others* who are motivated primarily by money; *our* motives are naturally of a higher order.

Victor H. Vroom (1964), a Yale professor who has specialized in motives involved in work, observes that the importance of money rewards to workers is a continuing source of controversy. Economists and business executives maintain that the size of the pay check determines both the satisfaction an employee receives from his work and the likelihood that he will stay on the job. Psychologists, however, argue that personal and social needs are the more significant motivators and that economic factors tend to be overemphasized by employers. Vroom points out that there is evidence for both sides in this controversy. When workers are asked to rank various aspects of their work experience, wages tend to be ranked mid-scale. But when employees are asked to indicate what causes them to be *dissatisfied* with their work, wages head the list time after time. Furthermore, when studies are made of the interrelationship of various aspects of the work experience, a higher degree of job satisfaction is generally reported by those receiving high wages, while a lower degree of satisfaction is characteristic of those who are paid low wages.

The fact that wages and satisfaction are correlated does not mean that wages necessarily influence the degree of satisfaction attained, any more than it means that satisfaction influences wages, but the suspicion remains that the two are involved in some way. The factor that links pay and work satisfaction is a persistent phenomenon in any research involving human motivation, namely, that a high degree of success seems always to be associated with many positive or favorable personal qualities and that a low degree of success is associated with unfavorable ones. People who rate above average in health and happiness also tend to rate high in other advantages, including income, while people who rate below average in health and happiness also tend to have below-average income and to lack other advantages. We will discuss this interesting phenomenon further in the chapter on Money and Mental Health.

The Question of a "Fair Wage"

Other research studies reviewed by Vroom indicate that the absolute amount of wage is not of most importance to the workers but rather the fairness of the wage with respect to what others receive. Workers estimate "fairness" in several ways. A psychiatrist on the staff of a mental hospital who is paid, say, $50,000 per year, may regard himself as underpaid if his psychiatrist friends with similar qualifications are making $75,000 in private practice. Consider the case of the migrant farm laborer, however, who has been hired by a farmer who is in a hurry to harvest and market his crop and who is therefore paying $50 per day instead of the $40 that is the going rate for field hands. In this instance, the worker considers his pay to be "more than fair."In other words, the "going rate for comparable employment" is one measure of "fairness."

The relationship between salary and status level is another measure. A foreman is likely to be satisfied with his wages if he makes less than his supervisor but more than the rank-and-file worker. If his salary is close to the top wage of the people he supervises, he will feel underpaid and will complain: "I don't know why I put up with all the headaches on this job. For a dollar an hour less I would just as soon be back on the assembly line without a care in the world. There I'd have a chance to make it all back in overtime."

The foreman's higher status and prestige are irrelevant for him, if his pay is not significantly higher than that of his subordinates. In the society we have constructed, money rewards are *supposed* to keep pace with differences in status and prestige. A disparity is viewed as a clear indication that *something is wrong.*

In the chapter on Money, Status, and Power, we noted that we view our pay as a form of social approval. If we are paid appropriately (according to our expectations) we take this as evidence that we have performed correctly and are living in a just world. But if we are paid less than we think appropriate we take this fact as evidence either that we are not performing correctly—are *failures*—or that the world is not as just as we had believed.

Which of these two conclusions we come to is partly a matter of personality. A person who has a low opinion of himself or who is characteristically depressed or apathetic takes the underpayment as a matter of course, as confirmation of his self-concept. People with normal self-esteem or ego-strength who are underpaid generally look for ways to correct the situation: perhaps the authorities are unaware of the disparity; perhaps they are uninterested; perhaps the matter must be brought to their attention by sending representatives to inform and persuade them; perhaps if that fails the workers must strike. But there is always the lingering thought that the system *may* be just and that the disparity in pay means that the workers are inferior after all. Such thoughts are disturbing. When they occur, they are denied and suppressed.

Money "Needs" as Smokescreens

Workers who feel that their pay levels are too low go on strike. Those concerned with such actions may believe that the strikers' motives are entirely economic. Strikers often claim that they cannot support themselves and their families on the wages they receive and hence need more money. Unfortunately for this argument, the need for more money is universal. Rare in today's world is the man, woman, child, family, state, or nation that does not need more money. Thus, even when strikes have been called to protect working conditions or for some other nonwage issue, the "package" that settles them often includes an increase in wages. This practice makes it appear that money is an important issue in strikes. But is it?

From the psychologist's view, the "need for money" is often a psychological smokescreen that conceals other motives— motives whose exposure would make the striker appear ridiculous to others and to himself as well.

Let us say, for example, that the workers' relations with their employer before the strike led them to believe, rightly or wrongly, that he viewed them as inadequate, incompetent, and irresponsible. They felt he was uninterested in hearing what they had to say about working conditions; he failed to consult them when he made decisions that affected them. Their resentment grew until an incident, probably of minor economic importance but of great symbolic value, brought the matter to a head. They went out on strike.

The "official" demand is given as "higher wages," but the underlying reason is the desire for respect from their employer. Workers cannot say "We are going on strike because we are not appreciated." There is no place for such an explanation in the ritual language of labor negotiations. It is also quite likely that the workers, like the rest of us, are unwilling and probably unable to confront motives that are potentially embarrassing. Money is therefore brought into the picture as symbolic payment for hurt feelings.

The fact that money and not the need for respect is made the main issue may keep both employer and workers from facing and dealing with the main problem, however. The negotiations that follow will be concerned with determining whether the workers' demands for more money are unreasonable and inflationary or whether the employer's refusal to raise pay rates is unreasonable and exploitive. The issue of whether the employer has behaved in an inconsiderate way or of whether the workers have been unrealistic in their expectations of how employers should or should not behave, is seldom if ever examined.

When the strike is settled, money issues will have been resolved, but the matter of bruised feelings and injured pride may continue to fester. Agreement in terms of money may be a merely cosmetic resolution.

Satisfactions and Dissatisfactions in Work

As this example illustrates, people live at several levels—private levels, which involve significant and compelling motives difficult to identify and even harder to talk about; and public levels, which involve stereotyped issues and symbols that form the media of everyday social interactions.

Frederick Herzberg (1966) of the University of Utah, one of the leading figures in the field of industrial psychology, has for many years maintained that the chief satisfactions people get from working involve the private motivational factors, while other elements in the working environment, which figure so prominently in labor negotiations, have little real bearing on satisfactions. The motivational factors underlying job-satisfaction are all intrinsic, for they include the opportunity to achieve, recognition for work accomplished, interest and involvement in the work itself, responsibility, and opportunities for personal growth and advancement. Although these are aspects of behavior that we all have difficulty pinpointing, psychologists can identify and measure them by means of well-designed interview and questionnaire methods.

Herzberg says that the causes of job *dis*satisfaction are not simply the direct opposites of the causes of job satisfaction. Whereas the causes of satisfactions are internal and self-generating, dissatisfactions are focused on the external work environment—what Herzberg calls the *hygiene* of the job. Hygiene includes such extrinsic factors as pay, employer policies, the amount and kind of supervision, relations with fellow employees on and off the job, and job security.

Our feelings about intrinsic motivational and extrinsic hygiene factors can be evaluated separately. For example, Peace Corps workers in the jungle villages of Central Africa might report that their work is exciting, demanding, creative, fulfilling, and deeply involving—all motivational factors. At the same time, they might complain about the low pay, the lack of support they receive from Washington, their frustrations in trying to communicate in a strange language, their difficulties in adapting to a strange culture, health problems, and homesickness—all environmental or hygiene problems.

Conversely, even when the environmental elements of a job are fantastically favorable the employee may find he has no heart for his work. Shortly before this chapter was written, a news story reported that James Abourezk, Senator from South Dakota, complained loudly and bitterly to a group of educators that the frustrations of his job were more than he could tolerate and that he was therefore not going to run for reelection. Few jobs offer more in the way of pay, status, and fringe benefits than does a seat in the United States Senate, but the abiding and intrinsic motivational satisfactions that come from a job well done were obviously lacking for Senator Abourezk.

Research demonstrates that Herzberg's theory of the primacy of intrinsic rewards is most applicable to white-collar workers—especially to those who work at managerial and professional levels (Gurin, Veroff, & Feld 1960; Ronan, 1970). Blue-collar workers, particularly those in metropolitan areas, seem more concerned with the hygiene or extrinsic aspects of their jobs than the theory predicts. Psychological studies of blue-collar workers' attitudes toward promotion to supervisory positions are most revealing. Blue-collar workers in small towns and rural areas, like white-collar workers, are more inclined to identify with managerial values and hence to find the responsibility and opportunities for self-development that come with promotion exciting and challenging. But most blue-collar workers in metropolitan areas seem to derive little satisfaction from being promoted to supervisory positions and often report that their responsibilities create more anxieties and other psychological disturbances than they are willing to tolerate (Hulin & Blood, 1968).

The assembly-line worker in an urban factory who is offered a promotion to the rank of foreman may be attracted by the higher pay, but once on the new job he finds that his power to supervise, to control, and especially to discipline his former workmates arouses resentment, envy, and even outright hostility. He has also violated an unwritten rule of the working-class poor,[1] which penalizes individual attempts to do anything out of the ordinary, especially when it permits escape to higher

---

[1]See the discussion in Chapter 6.

social levels. Some former assembly workers are able to tolerate the psychological pressures of promotion and hence move on up the status ladder; but the majority, according to research studies surveyed by Hulin and Blood (1968), regard their promotion primarily as a source of anxiety. Many, indeed, resign their jobs with a sigh of relief and return to their lower-paid, but psychologically more comfortable, former jobs.

The Enjoyment of Sheer Monotony

Ex-foremen have been willing to return to what would appear to be lives of monotony because the production-line possesses attractions unknown to the middle-class worker. Research by industrial psychologists has shown that assembly-line workers do not find their jobs to be dreary, unremitting drudgery. In one plant over 80% of the work force said they preferred to have their work paced mechanically, as by a moving assembly line; only 10% wanted to work at their own speed (Kilbridge, 1960). (Presumably, this 10% would most appreciate promotion to the position of foreman.) In another manufacturing plant assembly-line workers reported that they enjoyed their repetitive work. They complained only about the interruptions by supervisors and staff employees—these, they said, interfered with their attempts to maintain standards of quantity and quality (Turner & Miclette, 1962).

The results of such studies are consistent with the conclusions of Hulin and Blood, who found no support for the middle-class assumption that everyone must find routine, repetitive work boring. Their evidence made it clear that most blue-collar workers prefer such work because it is simple, straightforward, and involves a minimum of personal responsibility.

A few years ago, a team of six Detroit auto workers accepted an invitation to work for a few weeks in the plant of a Swedish automobile manufacturer, Saab. In most industrialized countries, as in the United States, auto workers perform the same operation repeatedly as each engine or chassis comes down the assembly line. The Saab plant functions quite differently; it has no routinized assembly line. Employees working in teams of three assemble complete engines. Each team decides how the work is to be shared and how it is to be done.

The system encourages workers to learn and practice a wide variety of skills and to develop a sense of pride about what they are producing.

Only one of the American workers liked the Saab approach, however. The other five, expressing the attitudes that Hulin and Blood had found to be typical, preferred their work on the assembly line at home because it proceeded at a slower and more relaxing pace, which permitted them to lose themselves in their thoughts. They complained that the Saab team-assembly method required continuous concentration and was more tiring. If Herzberg's theory applies to blue-collar workers, it seems to explain the attitudes of Swedish automobile workers better than it does those from Detroit.

It thus appears that monotony is not the major source of dissatisfaction for the blue-collar employee. Tedium and boredom are seldom mentioned in surveys. Instead, the dissatisfactions are likely to involve money matters, especially pay (see, for example, Smith & Keer, 1953). Money is of course a matter of common interest for blue- and white-collar workers. Although white-collar workers characteristically say that hygiene factors, such as pay, rank low in their scale of work motivators, the objective observer wonders what would happen if physicians, CPAs, and lawyers routinely received the same salaries as assembly-line workers. They do not, of course, nor is this likely to occur, so we shall never have the answer to that intriguing question.

Keeping in Step with Status and Income

White-collar professionals' average incomes will never drop below those of blue-collar workers because we as members of society have made three kinds of status—occupational, monetary, and social—roughly equivalent. In modern American society individuals may acquire status by moving up an occupational status ladder that reaches from the occasionally employed day laborer at the bottom to the physician at the top. Status, as we noted in Chapter 4, is expressed through the power to influence the behavior and attitudes of others. The possession of one form of social power provides the means to acquire other forms. Individuals who rise in occupational status, for example, acquire the money that goes with the new position. Hence the business executive who promotes a junior automatically includes an increase in salary, and civil service commissions set wages and salaries in accordance with the status of the positions to be filled.

This relationship between monetary rewards and status is, incidentally, not confined to capitalistic countries; it prevails in communistic countries as well, with some intriguing differences. Wage differentials between occupational status levels exist in the Soviet Union, but they are smaller than in capitalistic countries. However, individuals occupying top positions are rewarded with privileges worth more than mere rubles— i.e., in terms of goods and services not available to lower-status citizens: the right to buy scarce consumer goods at special commissaries, low-rent condominiums and *dachas* in specially designated and highly guarded resort areas, permits to travel abroad, and chauffer-driven limousines.

The fact that middle-class people generally rate the intrinsic or motivational aspects of their work as more important than monetary rewards may very well be due to their feeling that the economic side of their work will take care of itself. This does not mean that middle-class people are not anxious about money but rather that the social system provides more economic security for them than it does for the blue-collar workers. The accountant who receives his B.S. degree on graduation from college knows he has an excellent chance to get a job at the prevailing rate. He expects periods of unemployment during his working life to be brief, should they occur at all. In contrast, the carpenter who has recently completed his apprenticeship or graduated from a trade school has no such assurance. He faces a world in which layoffs, strikes, and long periods of unemployment are a common experience. His daily wage may actually exceed that of the young accountant; but unless he is unusually successful in finding steady work, his annual income will be lower.

The Search for Freedom

As workers we tend to be most concerned with obtaining whatever our jobs leave in shortest supply. Most blue-collar workers live in a social world where money supplies are chronically unpredictable and precarious. They may enjoy working for a number of psychological reasons—the job of being active and productive, or the social rewards of work-group membership and interaction with fellow workers, for instance—but the specter of unemployment, with no money in the bank and the rent overdue lurks always in the background.

The middle-class workers, on the other hand, are less likely to share this preoccupation with the economic side of life. Instead, they express concern about what seems to them to be in short supply: freedom. Freedom to them means more scope to make their own decisions, to be creative, to innovate, to arrange their work schedules to meet their unique needs. Blue-collar workers are even less free than white-collar workers are, but their anxieties about money force them to give freedom a lower priority. Besides, blue-collar workers are less likely to share the middle-class romance with work.

In the middle-class world, work is often mentioned in excited, even glowing, terms, for it is considered a major form— if not *the* major form—of self-expression. To those eager to express themselves, there is never enough freedom. Self-expressive persons are impatient with bureaucratic regulations, with deadlines and standards imposed by insensitive bosses and clients, and with unnecessary interruptions, minutiae, and trivia. Although work provides opportunities for self-expression it also exacts a price: one must conform to the demands and expectations of supervisors, co-workers, and clients or customers. Coping with these demands and expectations restricts the freedom of the individual worker. Facing such restrictions, individuals strive after jobs higher up the ladder, recognizing that increased power and status provide the means to create more freedom for oneself. Others find freedom only during time spent off the job—on weekends, for example, or in extended two- and three-martini lunch breaks. Some find freedom only when they retire; some never find it.

One reason for this concern about the on-the-job freedom for self-expression may be found in the early experiences of middle-class people. Psychological studies of child-rearing patterns have shown that middle-class and working-class parents behave in fundamentally different ways. Melvin L. Kohn (1969), who directs socio-environmental research at the Federally funded National Institute for Mental Health, has reviewed hundreds of such investigations. He observes that working-class parents characteristically want their children to conform to the demands and expectations of others, especially of people in authority. For them, the best thing that can possibly be said about a child is that he or she is obedient. Middle-class parents, on the other hand, want their children to think problems through and make their own decisions. Self-direction and independence, coupled with self-control, are the characteristics they rate as most important in children.

Middle- and working-class parents view the world differently. The jobs of working-class parents seldom afford the luxuries of independent problem-solving, freedom for self-expression, and personal development. Most blue-collar workers are paid to do what they are told; how the job is to be performed is laid out in specific detail. The worker who follows orders is a good worker; the worker who does not is fired, his money supply is cut off, and he becomes one of the unemployed, a candidate for public welfare. Working-class parents therefore teach their children what they consider to be the formula for economic survival: don't argue; don't ask questions; do as you are told.

Middle-class parents likewise prepare their children for the world *they* know. Jobs in their world call for individual initiative, independence in thinking, and responsibility. As a result, middle-class parents work hard at involving their children in problem-solving activities that they hope will develop qualities of independence and self-direction. They consider self-control important, because anger and aggression interfere with the decision-making process and alienate others whose help is needed in getting the job done. Kohn notes that middle-class parents are more likely to punish their children for loss of self-control, whereas working-class parents are more likely to punish them for disobedience.

Psychic Income: A Challenge to the Status = Pay Rule

We have so far said nothing about middle-class people who

possess relatively high status but are poorly paid, a combination that seems to deny the close relationship that we have claimed for occupational status and monetary reward. Two prominent groups in this category are the clergy and the artists, using the latter term to apply collectively to painters, potters, sculptors, musicians, actors, and freelance writers. Teachers, too, seem to challenge the status-equals-money equation to some degree, for the average male teacher receives less than the median wage received by men in all occupations. (The average female teacher is paid somewhat more than the median wage for all employed women.) Much the same may be said for social workers.

One explanation for this anomaly is that the psychological rewards received by the clergy, artists, teachers, and social workers supplement their subnormal pay.

The Governor of the State of California, Jerry Brown, expressed sentiments consistent with the foregoing when he trimmed a budgetary request for increases in state college and university professors' salaries on the grounds that their "psychic income" was greater than that received by most state employees. Governor Brown's explanation outraged the professors, of course, but it possessed considerable popular appeal.

The logic of such an argument is leaky, however, as a glance at the relative balance between psychic and monetary rewards at various other occupational levels will show. The psychic income of ditch-diggers and stoop laborers on farms is abysmally low, as are their wages. Indeed, one is hard pressed to find much in the way of either psychic or monetary reward at the lower end of the occupational scale. People do jobs at this level because they have little choice: it is a matter of survival in physical, economic, and social terms. At the upper end of the status ladder we find jobs rich in both psychic and monetary rewards. Physicians, for example, are admired and respected, perform medical miracles, deal with vital problems, plan their own work, make their own decisions, and receive more money on the average than individuals in any other occupational category. Business executives, too, are bountifully blessed with both psychic and monetary income.

The idea that college professors should receive less money because they reap copious psychic rewards seems inconsistent with the way the status system operates. Indeed, if professors were paid according to the usual status-income formula they would get as much as physicians, with whom they are virtually equal in status according to national opinion polls (Treiman, 1977).

But the plain fact is that professors are *not* paid as well as physicians. Why not? A major reason for the low income of professors and members of the other underpaid professions is the disparity between the number of people who seek psychic rewards in their work and the number of jobs in the appropriate occupations. The number of people who want to reap the psychic rewards of teaching exceeds the number of teaching positions at all levels of education, especially in colleges and universities. This means that colleges wishing to hire professors can get them for almost whatever they want to pay. In many colleges half the courses or more are taught by part-time instructors who not only receive less money than full-time faculty members but are also deprived of the usual fringe benefits: health insurance, retirement, unemployment compensation, and tenure.

The plight of the part-time instructor is clear evidence that a sizable number of middle-class people are willing to forego reasonable monetary rewards in order to perform even small amounts of intrinsically motivating work. A similar situation prevails in the arts, where the imbalance between money received and effort expended is much greater than in college teaching and has a much longer history. Irrespective of which of the several artistic fields we consider, the story seems to be the same: more art is produced than can possibly be consumed, even at very low prices, and the number of practitioners who struggle to make a living by their creative efforts is far greater than the number the market can employ at a reasonable wage. Robert Hughes (1979), a *Time* essayist, notes: "The American art education system, churning out as many graduate artists every five years as there were *people* in late 15th century Florence, has in effect created an unemployable art proletariat whose work society cannot 'profitably' absorb."

After a few years in the field, most artists realize that they are unlikely to receive what society calls a normal income from their work. Some drop out altogether, discouraged and disillusioned; a larger number remain, supporting themselves by part-time work often unrelated to their artistic field. Many devote themselves exclusively to their art, eking out a marginal existence through handouts from friends and relatives, unemployment compensation and welfare payments, and the earnings of spouses. For many active artists the economic facts of life are bruising and often humiliating, but the drive to do work that is psychologically satisfying—intrinsically rewarding—is such that the cost seems justified.

High Status, High Pay, High Motivation—the Best of All Worlds

The work situation of most high-status individuals in our society—lawyers, business and governmental executives, physicians, certified public accountants, consulting engineers—provides high levels of *both* intrinsic and extrinsic rewards. Why are extrinsic rewards high for them but low for the helping and artistic professions?

One explanation is the economic one, the supply-and-demand relationship we have noted—namely, that the high-income professions have a better control over the supply of job candidates. The number of new practitioners is kept low by training schools that reject all but a small proportion of applicants and that further reduce their ranks by requiring them to complete long years of preparation. In some fields, notably law, large numbers also fail licensing examinations. The procedure is not air-tight, of course. Some years produce too many engineers, and today there is a surplus of young lawyers. But the demand for the services of experienced, prestigious lawyers is sufficient to keep the monétary rewards of established lawyers high.

High-level executives do not have the influence over the supply of aspirants that physicians and other professional workers enjoy, but their control of the avenues to promotion in their organizations enables them to achieve much the same result as that attained by members of the licensed professions.

Are Extrinsic and Intrinsic Rewards Compatible?

The combination of high intrinsic satisfaction and low pay that characterizes the helping and artistic professions is sometimes rationalized in terms of the incompatibility of intrinsic satisfactions and extrinsic rewards, especially in the form of money. This thought may have been in the mind of California Governor Brown when he told the state college and university professors that "psychic income" should suffice them. Such an idea would be consistent with his background and training with the Jesuit order, whose vow of poverty was intended to free them from concern for extrinsic satisfactions, at least worldly ones, such as money.

The rejection of extrinsic goals—money in particular—has a long history. It played an important part in the daily life of Europeans during the Middle Ages, as we noted in Chapter 3, and it also has a firm place in the value systems of Asiatic cultures that revere those who have abandoned wordly goals for religious or philosophical contemplation.

The idea that extrinsic considerations might interfere with intrinsic motives has also been explored by psychologists. Richard DeCharms (1968), a social psychologist at Washington University in St. Louis, has defined intrinsic and extrinsic motivation in perceptual terms. He says that individuals are intrinsically motivated in their work to the extent that they see themselves as the cause of their own behavior, and that they are extrinsically motivated to the extent that they see the causes of their behavior external—when they see themselves as pawns, so to speak.

DeCharms maintains that extrinsic rewards interfere with the intrinsic enjoyment of a task because they make the individual dependent upon the source of the rewards. Being dependent on others limits the individual's freedom to choose and act for himself. His commitment deteriorates, as does his task motivation.

The DeCharms theory was put to the test by Calder and Staw (1975), social psychologists at the University of Illinois in Urbana. They divided their subjects—all male undergraduates—into four groups. Members of two of the groups worked individually at assembling jigsaw puzzles made of pictures with a high degree of intrinsic interest—action photographs from *Life* magazine, together with a few *Playboy* centerfolds. The other two groups worked on jigsaw puzzles that were blank. Half the participants in the jigsaw-puzzle sessions were told they would be paid for their work, and the money was placed in plain sight at the end of the row of puzzles they were to assemble. The other group was not paid.

At the end of the experiment, the men filled out questionnaires designed to elicit their feelings and attitudes toward the task they had completed. As might be expected, the men who assembled the picture puzzles reported greater interest in their work than did those who assembled blank boards, but the presence or absence of money made an interesting difference in their reactions. The men who were paid for doing picture puzzles declared less interest in the task than did those who were not paid. The opposite effect occurred with the men who assembled the blanks. Those who were paid found the job much more interesting than those who were not.

The parallel to the real world of work is an obvious one. Work that has little intrinsic interest becomes more enjoyable if an extrinsic reward, such as money, is introduced. The money is not received while the work is going on; it enters the scene only at the end. But the worker knows he will be paid, he anticipates the happy moment when the money is put in his hand, and he works contentedly, thinking of the reward he will receive and how he will spend it. As we noted in Chapter 9, it is the *expectation* of money that quickens and sustains the spirit, more than money itself. It is this expectation that keeps people at work doing all kinds of dreary but absolutely essential chores—cleaning clothing, streets, and toilets; changing the sheets and bedpans of the ill; and doing night guard duty in warehouses and empty buildings. But the motivation is still extrinsic.

When a job is rich in intrinsic interest—enjoyable for its own sake—the offer of an extrinsic reward seems irrelevant. Not only does such an offer introduce an unwanted state of dependency, but it also distracts and confuses. We can understand that the subjects who assembled picture puzzles may have had some difficulty in determining whether they were there to enjoy *Playboy* centerfolds or to earn money.

Real-life parallels to this situation are not common, but they do exist. Imagine Julie Roxas, a painter critics say is "somewhere between merely competent and really great." Ms. Roxas has taken this evaluation to heart and has become absorbed in the process of artistic self-discovery. She is barely launched into her work, when the telephone rings. A gallery owner is on the line saying that he has a customer who will pay a thousand dollars for the next picture she paints—whatever it may be. The money is attractive, for the rent is almost due and there are the usual expenses of the professional artist, but what will the intrusion of this extrinsic motivator do to her search for her artistic identity? She may be delighted at the commission, but at the same time it will probably distract her as she returns to her self-appointed task. Whereas before she was painting for Julie Roxas, now she is painting for an unknown person whose only attractive feature is a willingness to pay a thousand dollars for a picture.

To return to the jigsaw experiment, however, its results do seem to be contradicted by the fact that a good many professionals and executives enjoy their work and are also well paid.

The explanation of this seeming contradiction may be found in workers' perception of their situation. DeCharms said that the extrinsically motivated regard themselves as pawns. It seems hardly likely that successful professionals and executives view themselves as pawns. On the contrary, they conceive of themselves as "origins," to use the word DeCharms employs to characterize the intrinsically motivated person. People in these positions have a great deal of freedom to determine what they should do and how they will do it. Does this mean that money is irrelevant? It hardly seems likely. It is, rather, part of the "package" of status, prestige, power, and wealth that is theirs as a result of a combination of successful striving and good fortune. Money is not a major goal, but they would miss it if it were not there.

The Profit Motive and the Need to Achieve

The role played by money in the reward system of a good many hard-working, energetic people has been analyzed by David C. McClelland (1961), a Harvard psychologist specializing in the study of personality. McClelland maintains that the so-called "profit motive" is actually only a minor aspect of the need to achieve. Individuals strongly motivated to achieve are interested in money primarily because it is a universal measure of accomplishment, a measure they can use to provide themselves with "the concrete knowledge of the outcome of their efforts that their motivation demanded."

McClelland (1975) views the need to achieve as one of the keys to economic growth, in the sense that individuals who are concerned with doing things better become active, energetic entrepreneurs who create the business and industrial firms that serve as the foundation of developing economies. In later developmental stages, engineers, planners, and managers employed by government agencies can also make contributions as a result of their strong need to achieve. Still other individuals in managerial positions may not share this motive, but are, because of their strong need to succeed (a motive associated with the need for power, rather than achievement, according to McClelland), able to stimulate achievement motivation in others. But money is not a major incentive to achievement-oriented individuals, McClelland says, for they want it principally as a way of keeping score—as a *symbol* of higher achievement. And he concludes his discussion by noting that "gallons of ink and acres of paper might have been saved if economic and political theorists had understood this distinction" between money as a measure of achievement and money as a goal either for its own sake or as a means of controlling others.

An achievement-oriented person would probably have little difficulty in understanding McClelland's reasoning, but most people, when exposed to this view, are inclined to be skeptical and to prefer the more conventional interpretation of the highly motivated achiever's devotion to work: his hunger for money. A successful achiever inevitably arouses envy in us, and if we can tell ourselves "He is only interested in money," we have delivered the ultimate put-down.

When the achiever already has a great deal of money, however, this popular explanation does not make sense. As this is written, the fabulously wealthy Bob Hope is appearing in televised commercials on behalf of a savings and loan association. The question that must have been on the minds of a good many viewers who watched Hope deliver his sales pitch was put to me by a friend who asked wonderingly, not expecting an answer: "Why do you suppose he does it? With all *his* money he certainly can't need any more."

11 Money and mental health

It is better that a man tyrannize over his bank balance than over his fellow-citizens.   —JOHN MAYNARD KEYNES

Annual income twenty pounds, annual expenditure nineteen nineteen six, result happiness. Annual income twenty pounds, annual expenditure twenty pounds ought and six, result misery.   —MR. MICAWBER,
IN CHARLES DICKENS' *David Copperfield*

If you throw money away idly, you lose your great support. If you hug it too closely, you lose it and yourself too.   —JOHN LOCKE

Money is a social invention that enables us to strike a balance between the costs and benefits of life. It is a device that works reasonably well, especially if it is operated judiciously. The optimal functioning of modern society requires that the costs/benefits balance be maintained with maximum fairness to all. At the personal level, maintaining a reasonable and equitable balance is generally considered to be a significant clue to mental health—that is, an indication of the extent to which an individual may be considered to be a supportive, cooperative, nonexploitive, reliable, and worthy member of society. And there is a well-founded and widespread suspicion that anyone who cannot be trusted with money cannot be trusted in other respects. Inasmuch as interpersonal trust is the "gluon" that holds societies together and enables them to function, we are likely to observe carefully how others behave toward and with money.

But no one wants a really perfect society, for there would be nothing left to improve, nor do we want the system to work perfectly and on all occasions. Thus we are tempted at times to make it malfunction—in our favor, of course—by reducing costs relative to benefits, or increasing benefits relative to costs. This temptation is especially strong when we have been victimized by a successful manipulator, or believe that such has occurred. The fact that many do contrive, with apparent success, to tip the balance in their favor is enough to keep most of us on the defensive and also eager to redress real or fancied wrongs by taking advantage of swings and fluctuations in the shifting balance between costs and benefits. My clinical colleagues tell me that the tactics and maneuvers generated by strategems of defense and retribution cause more interpersonal trauma than the actual acts of exploitation they are intended to prevent or rectify. The same observation probably applies in the broader social scene of intergroup and international relations.

The widespread temptation to play games with the money part of the costs/benefits balance is intensified by two important considerations. One is the ambiguity that cloaks the operation of the system. Costs, benefits, and their value in money terms are in constant flux in their relation to one another as they attempt to reflect the give and take of everyday living. Hence it is difficult for us to determine at any given moment how we stand relative to others or relative to where we have been. This uncertainty is a major cause of the general insecurity that most of us feel about money, which is in turn a reflection of the pervasive insecurity that underlies our encounters both with specific others and with society in general.

The second consideration that lays us open to temptation is to be found in a condition that Rollo May (1950) says is endemic to modern society: anxiety.

Anxiety in Modern Life

To speak of anxiety is to speak of an ailment that is far more widespread than the common cold. It afflicts most of us several times a day; it attacks certain individuals every hour of their waking lives. The ailment is psychological, and it is so much a part of everyday living that those few who are immune from its effects are really not quite normal.

Anxiety is born of our need to make sense of life and the world around us. Things that do not make sense—that have no meaning—are troublesome. We do not know how they are affecting or will affect our lives and hence are at a loss as to how to deal with them. Anxiety is an emotional state that results from our inability to understand and deal decisively with problems, issues, and events that affect us.

Social interaction is certain to generate some anxiety for us because of the unpredictable element in all human relations. We are never absolutely sure of where we stand with others. As a consequence, we are never quite certain of how to behave toward them. When we suppress our qualms and barge right ahead, things usually work out. But sometimes they don't, and this is enough to keep our anxieties alive. The fact that our success or failure as members of society depends upon the judgments of others also feeds our anxieties.

The hidden future is an additional source of anxiety. Uncertainty about what will happen next and the feeling that we may have little control of future events keep us on edge—tense and apprehensive. It is a common observation that this is the "Age of Anxiety." The world changes more rapidly than it used to, as Alvin Toffler pointed out in *Future Shock* (1970), and we are continually kept off balance when a new turn of events catches us before we have adapted ourselves to the last one.

Anxiety and Its Ploys

Anxiety is the most painful of emotions. It is hardly surprising that we sometimes go to extreme lengths in building defenses against it. Some of our defenses are practical and sensible: we learn social conventions, for example, that enable us both to anticipate how others will behave toward us and to deal with them in ways that will invite their respect and acceptance instead of their antagonism or disdain. We attempt to cope with the anxieties of a chartless future by putting money aside for emergencies, preparing for work that will support us economically, taking out health and casualty insurance, and enrolling in pension plans. These sensible and realistic steps are designed to deal with potential threats to our well-being and thus enable us to forestall present and future anxiety.

But we also engage in activities that are less reality-oriented—attempts to deflect our attention from situations and events that are actual or potential sources of anxiety. Some of these activities are harmless forms of escape—e.g., collecting old china, reading, traveling, or watching television. Others are more or less neurotic and pathological—e.g., drinking too much, picking fights with family members, going on shopping sprees we cannot afford, or humiliating subordinates. Not a few of these involve money.

In their book *Money Madness* clinical psychologists Herb Goldberg and Robert T. Lewis (1978) discuss a variety of irrational ways of dealing with money. We are likely to have neurotic problems involving money, according to Goldberg and Lewis, if we:

Put money ahead of everything else in life.

Buy things we do not need or want, simply because they are on sale.

Feel guilty about spending money even when we have sufficient funds.

Spend money freely and even foolishly on others but grudgingly on ourselves.

Automatically say "I can't afford it," whether we can or not.

Know to the very penny how much money we have in our purse or pocket at all times.

Feel inferior to those who have more money than we do.

Feel superior to those who have less money than we do.

Feel anxious and defensive when asked about our personal finances, even by people who have a right to know.

Feel disdainful of money and look down on those who have it.

Prefer cash in the banks to investments, because we're never sure when everything will collapse.

Feel that money is the only thing we can really count on.

These symptoms are an expression of the "mechanisms" we all

use to defend ourselves against anxiety. The basic defense mechanisms as outlined by Freud and his followers are:

Repression: denying or overlooking embarrassing thoughts, feelings, and memories. Every form of defensive behavior involves repression in some way or other.

Rationalization: trying to make meaningless, stupid, or irrational actions appear reasonable.

Projection: criticizing others of being stingy, grasping, or greedy, for example.

Displacement: blaming an imputed but not the real source of our troubles, thereby absolving ourselves of responsibility.

Overcompensation: exaggerating our attempts to make up for some real or fancied personal deficiency, for example, throwing ourselves into the pursuit of money because we feel unloved or friendless.

Reaction formation: overreacting to fear or anxiety by going too far in the opposite direction (overcaution about investments, for example).

Compulsiveness: being unable to depart from a counterproductive behavior pattern (unable to resist items on sale or novelty items that are "the latest thing," for example).

Money-related defense tactics are often employed to deal with anxiety caused by real or imagined personal inadequacies. For instance, a person to whom we are strongly attracted may treat us in a casual, offhand, or detached manner. Feeling disappointed and hurt because our love or friendship signals are not reciprocated we decide that "people are no damn good." We therefore pursue conspicuously a lifestyle in which "only money matters."

Money-Related Defenses Against Anxiety

What I have just described are all fairly straightforward examples of our attempts to deal with anxiety through defense mechanisms. The interplay between anxiety and defensive behavior is usually quite complex and often takes forms that seem bizarre—even among quite normal people who are functioning reasonably well in other respects. Here is one example of the sometimes convoluted way money becomes interwoven with defensive behavior.

Philip Shotsky got into a heated argument with Ellen, his wife of ten months' standing, over the amount of time she spent at her job as a real estate salesperson. She left him and went to stay with her employer and his wife, Bob and Norma Gash, who had been extremely understanding and had encouraged her career. Philip had always been jealous of Ellen's relationship with the Gashes. Her decision to stay with them seemed a low blow.

Two days after Ellen left, Philip sold his year-old Porsche to a used-car dealer, accepting an offer far below the car's real value. He had cherished his Porsche, polishing it and fine-tuning its engine on weekends. When his friends expressed amazement and asked why he had sold his prized possession, Philip answered "I needed the money." He refused to give further explanations.

Clinicians would differ in their interpretations of Philip's actions. Those with Freudian leanings might call the sale a symbolic self-castration, observing that a powerful sport car is a fetish symbolizing the penis. When Ellen "emasculated" Philip by leaving him for the Gashes, he realized that he was defeated and completed the process by lopping off this prized extension of his masculine ego.

Clinicians of other persuasions might view Philip's gesture as symbolic suicide. By sacrificing the thing he loved second only to Ellen, he tells the world how deeply he has been hurt. Secretly he hopes she will learn of his dramatic gesture, will feel guilty for the way she has hurt him, and will return to him, repentant. But he has enough grasp on reality to know that his gesture is really ridiculous; hence he cloaks it with respectability by giving the one reason *anyone* would understand: "I needed the money."

Philip's behavior is neurotic and immature. It is not as bad as a real attempt at self-destruction; but it is bad enough, for it prevents him from gaining any insight into his relationship with

Ellen, finding some sensible way to work things out with her, or using the car to court another potential partner.

Clinicians of all schools would probably agree that Philip has been overwhelmed by anxiety and that an attempt to probe the causes of the difficulty would create even more anxiety for him. Hence the gesture of selling his car is a way of sealing off the affair. He probably even convinces himself that she made him sell his Porsche. The sacrifice of the car thus comes to make (neurotic) sense to him.

Especially interesting to this discussion is the excuse Philip gives: "I needed the money." He acts as if this explained everything. It explains nothing, of course, but he puts it forth because in our culture the need for money has become the umbrella explanation for everything.

"Money Need" as a Rationalization

In the last chapter we noted how striking employees use the need for money as a camouflage for motives they do not want to face squarely. Employers make similar excuses—the "bottom line" is the current phrase—to hide their motives from themselves.

The need for money can also conceal more positive motives, motives that are too complex to examine in detail. It is used in this sense by people who strive for higher positions at work, as well as by married women who decide to seek paid employment. In these instances the underlying motives are needs for self-fulfillment, the desire for freedom to make decisions regarding one's work and one's identity, the enticement of positions offering higher status and greater power, the urge to put one's capabilities to the test, and so on. These are all complex motives; it is simpler to say "I need more money" and let it go at that.

On the darker side of life the need for money is used to explain a wide variety of sociopathic behavior—e.g., the activities of the prostitute, the drug smuggler, the mugger, the seller of state secrets, the arsonist, and the embezzler. Society rejects and punishes such offenders, but its deepest scorn is reserved for those who cannot give "need for money" as an excuse.

Life is replete with ambiguity; ambiguity creates doubt

and indecision; doubt and indecision breed anxiety. Hence anything we can introduce into a situation that makes it seem less
ambiguous saves us from eventual anxiety. Money performs that
function well. It enables Philip to explain his obviously ridiculous behavior to his friends and, more important, to himself. It
performs the same function for ambitious young employees,
working wives, seekers for graduate degrees, and law-breakers.
Disagreements over money are a major cause of divorce, but
money problems are only the surface manifestation of personality clashes that are looking for an arena in which to do battle.

In earlier eras, personal disputes were settled by hand-to-
hand combat. In our more-or-less civilized world people are
more likely to resolve them in symbolic ways—through financial
suits in the courts, for example. Money was invented to facilitate
the exchange of goods and services, as we noted in Chapter 2,
but it works equally well as a facilitator of quarrels. Disagreements involving money are a starting point for disputes in many
areas of life, and the resolution of disputes often involves the
payment of money on the part of the loser. Even when disputes
do not directly involve money—questions of property rights,
personal injuries, and damage due to negligence, for example—
they are often settled by requiring the offender to pay a money
indemnity to the plaintiff. Individuals quick to take offense are
always suing someone for real or fancied grievances.

Neurotic Money Games

Psychotherapists often encounter the "scenario" of the individual who behaves irresponsibly, gets into trouble, blames others
for his mishaps, and attempts to manipulate those he blames
into retrieving the situation for him. Money frequently figures
in neurotic games of this type. The founder of transactional
analysis, Eric Berne (1972), described a classic example:

> Wanda, a patient in group therapy, was preoccupied
> with money problems because her husband kept getting
> into financial scrapes with his employers. He made good
> money, but somehow each month he would make an error
> of judgment (he overspent his entertainment and travel
> budget, or gave an unauthorized refund) that resulted in

his bringing home far less than expected. Each month Wanda would run up bills based on the anticipated income, and each month she was faced by the need to reduce expenditures drastically. On a number of occasions even severe economies did not suffice, and she had to turn to her parents for financial help.

When Wanda complained to the therapy group about her thankless role in life—scrimping and saving, never having enough money, having to go through the humiliating task of asking her parents for money—the members raised rather pointed questions about her husband's actions, which seemed to them to be at the heart of the problem. Wanda angrily defended her husband, saying that his difficulties were all caused by his employers, who were taking advantage of his honest mistakes, his minor errors in judgment, and his easygoing lack of attention to details. The penalties they exacted, she claimed, were always far in excess of the amounts his mistakes had actually cost them.

Wanda's arguments with the other members of the group had always ended in a standoff until the day she reported a dream. She had dreamed she was living in a concentration camp run by certain rich people living at the top of a nearby hill. The inmates of the camp could get enough food only by following the orders of the rich people or by tricking them.

After the dream had been interpreted to her, Wanda found her way of life easier to understand. It became apparent to her that her husband was really playing the "Let's Pull a Fast One" game with his employers so that Wanda could play the game of "Making Ends Meet." Whenever he was about to come out ahead in money terms he would quickly arrange to reverse matters so that both games could continue. When things really got bad he would collaborate with Wanda in the game of "Let's Pull a Fast One" against her parents. Much to the chagrin of Wanda and her husband, however, both employers and parents always managed to end up in control of the situation.

In the earlier stages of her therapy, Wanda had been impelled to react with angry defensiveness when she was challenged by the group: if she had admitted that her husband was a trickster, both his game and hers would have collapsed. Like many a neurotic, Wanda had come to depend on the game to help her suppress, and thus cope with, anxieties generated by self-doubt. Although money seemed at first glance to play a key role in Wanda's problems, it was actually only incidental to the main action. Money made the games possible if only because the players kept score in monetary terms, but the basic script dealt with the attempts of people to use one another in neurotic and destructive ways.

Berne described a number of other money games that are essentially neurotic ways of dealing with others and of interpreting one's own behavior. One of these is the "Try and Collect" game. It is often played by young married couples who use credit to buy goods and services. (The scale of their purchases depends on their social backgrounds and how they have been taught to play the game by their parents.)

Let us say that a couple, Louise and George White, have been taking advantage of the "easy credit" terms urged on them by eager retailers and are now behind in their "easy monthly payments" to a credit-card company. If the creditor makes only a few ineffectual attempts to collect, the Whites are able to enjoy their gains. If this occurs, they win the "Try and Collect" game. But let us presume that, as is customary, the debt is turned over to a collection agency. This outfit goes to the Whites' employers, makes nuisance telephone calls, threatens a law suit, and drives up to the couple's home in a truck boldly labeled **COLLECTION AGENCY**.

At this point in the game the Whites realize that they will have to pay eventually, but the coercive element in the creditor's tactics in their view justifies anger. They now switch over to the game that Berne called "Now I've Got You, You Son of a Bitch." This game enables the Whites to feel virtuous and above criticism, because the creditor has shown how greedy, ruthless, and grasping he really is. They abuse the creditor to their friends and acquire virtue in their eyes by revealing themselves as hapless victims of a vicious "system." They feel vindicated for having "ripped-off" the Establishment,because the Establishment showed that it deserved to be looted.

Should one of the friends before whom the Whites have acted their little charade also be a creditor, and should that friend visit them privately to collect something on the debt, the game is quickly changed to "You Only Want to Kick Me Because I'm Down and Out." The Whites reply to the request with cold scorn: "We told you how we are being harassed by the credit union, how we are on the brink of bankruptcy. Now you have the gall to ask us for this piddling little sum? With friends like you, who needs an enemy?" The creditor-friend is now neatly boxed in. If he insists on payment, he is not a friend; he is an enemy, like the credit-card firm. As an enemy, he is not entitled to be paid. But if he is to remain a friend, he won't be paid, either. He is made to feel guilty about having brought the matter up at all. He apologizes and slinks away, his tail between his legs.

It is clear that the Whites' game with their creditors enables them to overlook their own underlying motives. These motives are rather sordid and despicable, and the Whites could not easily tolerate seeing them for what they are. Secretly they may sense that they, not their creditors, are the exploiters. But whatever misgivings they have are extinguished by their all-compelling need to dramatize themselves before their friends and by the almost sensuous enjoyment they derive from playing the role of the martyr. The remedy is obviously psychotherapy, but the chances of the Whites' seeking help remain poor until they are ready to accept some responsibility for the misfortunes that befall them. Perhaps this readiness will come on the eve of their second bankruptcy.

Anti-Money Games

There are other money games in the guerrilla warfare troubled people wage against society and, in the final analysis, against themselves. In his book on the neurotic manifestations of the money motive, Thomas Wiseman (1974) describes an anti-money game played by Simon Dee, an English radio personality.

Dee began his adult life as a drama student, was unemployed for long periods, and worked briefly as a vacuum-cleaner salesman. He got his big opportunity as a disk jockey on Radio Caroline, a "pirate" radio station located in international waters to evade British laws, which at one time banned commercial broadcasts. When commercial radio became legal, Dee was much in demand as a host on televised talk shows and was making a thousand dollars and more a week, which was very good money in the London of the late 1960s. Within a year or so, however, Dee argued with his employer and walked off the job. Thereafter Dee was singularly ineffective in getting work of any kind. During his heyday he had not accumulated any assets that could have seen him through hard times.

In a newspaper interview after his fall from popularity, Dee expressed some interesting views about money. He said that he had not invested any money during his period of affluence because to do so would have forced him to trust other people's decisions. Nor had he bought any insurance. Insurance could not protect anyone against acts of God, he said, and he himself could deal with acts of man. He said, furthermore, that investing and buying insurance help to build "incredible financial empires that are hopelessly out of control, that are distorting our way of life."

Dee had not bought a house either, because the payments on the mortgage would in the end amount to much more than the sale price of the house. He thought it ridiculous to pay more for a house than it was worth. Payments on the mortgage would only put more money in the coffers of the banks and insurance companies, which he both feared and despised.

In his analysis of the psychological background to Dee's behavior, Wiseman pointed out that Dee's ignorance of money matters was only a minor part of the picture. He could have secured the advice of a professional who would have explained the advantages of using a mortgage to buy a house. Instead, according to Wiseman, Dee's deep-seated suspicion and resentment of money and the power it represents led to its eventual loss.

Dee's beliefs about money were completely consistent with his behavior toward the persons he worked with. He trusted no one but himself to make decisions about his talk show. When his co-workers objected to this, he quit. Such a rigid approach to the world is frequently encountered in teenagers, who make impossible demands on others but none on themselves; who mistake anger and aggressiveness for honesty; and who express a view of social insitutions so suspicious and cynical that it borders on the paranoid. Teenagers use this façade to conceal from themselves and others a welter of insecurities, self-doubts, and anxieties. They are unable to trust anyone because they cannot trust themselves. With time and experience, the rigidity, suspicion, and hostility usually fade. In people like Dee, however, self-doubts become so patterned and firmly set that they persist throughout life.

Dee was what Wiseman calls a "loser"—someone who finds success and dealing with the money it generates so stressful that he prefers failure. Dee reported that although his reaction to the abrupt termination of his career was one of "total shock and horror," he also sensed a feeling of happiness and relief. Life had been confusing when he was a well-paid member of the entertainment world, he said, but the long period of unemployment that followed his departure from television enabled him to sort out his priorities and determine what was really important and valuable in life. The happiness he had experienced in his work had actually been false, he said, because it was based on money; when the money was gone, he found true happiness.

Clinical psychologists recognize two types of rationalization employed by those who are trying to cope with the anxieties engendered by disappointment: "sour grape" and "sweet lemon." Dee used both to deal with his feelings after his fall from the top of the success ladder. He could no longer command the high wage that had been paid him by an admiring television industry; therefore he claimed that the values associated with large amounts of money are tarnished. The grapes he used to enjoy, in other words, were actually sour. On the other hand, life had, as it were, handed Dee a lemon by knocking him out of a much envied position and preventing him from making his way back to the top. Rationalizing, Dee tasted the lemon and pronounced it sweet. "How lucky I am," he said, in effect, "for now I need not use a value system corrupted by money. Instead I can relate to life as it really is."

If this kind of rationalization seems familiar it is because we have encountered it again and again in the conversation of those who have little money. Indeed, we may have used it ourselves from time to time. It is easy to sneer at the rationalizer who has no money and makes a virtue of it, but we should recognize that the purpose of rationalization is to make a difficult situation tolerable. Let us rather be concerned about the sufferer who does not rationalize, who believes that he is helpless in an impossible situation, and who hence becomes depressed and apathetic or, what is worse, openly hostile, aggressive, and destructive. If Dee found the peace and self-fulfillment in poverty that he had missed in affluence, let no man jeer at his good fortune.

Gambling: Losers' Choice

Although Simon Dee did not gamble, Wiseman felt that his tendency to prefer losing to winning was essentially the same motivation that plays a major part in the behavior of habitual gamblers. Gamblers sometimes say that if gambling and winning is the greatest of all thrills, then gambling and losing is the second greatest. Indeed, the fact that most gambling ventures produce losses has led some psychologists to view the need to lose as the chief motive in gambling. They thus see gambling as a masochistic exercise.

Wiseman describes the fate of the beautiful Polish actress, Bella Darvi, who was the mistress of Darryl F. Zanuck, the film producer. A compulsive gambler, Darvi was unable to stop once the mania had captured her. When she had lost all her money she would strip off her rings and jewelry and throw them on the gaming table in order to keep playing. On one occasion she lost so much money gambling on credit that the French government confiscated her passport. Zanuck bailed her out on this and other occasions, but eventually his patience ran out. When there was no one left to pay her debts and finance her addiction she committed suicide.

Few habitual gamblers have so dramatic and tragic a career as Bella Darvi's, but their addiction nevertheless creates severe problems for them and their families. The chronic gambler may become as undependable and unpredictable in his behavior as a person addicted to alcohol or heroin. He seems unable to stop gambling, even though aware of the harm he is doing his career, his family, and his friends.

The truly addicted gambler lives in a state of tension and suspense, which he hides behind a mask of calm stoicism—the well-known "poker face." He is unable to relax because he is continually reading racing tip sheets, arranging card or dice games, making bets, or raising funds to gamble or to pay off debts. Just as the alcoholic hides bottles of liquor in secret places to get through some future "dry period," the addicted gambler maintains a reserve fund—his "betting money"—which he will not use for other purposes even though his personal or family needs may be desperate.

Most people who gamble are not addicted to it, of course, but nevertheless a kind of pathological ferment seems to grip many otherwise healthy individuals when they enter a gaming casino. The sight of huge amounts of money in itself stimulates and arouses, and watching people bet, win, and lose these large amounts generates excitement and the desire to become a participant. No one wants to be left on the sidelines when there is a party in progress, and the casino management makes it exceedingly easy to join the party. Some clubs provide visitors with an initial roll of nickels or a short stack of poker chips to start the process of involvement.

The "house odds" in a casino are such that most players lose, but losing one's initial stake usually takes a number of plays, some of which result in wins. All that is required to keep a gambler playing is the intermittent reinforcement of an occasional win. We have met up with intermittent reinforcement already in Chapter 9.

Gambling fever is not confined to casinos. It operates in

the stock option and commodity futures markets, and, less often today, in the stock exchanges. The individual who gambles in these seemingly more legitimate precincts usually plays for larger stakes then prevail in the action at a Las Vegas gaming club. He often rationalizes his behavior by saying that he is a speculator, not a gambler, the difference being that the speculator knows what he is doing and can choose situations in which the odds favor him, whereas the gambler entrusts his fate to pure chance.

The difference, however, is academic. Most people who play stock-option and commodity-futures games lose just as certainly as if they were bucking a black jack dealer at Harrah's Club in Reno. Except for an elite few who have a phenomenal grasp of economic movement and mass psychology, the only consistent winners are the brokers, who collect impartially from both winners and losers.

The individual who gambles on stock options or commodity futures may convince himself, and others as well, that he is not speculating but investing, because he "knows for certain" that Magnum is going to take over Consolidated Lintels, or that the current subzero weather will delay spring planting and thus make a shambles of the grain markets. He holds this conviction so firmly that he blindly ignores the many other factors that may affect the future price of the stock option or commodity he is interested in.

The Speculator's Neurotic Omnipotence

According to Sandor Ferenczi (1916), a member of Freud's group in Vienna, the feeling of absolute certainty, which is familiar to anyone who has ever speculated or gambled, is a lingering form of "infantile omnipotence." Ferenczi maintained that infants do not look upon themselves as weak and helpless but rather as all-powerful, omnipotent beings, whose needs are met by adults who have no voice in the matter. Infants, he said, are able to maintain this wholly unrealistic self-concept because they lack the means to find out how weak, dependent, and helpless they really are. With time, they encounter the rough edges and hard surfaces of reality; disillusioning experiences teach them the facts of life.

Maturity means learning not only what you can do but also what you cannot do. Most of us have lost the feeling of omnipotence by the time we became preschoolers, but it reemerges from time to time in later years, especially when we want something very much and are convinced that we can have it—no matter what.

The speculator, for example, knows a few things that may affect the price of his desired option or commodity, but he does not know everything. Most important, he does not know how significant his bits of information are, relative to all other relevant information. Hence he does not know what the odds are for success. Not knowing the odds permits him to place an exaggerated value on what he knows. He wants very much to play and so he calls upon the magic of his never-quite-forgotten infantile omnipotence to rationalize the plunge. This feeling of infinite power is characteristically strongest after he has had a string of losses. The weaker his financial position, therefore, the more convinced he is that he is *certain* to win this time.

Sir Walter Raleigh did not speculate in stock options or commodity futures, but he did, according to Wiseman, have occasional feelings of certainty so absolute that he tossed all caution to the winds. When Raleigh was sixty-four years old, he was as sure of finding El Dorado as "of not missing his way from his dining room to his bedchamber." The expedition he had led twenty years before had ended in failure. At that time he had not been alone in his conviction that El Dorado, the City of the Golden Man, was somewhere in the Americas, just waiting to be discovered. Others had tried to find it and failed. Now almost everyone but Raleigh was convinced that its existence was a myth. But Raleigh was absolutely certain that he would succeed. He sold all his property, and his wife's as well, and set off for South America. For twenty years he had cherished a vision of a high, cold city decorated with golden eagles and jackals, its walls and roofs studded with precious stones. He had mapped the route in his imagination—the trail up the Orinoco River, which led to a high pass over a mountain of crystal—he could see it all in his mind's eye.

As Wiseman says, "This is exactly the gambler's passion; whipping himself up into a state of hallucinatory *knowing,* whereby he can actually see the numbers that will come up. One is bound to see in such ill-judged ventures—that so patently go against the laws of probability, and yet are attended by the certitude of success—the workings of the losing drive."

Raleigh, then, was a compulsive loser. His grand illusion was an elaborate rationalization of his neurotic infatuation with losing. Similarly, the infantile omnipotence that makes commodity and option speculators, as well as horse players, so sure they have the key to winning serves to hide from them the fact that they are members of the Secret and Psychological Fraternity of Losers.

The Happy/Sad Fate of Big Winners

To those who gamble, the epitome of happiness is "winning big." Otherwise, why put dollar after dollar into lottery tickets, or spend endless hours poring over racing form charts in the hope of hitting a daily double?

But does "winning big" really bring happiness? A study of people who "won big" in the Illinois State Lottery indicates that the windfalls brought about changes in their lives, but that an increase in happiness was not one of them. A team of psychologists located twenty-two lottery winners who had won prizes ranging from fifty thousand to one million dollars, with an average gain of about five hundred thousand.

The winners were asked how they rated their past, present, and probable future happiness, and how enjoyable they found everyday pleasures, such as talking with a friend, eating breakfast, watching television, hearing a funny joke, and so on. Contrary to what we might expect, the winners' ratings of their past, present, and future happiness were not significantly different from the similar ratings made by a comparison group of nonwinners living in the same neighborhoods. The people in the comparison group did, however, rate their enjoyment of everyday pleasures higher than the winners did. Indeed, the winners rated everyday pleasures even lower than did a group of patients who were wholly or partially paralyzed as a result of accidents.

The psychologists explained the winners' tendency to experience less pleasure in mundane activities as an effect produced by their "peak experience"—winning a major prize—which made ordinary pleasures pale by comparison. "Winning big" was also fatal to the great expectations that keep lottery players buying tickets. Once they "made a killing," most of the pleasure was drained from the lottery game. The greatest excitement lies in perennial hopes and dreams about big money prizes that never get realized.

The fact that the winners' happiness was no greater than that of the comparison group can be explained partly in terms of the fact that people quickly adapt themselves to improvements in their life style and readily take them for granted. Furthermore, as the winners told the interviewers, the favorable changes in their lives were balanced off by unfavorable ones. Although they now had more financial security and leisure, they experienced some strain in their social relationships. Some complained, for example, about seeing less of their former associates. Evidently, friends who do not have money tend to shun a winner in order not to appear wanting money or simply to avoid experiencing social comparison (Brickman, Coates, & Janoff-Bulman, 1978).

The results of this study are probably not very surprising. Most people know that "money won't buy happiness," although they often rationalize their vigorous and persistent efforts to acquire it on the grounds that happiness will somehow result when money needs are met. In all probability, what really motivates money-seekers is not so much the belief that money will bring happiness, but the expectation that money will relieve their current anxieties about solvency and economic security. Most of us are too realistic to hope for a major windfall, but we do believe that the augmentation of our resources with "a little more money" will go a long way toward making life easier.

The "Little More Money" Delusion

The belief that "a little more money" will solve one's problems is a delusion, but it is one that is cherished by almost everyone. The delusion is held more strongly by some than others, but in any event it is firmly supported by popular belief and reinforced by sympathetic social approval. Most of us are victims of the conviction that our problems would be solved if we could just get our hands on a little more money. The validity of this conviction seems incontrovertible. We sit down to pay bills after the first of the month and find that there just isn't enough money to go around. What we obviously need is "a little more money." Lacking it, we pay the urgent bills and distribute the residue in the form of partial payments to the other creditors. In this we are encouraged by department stores, oil companies, and credit-card agencies. They like to receive partial payments, in order that they might charge us 18–22% interest on the unpaid balance.

In many—perhaps most—American households this procedure is routine. Each month sees payments on some debts postponed and thus added to the accumulating mortgage on the future. Each month someone thinks or says, "If we only had a little more money."

Some families keep their purchases firmly in check and have no debts other than the mortgage on the house, a loan on the car, and current bills. The members of such families are able to attain this blessed state only by stern self-restraint and self-denial, by refusing to buy or contract for goods and services whose costs cannot be accommodated in the monthly budget. Such decisions may mean that Dad does not get a dental bridge, that the family has to walk or take public transportation for a week while the engine of their aging car is overhauled, that the children do not get to summer camp, and so forth, on and on. The economical family is less likely to incur debts on which they must pay 18–22% interest, but they experience all the other problems that less frugal families have. And they are equally inclined to sigh, "If only we had a little more money."

The income of the household does not seem to matter; the feeling that "just a little more money" would solve current problems seems universal. We live in a society in which the opportunities to spend are limitless. There is always something desirable that we do not have. And in a threatening and unstable world we can always buy more security: increased insurance, a broader pension plan, or a burglar alarm system. We should never forget that money is a form of power. The person does not exist who cannot use a little power—power to make life richer, more interesting, and more exciting, and power to take some of the uncertainty and risk out of the future. Our needs to achieve or "self-actualize" demand more power to provide the freedom and opportunity for self-expression and self-development, while the anxiety that lurks in the background demands more power to provide protection and security.

Most people do not realize that the need for "a little more money" is a universal experience. They think their situation is unique. They do not foresee the inevitable result of obtaining "a little more money:" they will shortly need still a little *more*. Many treat the need for "a little more money" as a problem that can be solved, once and for all. Families embark on attempts to deal with this " problem." The breadwinner quits a job he likes and takes one he dislikes because it pays more money. The mother of small children may take a job that requires her to hire a babysitter. In this she is reinforced by the Internal Revenue Service, which allows tax deductions for baby-sitting fees under these circumstances. The IRS thus plays a dual role: It is the indulgent benefactor that makes it easier for the family to solve its financial problems, and it is also the heartless, impersonal bureaucracy that rakes in more taxes as the family's income soars to a higher bracket.

Some people deal with the problem of the "need for a little more money" by borrowing on their home or personal property and sinking deeper into debt. Some, attracted by the inflated value of real estate, sell their houses and move to apartments, only to find themselves at the mercy of landlord-speculators who raise the rent each time the apartment house changes hands.

Whatever our efforts, the "little more money" we find is never enough. Most people never learn that "enough money" is the pot of gold at the end of the rainbow, an incentive that keeps us racing on and on but never catching up.

From time to time, of course, most people do seem to get "a little more money" in the form of higher wages, cost-of-living adjustments, and increases in fees and profits. We get these augmentations because our economy, like economies throughout the world, is geared to provide relatively steady increases in the supply of money which in turn shows up in higher wages, social security payments, dividends, and so forth.

A "Little More Money" and Inflation

Why governments keep putting "a little more money" into the pockets of their citizens is not hard to determine. Societies, democratic or otherwise, succeed only to the extent that they satisfy the needs of their members. And if the members feel a need for a "little more money," as they usually do, then national banking systems are manipulated, sometimes deliberately and sometimes without seeming awareness, to provide more money. The monetary inflations created by John Law, the Continental Congress of the thirteen American colonies, the revolutionary government of France in the 1790s, and the German government in 1923 are all examples of the eagerness of people in charge to give people what they want—"a little more money." The same may be said regarding the "creeping inflation" that has beset all industrialized countries during the years since World War II.

And, as we noted in Chapter 3, the optimism of people can also increase the velocity with which money changes hands, thus generating inflationary forces without any help from the national treasury.

Whatever the cause of the inflation—increased supply, increased velocity, or both—we quickly accommodate ourselves to our larger paychecks and look for more. The "little more money" inflation seems to put in our pockets cannot satisfy us. We are constructed neurologically to adapt readily to moderate changes in our environment.[1] The more pleasurable the change, the more rapidly we accommodate ourselves to it. Hence each increment in affluence—even the illusory affluence of inflation—is eagerly welcomed, but we quickly adjust to it and look for the next one. In Chapter 2 we cited the great urban planner, Constantine Doxiadis (1970), who observed that man is the only animal who always wants more. And the societies we have created are programmed to produce whatever "more" is wanted, be it excitement, pleasure, creature comforts, exotic diets, friendly social interaction, freedom in the form of more options, or just money.

---

[1]A phenomenon known to psychologists as "sensory adaptation."

An increase in the money supply relative to the supply of goods and services is called "inflation," of course, a topic we discussed at some length in Chapter 3. Historians and economists alike severely criticize economic policies that produce inflations and support their criticisms by citing reports of the social and economic difficulties they produce. They have ample data to draw from, beginning with the successive debasements of the currency by Roman emperors from Nero onward and continuing down the centuries to the present day, which finds inflation more prevalent than ever. The universal employment of debt money and credit today has given us unlimited powers to inflate the money supply, a matter that upsets economists and financial experts, who are not alone in their criticisms. The dentist, the plumber, and the grocery-store owner all condemn inflation when they say, apologetically: "I'm sorry to charge you more, but I have to, because of inflation. Since my costs are higher I must raise my prices." The union leader says inflation necessitates a 10–20% wage increase, and the political candidate promises to do something about inflation if he is elected. Inflation has become a whipping boy for everyone.

Inflation and Mental Health: A Surprising Relationship

Perhaps "scapegoat" is a better term than "whipping boy," for what would we really do without inflation? If the costs of living and doing business were not rising, how could any of us justify our claim to "just a little more money" for our goods and services? Without inflation, most of us would only rarely enjoy that pleasurable, though unfortunately transitory, thrill that comes when "a little more money" is handed over to us.

Whatever economic problems it causes, "a little more money" may be a good thing from a psychological point of view. It is one of the pleasant " strokes" that life provides. "A little more money" encourages, rewards, and reassures. It calms and anesthetizes the anxieties that stir fretfully in the background. The Irish saying, "Money won't buy happiness, but it certainly quiets the nerves," is more than a wry and cynical comment. It is a great truth. In any case, "a little more inflated money" is inevitable. Inflation is a fact of life in every country, though some governments are more permissive in this respect than others.

Does all this inflation have a demoralizing effect? Common sense suggests that it should; but, as sometimes happens, the logic of common sense is out of phase with the logic of reality, for some data suggest that monetary inflation may have a positive effect on morale and hence on mental health.

Psychologists are not in accord as to what all the components of mental health may be, but they do agree that an optimistic view of life is essential. Consider, then, the results of the Gallup poll conducted at the end of 1977 in eighteen countries, including the United States. Pollsters asked people whether they expected 1978 to be better or worse than 1977. No attempts were made to specify what "better" or "worse" meant—each respondent was permitted to make his own interpretation. A country-by-country analysis of the results shows an interesting trend: in countries that had experienced a high rate of inflation there were noticeably greater percentages of people saying they were optimistic about the future than in countries where inflation had been minimal.

If inflation is associated with[2] elevated degrees of optimism and, presumably, good mental health, then why is it without friends? Why is it universally decried as a form of legalized thievery?

The answer to these questions, according to Lester C. Thurow (1978), professor of economics and management at the Massachusetts Institute of Technology, lies in the disparity between the gains we have experienced in "money income" and those achieved in "real income." Money income gains between the end of 1973 and the first quarter of 1978 had increased an

---

[2]The fact that inflation and public optimism are associated (or positively correlated, to use the technical term) does not prove that one causes the other. The relationship may, in fact, result from other factors. However, that there is a causal linkage between the two is plausible because of the significant role played by money in our lives. Indeed, the relationship may be an interactive one: Having more money makes us optimistic and we spend more freely, which in turn causes money to circulate more rapidly, thus adding to the money supply. (See discussion of "velocity" in Chapter 3). Conversely, a deflation would lead us to be more pessimistic and hence more cautious. Money would circulate less rapidly, and the money supply would be diminished even further. The fact that the Great Depression of the 1930s was marked in its initial stages by both monetary deflation and pessimism further suggests that changes in the money supply and national mood are causally interlinked.

average of 50%. People whose income from all sources averaged $10,000 per year at the end of 1973 were averaging $15,000 during the first quarter of 1978. We all know, however, that much of this gain was illusory, for in 1978 we were all paying out a great deal more for goods, services, and taxes than we were some four years earlier—so much more that at times many of us have felt that we were worse off. According to Thurow, however, the average person was actually *better* off, for his "real" income—income adjusted to allow for increases in the cost of living and taxes—had in fact gone up 8.4% during the same period. In other words, money income grew six times as fast as real income during the four years in question.

This disparity between increased money income and real income creates an illusion. As Thurow points out, each of us imagines what life would be like if our income were rising 50% without inflation. The large gap between money growth and real income growth may even cause many to believe that their real standards of living have fallen when objectively they have not.

When we complain that inflation raises prices, Thurow continues, we are forgetting that it also raises incomes. Although every price increase is a reduction in the real living standard of purchasers of goods and services, it is at the same time a real income increase for those who provide the goods or services. He says, "The money that it takes to pay higher prices does not disappear. It goes to someone. And most of us have benefited by such inflationary increases."

Another economist who takes a sympathetic view of inflation is Joseph J. Minarik (1979) of the Brookings Institute in Washington, D.C. Minarik maintains that inflation benefits the poor but penalizes the rich. He points out that Social Security pensions, welfare payments, and unemployment compensation are all "indexed" in one way or another, with the end result that they increase as the cost of living goes up. Even middle-class families benefit from inflation. Increases in the values of homes have even exceeded the rate of inflation. Those who owe money benefit because inflation raises their income, while the dollar amount of their debts remain the same. Food prices do go up, but wages and salaries also go up, while mortgages are paid off in depreciated dollars.

Wealthy people who live off interest payments are at a disadvantage, because the fixed amounts they receive decline in buying power as a result of inflation. Even when they are able to increase the return on their investments, they still lose, as Minarik points out, because the additional income is taxed at rates that run as high as 70%. Nor are stocks any better; research on dividends and price appreciation indicates that they have, on the average, done poorly in recent years. And bonds, too, have been a disaster in this era of high interest rates. The wealthy can of course buy gold, antiques, and real estate, but each of these investments suffers from illiquidity, and their values are subject to the capriciousness of economic trends.

Inflation: Benefactor or Malefactor

The arguments are waged furiously among economists about the merits and demerits of inflation. The conservatives condemn it in the strongest terms allowed by their professional journals, while the more radical element, taking their cue from John Maynard Keynes, maintain that inflation is absolutely necessary to promote economic and social progress and keep unemployment at a minimum. Indeed, Galbraith (1975) looks upon monetary inflation as one of the better ways of financing social progress. He sees inflation as a hidden tax levied by progressive governments on the assets of their countries, a tax that has the effect of redistributing wealth and property, a necessary step in liquidating the power of social and financial oligarchies. Galbraith cites these outcomes as advantages. Some would see them as compelling arguments against inflation.

All the verbiage aside, what bothers conservatives is the fact that inflation smacks of dishonesty. We delude ourselves, they say, if we think that by increasing the money supply we are increasing wealth. When a government sells $1,000 bonds redeemable in ten years, the purchasers should suffer no loss in buying power, when they cash in their bonds on maturity. But if the government has manipulated the money supply so that the dollars with which it pays off its bonds have only half the purchasing power of the dollars it borrowed ten years earlier, it has engaged in a form of legalized larceny.

The argument of the conservatives is logically and morally

sound. But, say the radicals (shall we call them liberals? progressives?), it does no one any good if, during the ten-year period, the economy stagnated or deteriorated, bankruptcies rose to all-time highs, unemployment stood at ruinous levels, and people were starving in full view of warehouses filled with grain rotting for lack of buyers. A higher morality than quid-pro-quo and pay-what-you-owe, they say, is the morality of social responsibility.

And so the debate continues. The weight of public action, if not of public opinion, is on the side of the radical/liberal/progressive group. If production statistics mean anything, the expansion of the money supply over the last generation has made possible gains in real personal wealth. Costs have risen, to be sure, but production has risen even more.[3]

For his part, the psychologist notes that given the emotionally supportive and socially rewarding effects of "a little more money"—even taking into account its illusory nature—the evidence favors monetary inflation. In any event, inflation is inevitable—at least as long as people remain optimistic and hopeful about the future. However, in closing this discussion I would cite the Greeks, who not only invented silver coinage, but also learned to substitute copper for silver, thus inventing monetary inflation as well. On the temple of Apollo at Delphi they inscribed this admonishment: "Nothing to excess."

---

[3]From 1965 to 1975, the gross national product of the United States rose an average of 3% per year, after adjusting for inflation. During 1976-78, years of even greater inflation, the real gross national product increase averaged over 5% (Conference Board, 1978).

Appendix

Analysis of the Reader's Questionnaire

The twelve-item attitude scale that I have included in the Preface is, as I have indicated, an instrument that attempts to determine the extent to which people feel positively or negatively about money.

The negative items all say in one way or another that money is a bad thing. As statements, they are fairly extreme, and the professors and students who took the questionnaire tended to reject them more decidedly than they accepted the six positive statements.

Statement No. 1, "Money is the root of most evil," got the least rejection. The mean score was 3.1, which is almost neutral. This item is a watered-down paraphrase of the well-known "Money is the root of all evil," which is in turn a misquotation of *I Timothy VI, 10*, "The love of money is the root of all evil." As to the validity of the three versions, a better case can be made for the original than for the other two, especially if "love of money" can be considered a literary device that refers to all motives that are selfish, exploitive, and unconcerned with the welfare of others. But if we do not interpret "love of money" in that expanded sense, and most people do not, then the statements are invalid, even the less-inclusive Item No. 1. What we commonly recognize as evil—crimes against the individual or society, cruelty, unwarranted violence and destruction, and so forth—have their principal causes either in generally unfavorable environmental conditions or in selfish, inconsiderate, and immature motives. Which of these two types of explanations psychologists prefer depends on whether they are behavioristically oriented, in which case they look to the environment for the causes of behavior, or whether they favor personality theory, in which case they prefer motivational explanations. In either event, the explanation of whatever evil action we attend to is likely to involve a great many more factors than money. It would be difficult to pinpoint money as a basic cause of whatever evil we have in mind, although, as I have pointed out in a number of instances in this book, money may be involved incidentally and may actually be cited as a reason by the perpetrators of misdeeds, who seize on this made-to-order explanation because they really do not understand their own motives. A good many anti-social actions do have money as their stated goal (mugging, embezzlement, or forgery, for example), but their explanation goes much deeper. It lies in cultural norms that tolerate violence and aggression, the alienation of large segments of the population, the cult of self-centeredness, and so forth. "Money" is thus an excuse that gives people a reason to express their aggressiveness, alienation, and/or selfishness.

A slightly better case can be made for Item No. 3, "Most of the pathological problems of the world are either caused or aggravated by money." Money, as I have pointed out, facilitates social transactions, and it can facilitate the accomplishment of unworthy as well as worthy aims. In the light of what I have said above, however, "caused" is too strong, and "aggravated" is questionable.

The validity of Item No. 5, "The introduction of money into a human relationship inevitably worsens it," depends, of course, on what the relationship is. If it involves a purchase, the receipt of wages, or the paying of a pension, it would seem that money would facilitate rather than impede the transaction. If the relationship is characterized by love, friendship, or neighborly helpfulness, the payment of money would be inappropriate. As the research by Foa (1971) that I discussed in Chapter 4 indicated, love and money are incompatible in an exchange relationship. The same could reasonably be said for other interactions where altruism in one form or another is a significant element. Because the item can be interpreted either way, a "?" would seem to be the best response, but people who are especially negative about money would be inclined to agree with it, whereas those who feel very attracted to it would disagree with it.

If a questionnaire is to measure a full range of attitudes for and against something, it ought to include a few extreme statements. Item No. 7, "Money is or symbolizes the ultimate obscenity," is an example of such a statement. It evoked the highest degree of rejection among the faculty and students who took the questionnaire, and only one or two marked it "agree."

Item No. 9, "The abolishment of money is prerequisite to the establishment of the ideal society," received the second highest degree of rejection, after Item No. 7. It represents an ultrahumanistic position, of course. Many who have attempted to found ideal societies have tried to eliminate money, but inevitably they have had to create some means for exchanging and valuing goods and services. Money is of course the most efficient way of accomplishing such tasks.

Item No. 11, "Money corrupts whatever it touches," is a diluted version of Item No. 7, and most of those who completed the questionnaire rejected it.

The concepts represented in the even-numbered items were more diverse than those included in the odd-numbered ones. These are three that share a common factor—that money is good for society and helps it operate more efficiently and equitably. One is Item No. 2, "Money is an absolute necessity in the functioning of any modern society," an item that called forth a strong vote of approval among the test takers. The second, Item No. 8, "Whatever economic democracy we have in Western society is made possible by money," was accepted by students, but rejected by professors, who seemed unaware that money enables almost everyone to share in the costs and benefits of civilization. They may have been thinking of the great disparity in the size of shares that exists among society's members, but this is the result of the operation of status systems. Differences in social status are not created by money, as I pointed out in Chapter 4; they are reflected in differences in wealth. But most people believe that differences in social status are *caused* by differences in wealth, research results to the contrary. The world was certainly less democratic before the invention of money, when social power was centered in religious ideology and force of arms. As I indicated in Chapter 2, the invention of money created a new form of power, one that could be invested, saved, and expanded (in the form of credit). Over the last 2500 years money has afforded a great many people, who would otherwise have been without significant material assets, the opportunities to acquire them. Individual shares of goods, housing, and services today may be unequal, but most of them are much larger than they would be if money had not been invented. The third item to which the same comment applies is Item No. 12, "Thanks to money, the world is a better place," an item that was rejected by both faculty and students.

Item No. 4, "It is reasonable to put a money value on the responsibilities that employees bear toward employers," received a fair degree of acceptance from the test takers. Since it describes the employee-employer relationship accurately, we may wonder why it did not evoke a stronger degree of agreement. It may be that the test takers felt that some aspects of employees' responsibility go beyond what could be expressed in money terms—loyalty, concern for the employer's interest, or whatever. But the same could be said for the employer's responsibility toward employees. Therefore the statement as it stands seems to be reasonable in the light of everyday practice.

Item No. 6, "People who have money tend to be happier than people who do not have any," received a fair amount of agreement from the professors who completed the questionnaire, but proportionately fewer students agreed with it. Although the conventional wisdom holds that happiness and money are unrelated, and that the poor are just as happy as the affluent (perhaps even happier!), opinion polls of various types show that respondents with average or higher incomes tend to have fewer problems of all types and tend to be more positive and optimistic in their outlook than people with lower incomes. I mentioned these findings at a number of points throughout the book. This is not to say that "money causes happiness," for a similar relationship between "happiness" and both educational and occupational status also exists. People who are average or above on these types of status apparently have more resources with which to deal with problems and more freedom to enjoy the fruits of their work. This appears to be true in all countries.

Item No. 10, "Money provides a reasonable basis for a status system, if we are required to have one," was rejected by a majority of the respondents. As I pointed out in Chapter 4, status systems are inevitable in all societies, and thus it can be said, in a manner of speaking, that "we are required to have them." But I also said that the research of sociologists indicates that such systems tend to be based on mutual associations among people of similar occupational rank and educational status, and not on money. Money may aid us in acquiring education and thus in achieving high levels of occupational status; and it may also enable us to participate in the activities that are characteristic of the status level we have attained, but it seldom is the direct *cause* of status. This is the only even-numbered item for which a "disagree" response would seem appropriate.

For the benefit of those who would like an indication of the questionnaire responses that would be consistent with the arguments of this book, I propose the following:

1. disagree	4. agree	7. disagree	10. disagree
2. agree	5. ?	8. agree	11. disagree
3. disagree	6. agree	9. disagree	12. agree

Whether one wishes to add "strongly" to any of these responses is a matter of personal taste. But taking the responses at their more moderate level, the indicated total score on the questionnaire would be 45.

References

Abourezk, J. Reference to his not wanting to run for U.S. Senate appeared in *Education Today*, Dec. 26, 1977, vol. 1. No. 3, p.4.

Anonymous. Chrysler squeaks. (Editorial) *Wall Street Journal*, March 3, 1978.

Bergler, E. Psychopathology of "bargain hunters. In E. Borneman (Ed.), *The Psychoanalysis of Money*. New York: Urizen, 1973 (trans. 1976).

Berlyne, D. E. Curiosity and exploration. *Science*, 1966, **153**, 25-33.

Berne, E. *What do you say after you say hello?* New York: Grove, 1972.

Bickman, L. The effect of social status on the honesty of others. *Journal of Social Psychology*, 1971, **85**, 87–92.

Black, D. *The behavior of law*. New York: Academic, 1976.

Borneman, E. *The psychoanalysis of money*. New York: Urizen, 1973 (trans. 1976 from German).

Brehm, J. W. *A theory of psychological reactance*. New York: Academic, 1966.

Brickman, P., Coates, D., & Janoff-Bulman, R. Lottery winners and accident victims: Is happiness relative? *Journal of Personality and Social Psychology*, 1978, 36, 917–927.

Brown, N. O. *Life against death*. Middletown, Conn.: Wesleyan Univ. Press, 1959.

Bruner, J. S., & Goodman, C. C. Value and need as organizing factors in perception. *Journal of Abnormal and Social Psychology*, 1947, **42**, 3344.

Burke, R. J. Differences in perception of desired job characterisitcs of the same sex and of the opposite sex. *Journal of Genetic Psychology*, 1966, **109**, 37–46.

Calder, B. J., & Staw, B. M. The self-perception of intrinsic and extrinsic motivation. *Journal of Personality and Social Psychology*, 1975, **31**, 599–605.

Callahan-Levy, C.M., & Messé, L.A. Sex differences in the allocation of pay. *Journal of Personality and Social Psychology*, 1979, **37**, 433–446.

Campbell, D. T. On the conflicts between biological and social evolution and between psychology and moral tradition. *American Psychologist*, 1975, **30**, 1103–1126.

Cimbalo, R. S., & Webdale, A. M. Effects of price information on consumer-rated quality. *American Psychological Association Proceedings*, 1973, **8**, 831–832.

Coleman, R. P., & Neugarten, B. L. *Social status in the city*. San Francisco: Jossey-Bass, 1971.

Combs, A. S., & Snygg, D. *Individual behavior: A perceptual approach to behavior*. New York: Harper, 1959.

Conference Board. Major economies in 1978. *Economic Road Maps*, No. 1825, February, 1978.

Daviet, C., & Rotter, G. Development of a bargain-interest attitude scale. *American Psychological Association Proceedings*, 1973, **8**, 827–828.

Dawson, J. L. M. Socio-economic differences in size-judgments of discs and coins by Chinese Primary VI children in Hong Kong. *Perceptual and Motor Skills*, 1975, **41**, 107–110.

DeCharms, R. *Personal causation: The internal affective determinants of behavior*. New York: Academic, 1968.

Doob, A. N., et al. Effect of initial selling price on subsequent sales. *Journal of Personal and Social Psychology*, 1969, **11**, 345–350.

Doob, A. N., & Gross, A. E. Status of frustrator as an inhibitor of horn-honking responses. *Journal of Social Psychology*, 1968, **76**, 213–218.

Doxiadis, C. A. Ekistics, the science of human settlements. *Science*, 1970, **170**, 393–404.

Drucker, P. F. Is executive pay excessive? *Wall Street Journal*, May 23, 1977.

Ehrlich, D., et al. Post-decision exposure to relevant information. *Journal of Abnormal and Social Psychology*, 1957, **54**, 98–102.

Einzig, P. *Primitive money*. Oxford: Pergamon, 1966.

English, H. B., & English, A. C. *A comprehensive dictionary of psychological* terms. New York: McKay, 1958.

Ferenczi, S. Stages in the development of the sense of reality. In E. Jones (translator), *Sex in psychoanalysis*. Boston: Badger, 1916.

Festinger, L., & Carlsmith, J. M. Cognitive consequences of forced compliance. *Journal of Abnormal and Social Psychology*, 1959, **58**, 203–210.

Field, M. How voters would cut governmental spending. *California Poll*, May 29–31, 1978.

Fisher, J. D., & Nadler, A. Effect of donor resources on recipient self-esteem and self-help. *Journal of Experimental and Social Psychology*, 1976, **12**, 139–150.

Foa, U. G. Interpersonal and economic resources. *Science*, 1971, **171**, 345–351.

Foster, G. M.*Tzintzuntzan: Mexican peasants in a changing world*. Boston: Little Brown, 1967.

Freedman, J. L., & Fraser, S. C. Compliance without pressures: The foot-in-the-door technique. *Journal of Personality and Social Psychology*, 1966, **4**, 195–202.

Fromm, E. *The sane society*. New York: Rinehart, 1955.

Galbraith, J. K. *Money: Whence it came, where it went*. Boston: Houghton Mifflin, 1975.

Gallup, G. Where Americans place their trust. *Field Enterprises*, June 12, l978.

Goffman, E. *Interaction ritual*. Chicago: Aldine, 1967.

Goldberg, H., & Lewis, R. T. *Money madness: The psychology of saving, spending, loving and hating money*. New York: Morrow, 1978.

Goodman, G. J. W. See "Adam Smith."

Groseclose, E. *Money and man: A survey of monetary experience*, 4th ed. Norman: University of Oklahoma Press, 1976.

Gurin, G., Veroff, J., & Feld, S. *Americans View Their Mental Health*. New York: Basic Books, 1960.

Hagen, R. L., Foreyt, J. P., & Durham, T. W. The dropout problem: Reducing attrition in obesity research. *Behavior Therapy*, 1976, **7**, 463–471.

Hall, E. T, *Beyond culture*. Garden City, New York: Anchor Press/Doubleday, 1976.

Hawtrey, R. *Currency and credit*, 3rd ed. New York: Longmans Green, 1928.

Head, B. V. *Historia numorium: A manual of Greek numismatics*, 2nd ed. London: Clarendon, 1911.

Hebb, D. O. *The organization of behavior*. New York: Wiley, 1949.

Heilbroner, R. L. Inflationary capitalism *The New Yorker*, Oct. 8, 1979, 121–141.

Hendrickson, R. A. *The future of money*. Englewood Cliffs: New York: 1970.

Herzberg, F. *Work and the nature of man*. New York: World, 1966.

Hitchock, J. L., Munroe, R. L., & Munroe, R. H. Coins and countries: The value-size hypothesis. *Journal of Social Psychology*, 1976, **100**, 307–6.

Hodge, R. W. Socioeconomic differentiators. *Science*, 1979, **206**, 209–210.

Holtzman, W. H., Diaz-Guerrero, R., & Swartz, J. D. *Personality development in two cultures*. Austin: University of Texas Press, 1975.

Horney, K. *Neurosis and human growth*. New York: Norton, 1950.

Huck, S. W., & Gleason, E. M. Using monetary inducements to increase response rates from mailed surveys: A replication of previous research. *Journal of Applied Psychology*, 1974, **59**, 222–225.

Hughes, R. Confusing art with bullion. *Time*, 1979, **114**(27), 56–57.

Hulin, C. L., & Blood, M. R. Job enlargement, individual differences, and worker responses. *Psychological Bulletin*, 1968, **69**, 41–45.

Isen, A. M., & Levin, P. F. Effect of feeling good on helping: Cookies and kindness, *Journal of Personal and Social Psychology*, 1972, **21**, 384–388.

Jansen, R. F. Rapid growth of Eurodollar market prompts debate over the wisdom of imposing controls. *Wall Street Journal*, Aug. 3, 1979.

Katona, G. *The powerful consumer*. New York: McGraw-Hill, 1960.

Katona, G. *The mass consumption society*. New York: McGraw-Hill, 1964.

Katona, G. *Psychological economics*. New York: Elsevier, 1975.

Kilbridge, M. D. Do workers prefer larger jobs? *Personnel Journal*, 1960, **37**, 45-48.

Kluckhohn, C., & Leighton, D. *The Navaho*. Cambridge: Harvard University Press, 1946.

Koffer, K. B., Coulson, G., & Hammond, L. Verbal conditioning without awareness using a highly discriminable, monetary reinforcer. *Psychological Reports*, 1976, **39**, 11–14.

Kohn, M. L. *Class and conformity: A study in values*. Homewood, Ill.: Dorsey, 1969.

Kristol, I. The "new class" revisited. *Wall Street Journal*, May 31, 1979.

Laurent, H. Incentives study. *Social Science Research Reports, IV. Surveys and Inventories*. Standard Oil of New Jersey, 1962.

Lawler, E. E. III. *Pay and organizational effectiveness: A psychological view*. New York: McGraw-Hill, 1971.

Lee, A. McC. Social power. In H. P. Fairchild (Ed.), *Dictionary of sociology*. New York: Philosophical Library, 1944.

Maslow, A. H. *Motivation and personality*. New York: Harper, 1954.

May, R. *The meaning of anxiety*. New York: Ronald, 1950.

McClelland, D. C. *The achieving society*. Princeton, New Jersey: Van Nostrand, 1961.

McClelland, D. C. *Power: The inner experience*. New York: Irvington, 1975.

Minarik, J. J. as interviewed by Richard E. Meyer of the Associated Press, reported in the San Francisco *Sunday Examiner and Chronicle*, February, 18, 1979.

Morse, S. J., Gruzen, J., & Reis, H. T. The nature of equity restoration: Some approval-seeking considerations. *Journal of Experimental Social Psychology*, 1976, **12**, 1–8.

Moskowitz, M. Shopping—how the poor get poorer. In the weekly column, "Money Tree." *San Francisco Chronicle*, 1977.

Opsahl, R. L., & Dunnette, M. D. The role of financial compensation in industrial motivation. *Psychological Bulletin,* 1966, **66,** 94–118.

Osborne, J. G., Powers, R. B., & Anderson, E. G. A lottery to stop littering. *Psychology Today, 1974 (August),* **8,** 65–66.

Pepitone, E. A., Loeb, H. W., & Murdoch, E. M. *Social comparison and similarity of children's performance.* American Psychological Convention, San Francisco, 1977.

Pierce, R. E. *The effect of monetary rewards on improved academic performance.* Unpublished Ed. D. dissertation. University of Southern Mississippi, 1970.

Pliner, P., Hart, H., Kohl, J., & Saari, D. Compliance without pressure: Some further data on the foot-in-the-door technique. *Journal of Experimental Social Psychology,* 1974, **10,** 1–16.

Powers, R. B., Osborne, J. G., & Anderson, E. G. Positive reinforcement of litter removal in the natural environment. *Journal of Applied Behavior Analysis,* 1973, **6,** 579–586.

Pressley, M. M., & Tullar, W. L. A factor interactive investigation of mail survey response rates from a commercial population. *Journal of Marketing Research,* 1977, **14,** 108–111.

Raymond, B. J., & Unger, R. K. "The apparel oft proclaims the man:" Cooperation with deviant and conventional youths. *Journal of Social Psychology,* 1971, **87,** 75–82.

Reiss, M. L., Piotrowski, W. D., & Bailey, J. S. Behavioral community psychology: Encouraging low-income parents to seek dental care for their children. *Journal of Applied Behavior Analysis,* 1976, **9,** 387–397.

Rivera, A. N., & Tedeschi, J. T. Public versus private reactions to positive inequity. *Journal of Personal and Social Psychology,* 1976, **34,** 895–900.

Roethlisberger, F. J., & Dickson, W. J. *Management and the worker.* Cambridge: Harvard University Press, 1939.

Rogers, C. *Client-centered therapy.* Boston: Houghton Mifflin, 1951.

Ronan, W. W. Relative importance of job characteristics. *Journal of Applied Psychology,* 1970, **54,** 192–200.

Rosen, B. C. Race, ethnicity, and the achievement syndrome. *American Sociological Review*, 1959, **24**, 47–60.

Rosenberg, M. *Occupations and values*. Glencoe, Ill.: Free Press, 1957.

Rosenblatt, P. C., Fugita, S. S., & McDowell, D. V. Wealth transfer and restrictions on sexual relations during betrothal. *Ethnology*, 1969, **8**, 319–328.

Russell, J. B. *Medieval civilization*. New York: Wiley, 1968.

Schoeck, H. Envy: *A theory of social behavior*. New York: Harcourt Brace, Jovanovich, 1966.

Seligman, M. E. P. *Helplessness*. San Francisco: Freeman, 1975.

Shils, E. D. In J. A. Jackson (Ed.), *Social stratification. Sociological studies 1*. Cambridge: Cambridge University Press, 1968.

"Smith, Adam." *The money game*. Boston: Houghton Mifflin, 1969.

Smith, F. J., & Keer, W. A. Turnover factors as assessed by the exit interview. *Journal of Applied Psychology*, 1953, **37**, 352–355.

Snygg, D., & Combs, A.S. *Individual behavior*. New York: Harper, 1949.

Sowell, T. *Race and economics*. New York: David McKay, 1975.

Spivak, J. Hungary's Gypsies, poor and unpopular, embarrass regime. *Wall Street Journal*, June 11, 1979.

Spott, R., & Kroeber, A. L. Yurok narratives. *University of California Publications in American Archeology and Ethnology*, 1942, No. 35.

Stanton, H. F. Fee-paying and weight loss: Evidence for an interesting interaction. *American Journal of Clinical Hypnosis*, 1976, **19**, 47–49.

Swingle, P. G., & Coady, H. V. Social class, age, and the nature of incentive in children's lever-pressing performance. *Canadian Journal of Psychology*, 1969, **23**, 41–48.

Taylor, F. W. *The principles of scientific management*. New York: Harper, 1911.

Thurow, L. C. The real sources of economic pain. *Wall Street Journal*, July 6, 1978.

Toffler, A. *Future shock*. New York: Random House, 1970.

Treiman, D. J. *Occupational prestige in comparative perspective*. New York: Academic, 1977.

Turner, A. N., & Miclette, A. L. Sources of satisfaction in repetitive work. *Occupational Psychology*, 1962, **36**, 215–231.

U.S. Department of Health, Education, & Welfare, Division of Health Statistics. Blood pressure of persons 6–74 years of age in the United States. *Advance Data*, October 18, 1976.

Valenzi, E., & Eldridge, L. Effects of price information, composition differences, expertise, and rating scales on product-quality rating. *Proceedings of the American Psychological Association*, 1973, **8**, 829–830.

van Lawick-Goodall, J. *In the shadow of man*. Boston: Houghton Mifflin, 1971.

Vroom, V. H. *Work and motivation*. New York: Wiley, 1964.

Warner, W. L., & Lunt, P. S. *Social life of a modern community*. New Haven: Yale University Press, 1941.

Wernimont, P. F., & Fitzpatrick, S. The meaning of money. *Journal of Applied Psychology*, 1972, **56**, 218–226.

Whittlesy, C. R. Money. In *Encyclopaedia Brittanica*, Vol. 15, 701–707. Chicago: Enclyclopaedia Brittanica, 1967.

Wiseman, T. *The money motive*. New York: Random House, 1974.

Wolfe, J. B. Effectiveness of token-rewards for chimpanzees. *Comparative Psychological Monographs*, 1936, **12**, No. 5.

Index

Abourezk, James, 81
achieve, need to, 192–94
acquisitiveness, 62–63
"Adam Smith," see G. J. W.
  Goodman
Africa, 13
Aid to Families with Dependent
  Children (AFDC), 159–60
Alexander the Great, 18–19
Alfonso I, of Aragon, 36
almonds, as value standard, 12
alms-giving, 126–27
altruism, underlying motives of,
  124–25
ambition, 62–63
Anderson, E. G., 158
anti-money games, 205–8
antoninianus, 27
anxiety, in modern life, 196–97
  and money, 199–202
Arab workers, employment goals of,
  152
arousal, as universal human need,
  64–65
artists, occupational rewards of,
  187–89
assembly-line work, 182–83
assignats, 51, 52
Athens, ancient, 16–17, 23, 25
Attitudes toward Money
  (questionnaire), xi–xiii, 153–54,
  223–26

Augustus, 26
aureus, 27

Bailey, J. S., 114–15
Bank of England, 41
Bank of Scotland, 45
bankrupt, meaning of term, 39
banks, people's confidence in, 49
Banque Royale, 46
bargain-hunters, personality of,
  170–71
barrios, 117
Barron's, 3
barter, 8–14, 51
basic needs, Maslow's theory of,
  140–41
beaver skins, as value standard, 12
Bedouins, 135
Bergler, Edmund, 171
Berlyne, D. E., 63
Berne, Eric, 202–205
Bernhard, Hubert J., xvii
Bickman, Leonard, 71, 161
Bierce, Ambrose, 156
bills of exchange, medieval, 38–39
Black, Donald, 66–67, 110
Blood, Milton R., 181–83
blood pressure, and income, 88
Borneman, Ernest, 124, 146, 147
brassage, 42
Brehm, Jack W., 127
bribes, and effect on lying, 162–65

Brickman, Philip, 212–13
Brown, Governor Jerry, 187, 190
Brown, Norman O., 148, 172
Bruner, Jerome S., 113
budgetary problems, of rich and poor, 6–7
Bulwer-Lytton, Edward Robert, 83
Burke, Edmund, 58
Burke, Ronald J., 152
business executives, occupational rewards of, 187
Business Week, 3
Butler, Samuel, 144
butter, as value standard, 12
Byzantine Empire, 30–31, 34

Cabaret, 1
Calder, Bobby J., 190–91
Campbell, Donald Thomas, 155
Camus, Albert, 137
Canadian money, and self-esteem, 93
canvassing, for charitable causes, 165–66
capitalism, mood of, 55
caritas, 126
Carlsmith, J. Merrill, 162–65
Casanova, Giacomo, 143
cattle, as value standard, 12
Cellini, Benevenuto, 42
Center for the Study of Democratic Institutions, 148–49
charity, attitude on being objects of, 130–36
Charlemagne, 35
Charles I, of England, 40
Charles II, of England, 41
Chaucer, Geoffrey, 156
child-rearing, social class differences in, 185–86
children, and attitudes toward money, xiv
chimpanzees, sharing among, 128
Chimp-o-Mat, 137–38
China, Communist, 49
Chinese, 41

Chinese proverb, 1
Cimbalo, Richard S., 169
civilization, Greco-Roman, 29–30
clergy, occupational rewards of, 187
Clough, Arthur Hugh, 8
Coady, H. V., 114
Coates, Dan, 212–13
cognitive dissonance, 162–68
coinage, invention of, 15
    medieval debasement of, 38, 42
    Roman debasement of, 25–27
coins, copper, as fiat money, 23–25
    differences in size issued by wealthy and poor nations, 113
    gold, 38, 40
    medieval, 35, 37–38, 42
    portraits on, 18–20
    as propaganda, 16–20, 27–29, 38
    token, 23–25
Coleman, R. P., 112
Columbus, 42
Combs, Arthur S., 84–86
Comfort, Alexander, 148–50
commitment, price of, 167–68
communist government of Hungary, and attitudes toward Gypsies, 135
commodities, as value standards, 8, 11–14
commodity futures, gambling in, 210
commodity money, 41–43, 47
conditioning, psychological, 156
Consumer Sentiment, Index of, 55
Continental Congress, monetary policies of, 50–51
Coulson, G., 157
creativity, xvi
credit cards, 56
Crusaders, 22, 36–37, 38
cut-price fallacy, 169–70

Daviet, Charles, 170–71
darics, 17–18
Darius, 17
Darvi, Bella, 208–9
Dawson, John L. M., 113

deben, 13
debt, instruments of, 38–41
debt money, 38–57
DeCharms, Richard, 190, 192
Dee, Simon, 206–8
defense mechanisms, 120–21, 144, 199–202
deference, and prestige, 73
de Goncourt, Edmond and Jules, 100
de Levichine, A., 108
Delphi, Temple of Apollo at, 221
denarius, 25–27
deniers, 35
de Saari, D., 165–66
Diaz-Guerrero, Rogelio, 122–23
Dickens, Charles, 195
Dickson, William J., 173–75
dinar, 22
Diocletian, 27
direct-mail advertising campaigns, 161–62
dissatisfactions, in work, 176, 180–82
dollar, origin of, 43
dollars, American, repatriation of, 48
Doob, Anthony N., 72–73, 170
Doxiadis, Constantine A., 11, 216
drachm, purchasing power of, 23
Drucker, Peter F., 90–91
ducats, 38
dumps, as origin of coins, 15
Dunnette, Marvin L., 175
Durham, Thomas W., 167–68

Ecclesiastes, 1, 8, 83
economic growth, and need to achieve, 193
economists, predictions of, 54
education, and prestige, 74
efficiency experts, 172–73
Egypt, ancient, 13–14, 39
Einzig, Paul, 10–14
electrum, 15

End Poverty in California (EPIC), 107
envy, as reflected in progressive income tax, 107
as a universal experience, 106–9
Erasmus of Rotterdam, 156
Eurodollars, 56
exchange rates, and American dollars, 91–93
excrement, money as, 4, 146–47
Exodus, 100
expectations, monetary, 159–60

factory workers, prestige of, 89
fair wage, question of, 177–78
Farley, James, 58
Feld, S., 181
Ferenczi, Sandor, 146, 210
Festinger, Leon, 162–65
fiat money, 23–25
Fisher, Jeffrey David, 130–33, 135
Fitzgerald, F. Scott, 102
florin, 38
Foa, Uriel, 79–81, 143
foot-in-the-door technique, 165–67
Forbes, 3
Foreyt, John Paul, 167–68
Fortune, 3
Foster, George M., 108
France, 45–47
Franklin, Benjamin, 2, 8, 33
Fraser, Scott C., 166
Freedman, Jonathan L., 166
freedom, and middle-class occupational goals, 185
and money, 77–79
Freud, Sigmund, 4, 120–21, 125, 142, 143–48, 199, 200
Fromm, Erich, 147
Fugita, Stephen S., 159
Galbraith, John Kenneth, 44, 47, 50, 52, 220
garbage collectors, wages of, 112
German mark, 51–52
Gleason, E. M., 162
Goffman, Erving, 60

gold, 151, 21–22, 38, 40, 41
  as backing for currency, 53–54
Goldberg, Herb, 198–99
goldsmiths, as bankers, 40–41
Goodman, C. C., 113
Goodman, George J. W. ("Adam
  Smith"), xv, 101, 148, 150
Gould, Jay, 2
grain, as standard of value, 14
Greeks, ancient, 15–25, 221
Groseclose, E., 46
Gross, Alan E., 72–73
gambling, compulsive, 208–10
Gruzen, Joan, 94–95
guilt, as basis for charitable giving,
  127–28
  free-floating, 125–26
Gurin, Gerald, 181
Gyges, King, 15
Gypsies, Hungarian, 134–36

Hagen, Richard L., 167–68
Hall, Edward T., 142
Hamilton, Alexander, 50
Hammond, L., 157
Hammurabi, Code of, 14
happiness, and income, 88
  and affluence, 226
Hart, Heather, 165–66
Hawthorne effect, 173–75
Hawtrey, Ralph, 8
Head, Barclay V., 15
Health and Nutrition Survey, U.S.
  Department of Health,
  Education, and Welfare, 88
Hearst, Patricia, 67
Hebb, D. O., 139
Heilbroner, Robert L., 55–56
"helping professions,"
  unemployment in the, 151
Hemingway, Ernest, 102
hemitartemorion, 23
Hendrickson, Robert A., 47, 54
Herodotus, 15
Hertzberg, Frederick, 180–81, 183

high-status jobs, supply and demand
  relative to, 189
Hitchcock, Jan L., 113
Hitler, Adolf, 52
Hodge, Robert W., 75
"Holmgren, Pamela and Carl," 6
Holtzman, Wayne H., 122–23
Hope, Bob, 194
Horace, 58
Horney, Karen, 139
Hospitallers, 37
hubris, 105
Huck, S. W., 162
Hughes, Robert, 188
Hutchins, Robert M., 148–49
Hulin, Charles L., 181–83
"hygiene," of job, 180–81
hyperpyra, 22

income, and blood pressure, 88
  and happiness, 88
  and social activity, 75
India, 12
Indians, North American, 12
inflation, 44
  during the American Revolution,
  50–51
  and capitalism, 44
  as compared to growth in gross
  national product, 221
  creeping, 52
  and its effect on rich and poor,
  219–20
  in France, 45–47, 50–51
  as fundamentally dishonest, 220
  in Germany, 51–52
  psychology of, 54–56, 216–221
  as related to public optimism,
  218–221
  in Roman times, 26–27
  as scapegoat, 217
influence, social, 59–63
interest rates, 55, 56
Internal Revenue Service,
  apprehensiveness toward, 105

Iran, 47
Ireland, 12
Isabella of Spain, 42
Isen, Alice, 161

James, William, 84
Janoff-Bulman, Ronnie, 212–13
Jansen, R. F., 56
Jefferson, Thomas, 32
Jesuits, 190
Jesus Christ, 34, 102, 123
jewels, as backing for currency, 47
Jewish merchants, 37
Joachimstaler, 43
job characteristics, students' ranking
  of, 152–53
Johnson, Charles, xvii
Johnson, Lyndon B., 123
Johnson, Samuel, 143
Judea, Roman defeat of, 28
Julius Caesar, 123

Katona, George, 4, 55
Keynes, John Maynard, 195, 220
Kilbridge, M. D., 182
Kipnis, David, 124
Kluckhohn, Clyde, 108
Knights Templar, 35–37
Koffer, Kenneth Barry, 157
Kohl, Joanne, 165–66
Kohn, Melvin L., 186
Kroeber, Arthur L., 102–3
Kublai Khan, 41

laborers, occupational rewards of,
  187
language, 9
La Rochefoucauld, François de, 124
Laurent, Harry, 152
Law, John, 2, 44–47, 49, 52, 53,
  216
Lawler, Edward Emmett III, 139–
  40
lawyers, job market for, 189
Lazarus, 34

Lee, Alfred McClung, 61
"Let's Pull a Fast One" (neurotic
  game), 203–4
Levin, Paula, 161
Lewis Robert T., 198–99
Lex Didia, 107
libido, see sex drive
Lindgren, Fredi, xvii
"little more money," delusion of,
  213–15
  and inflation, 216–17
Locke, John, 195
Loeb, Helen Ward, 121–22
Lombards, 37
Long, Huey P., 107
"losers," attractiveness of, 151–53
lottery winners, feelings of, 212–13
love, as particularistic resource, 79–
  81
  as requiring commitment, 81
loyalty to group, in poor
  communities, 118–20
Lunt, P. S., 101–2
Luther, Martin, 145
luxury, as relative concept, 107
Lydia, ancient, 15–16

M1 and M2, 53, 56
Machiavelli, 83
"Making Ends Meet" (neurotic
  game), 203
mandats, 51
Marco Polo, 41
Marx, Karl, 123
Maslow, Abraham H., 140–41
Matthew, 32, 102
Maugham, Somerset, 1
McClelland, David C., 193
McDowell, D. G., 159
mental health, xvi
  and money, 195–221
Mesopotamia, ancient, 14
Mexicans, attitudes of lower- and
  middle-class, toward striving for
  success, 122–23

Michelangelo, 42
Miclette, A. L., 182
middle class, culture of, 111
  as preferred status, 103
millionaires, economical life style of,
  6
Minarik, Joseph J., 219–20
Mississippi Company (Compagnie
  d'Occident), 46–47, 52
Money (magazine), 3
money, its ability to make things
  interesting or important, 64–66
  and achievement, 172–94
  and anxiety, 197–202
  as catalyst, 57
  children's attitudes toward, xiv
  Christian disdain of, 34–35
  commodity, 11–14
  and common sense, 175
  as conditioner of mood, 160–62
  and costs/benefits balance, 195–96
  and creativity, xvi, 192
  as debt, 39–41
  and development of capitalism, 44
  and dissatisfaction with work, 176
  and envy, 77
  as excrement, 4, 146–47
  expectation of, 191
  as extrinsic motivator, 173–75
  and freedom, 73–79
  giving of, 124–26
  guilt feelings about, 154–55
  as manipulator, 156–71
  and mental health, xvi, 195–221
  and mental-health problems, 155
  as motivator, 172–75
  neurotic games involving, 202–10
  origin of term, 22
  and personal worth, 66–69
  and power, 58–82
  preoccupation with, 76
  psychohistory of, 8–57
  Questionnaire on Attitudes
    toward, xi–xiii, 153–54, 223–
    226

  as reinforcement or reward, 114–
    15, 139–40, 157–58
  as related to wealth, 100–102
  as not requiring commitment, 81
  and self-theory, 84–87
  and self-worth, 83–99
  as socioeconomic catalyst, 30
  and social-class-related attitudes
    toward, 111–13
  and status, 58–82
  as symbol of achievement, 193
  as universalistic resource, 79–81
  and urbanization, 11
  velocity of, 54–55, 218
  and work, 172–94
money games, of everyday life, 87–
  88
  neurotic, 202–10
money motive, 137–43
  and common sense, 175
  guilt feelings about, 154–55
  psychoanalytic views of, 145–48
  and sex drive, 142–50
money motives, as psychological
  smokescreens, 178–79
money supply (M1 and M2), 53, 56
Money Tree, 3, 119
Morgan, John Pierpont, 2
Morse, Stanley J., 94–95
mortgages, 56
Moskowitz, Milton, 3, 119
motherhood, unmarried, 159–60
motivation, intrinsic vs. extrinsic,
  173–75
Munroe, Ruth H., 113
Munroe, R. L., 113
Murdoch, Eleanor M., 121–22

Nadler, Arie, 130–33, 135
Navahos, 108–9
"need for money," as
  rationalization, 201–2
Neugarten, Bernice L., 12
neurotic needs, 139
Nero, 26–27

Newburyport, Massachusetts, 101
Norway, medieval, 12
"Now I've Got You, You Son of a
Bitch" (neurotic game), 204–5

obesity therapy, effect of fees on,
167–68
occuptional rankings, and prestige,
74
omnipotence, neurotic, of gamblers,
210–12
Opsahl, R. L., 175
optimism, and inflation, 54
Order of St. John of Jerusalem
(Hospitallers), 37
Osburne, J. Grayson, 158
overpayment, reactions to, 94–96

paper currency, 41–49
particularistic resources, 79–81
Pax Romana, 32–33
pay, relative importance of, 175–77
pecuniary, derivation of word, 13
penny, silver, 38
Pepitone, Emmy A., 121–22
Persia, ancient, 17
physicians, occupational rewards of,
187–88
Piacenza, 37
pieces-of-eight, 43
Pierce, Robert E., 113–14
Piotrowski, W. D., 114–15
Pliner, Patricia, 165–66
poker face, 209
poor, elusiveness of the, 103–5
euphemisms for, 104
poor people, alienation of, 111
alleged laziness of, 109–10
and attitudes toward creativity,
121–22
and attitudes toward success,
116–17
as deviates from the norm, 110–
111
difficulties encountered in
helping, 126–27
higher food prices paid by, 116,
119
as more influenced by advertising,
119–20
as targets for hostility, 109–10
Pope, Alexander, 124
Porter, Sylvia, 3
poverty, as associated with virtue,
127
Christian glorification of, 34–35
as contrasted to wealth, 100–23
as menace to society, 132
poverty level, official, 104
power, as centered on position, 60
and financial status, 69–70
and money, 58–82
of money, 1–2
as social influence, 59–63
power structure, and financial
status, 69–70
Powers, Richard B., 158
pregnancy, among teenagers, 159–
60
prestige, and deference, 73
and education, 74
and money, 73–76
and occupation, 74
Pressley, M. M., 162
price, as related to value, 90, 168–
69
professors, occupational prestige of,
89
and psychic income, 187–88
salaries of, 112
profit motive, and need to achieve,
192–94
promotion, foremen's anxieties
about, 181–82
propaganda, on coins, 16–20, 27–29,
38
Proposition 13, 109
prosperity of others, peasants'
anxiety about, 108
psychic income, of high-status jobs,
186–88
Ptolemies, 14

Questionnaire on Attitudes toward Money, xi–xiii, 153–54, 223–26

Raleigh, Walter, 211–12
ratebreakers, 117–18
Raymond, Beth J., 71
real income, as compared to money income, 218
reality, and the self-system, 86–87
reinforcement, 139–41
    intermittent, 209
Reis, Harry T., 94–95
Reiss, Maxine L., 114–15
Rentenmark, 52
repetitive work, enjoyment of, 182–83
rewards, extrinsic and intrinsic, 190–92
rich, euphemisms for, 105
    elusiveness of the, 103–5
rich people, as deviates from the norm, 110–11
    "low profile" of, 111
    as targets for envy, 109
Rio de Janeiro, 116–17
rituals, in interaction, 60
Rivera, Alba, 95
Roethlisberger, F. J., 173–75
Rogers, Carl, 84
Roma Eterna, veneration of, 34
Roman Empire, barbarian invasion of, 32–33
    monetary policies of, 26–31
romance with work, middle-class, 185
Romans, 20–21, 25–31, 32–33
Rosen, B. C., 115
Rosenblatt, Paul C., 159
Rotter, George, 170–71
Rousseau, Jean-Jacques, 142
"Roxas, Julie," 192
Rukeyser, Louis, xv, 3
Runyon, Damon, 67
Russell, Jeffrey Burton, 34–35
ryal, Iranian, 47

Saab (auto company), 182–83
Saari, Dory, 165–66
St. Patrick, 12
salary, and rank in corporations, 90–91
    and seniority among teachers, 89–90
"Santos, Maria," 5, 7, 119, 120, 121
Sardes, 15
satisfctions, in work, 180–82
Savonarola, 34
Schoeck, Helmut, 106–9, 150–51
Schweitzer, Robert N., xvii
Seleucus, 19
self-esteem, and money, 66–69
self-help books, 76
selfishness, universality of, 124–26
self-system, 85
self-theory, 84–87
self-worth, and exchange value of American dollar, 91–93
seniorage, 42
sensory adaptation, 216
sequins, 38
Sermon on the Mount, 102
sex differences in self-worth, as reflected in pay, 96–99
sex drive, and money motive, 142–50
    psychoanalytic view of, 143–45
sexual behavior, and monetary incentives, 159–60
sexual freedom, and mental-health problems, 154–55
Shaw, George Bernard, 32, 100, 172
Shils, Edward, 73
"Shotsky, Philip," 200–201
sigloi, 17
silver, as standard of value, 14
    as monetary standard, 21–23, 26, 42
Sinclair, Upton, 107
slave girls, as value standard, 12
social needs, 9

Snygg, Donald, 84–86
social-class differences, in attitudes
 toward money, 112–15
 in attitudes toward striving for
  success, 122–23
 in child-rearing, 185–86
 and job security, 184
 in perception of coin sizes, 113
 in reward-value of money, 113–14
 sociologist's view of, 101–102
social cohesiveness, in Roman
 Empire, 33
social norms, power of, 59–60
social rules, explicity and implicit,
 91–92
social workers, occupational rewards
 of, 187
socioeconomic status, as reflected in
 automobiles, 72–73
 and dress, 58–59, 70–71
 and the power structure, 69–70
 research on, 101–102
sociopathic behavior, as rationalized
 by "need for money," 201–202
Somerville, William, 83
Sowell, Thomas, 116
Soviet Union, 49
 perquisites in, 184
Spivak, Jonathan, 134–36
Spott, R., 102–103
status, equivalency of various types,
 183
 and money, 58–82
 as particularistic resource, 79
 and seniority among teachers, 89–
  90
 and its effect on lawbreakers'
  treatment, 66–67
Stanton, H. F., 167–68
Staw, Barry Martin, 190–91
stimulation, need for, 9, 63–64
stock-market game, 130–33
stock options, gambling, 210
street sweepers, "overpayment" of,
 75

students, as college "dropouts,"
 150–51
suicide, 68
Swartz, Jon David, 122–23
Swingle, Paul G., 114
sympathy, among chimpanzees, 128
Syria, kings of, 19–20

Tain, 12
talers, 43
Taylor, Frederick Winslow, 172–73,
 174
teachers, occupational rewards of,
 187
Tedeschi, James, 95
tetradrachms, 18, 20
Thackery, William Makepeace, 137
Thurow, Lester C., 218–19
time restraints, and human
 behavior, 142
Timothy, I, 100
tipping, attitudes toward, 128–30
Titus, 28, 81
tobacco, as value standard, 12
Toffler, Alvin, 197
token economies, among
 chimpanzees, 137–38
Toupin, Arthur V., ix–x
Trajan, 28
Treiman, Donald J., 73–74, 89, 188
Trollope, Frances, 144
"Try and Collect" (neurotic game),
 204–205
Tullar, William L., 162
Turner, A. N., 182
Tzintzuntzan, 108

unemployment, and self-worth, 88–
 89
Unger, Rhoda Kesler, 71
U. S. Bureau of the Census, 159–60
universalistic resources, 79–81
upper class, size of, 112
urban life, 11
 and anonymity, 80
usury, 35–37

value, as related to price, 90
van Lawick-Goodall, Jane, 128
Vencill, C. Daniel, xvii
venereal disease, 154–55
Veroff, Joseph, 181
Vespasian, 28, 81
Virginia, colonial, 12
Voltaire, 172
Vroom, Victor H., 176–77

Wall Street Journal, 3
Wall Street Week, xv, 3
Walpole, Robert, 124
"Wanda," 202–204
Warner, W. Lloyd, 101–102
wealth, as associated with sin, 127
    as contrasted with poverty, 100–23
    as related to money, 100–102
Webdale, A. M., 169
welfare costs, public's desire to
    reduce, 109–10

welfare recipients, relative prestige
    of, 89
Western Electric study, 173–75
"White, Louise and George," 204–205
Whittlesy, Charles R., 8
winning big, reactions to, 212–13
    risks of, 115–17
Wiseman, Thomas, 101, 146–47,
    206–208, 211–12
Wolfe, John B., 137–38

Xerxes, 17

Yuroks, 102–103
"You only Want to Kick Me because
    I'm Down and Out" (neurotic
    game), 204–205

Zanuck, Darryl F., 208–209